CHRISTIAN BY DEGREES

CHRISTIAN BY DEGREES

*Masonic Religion
revealed in the
Light of Faith*

BY

WALTON HANNAH

With a Foreword by
DR. E. L. MASCALL
OF CHRIST CHURCH · OXFORD

LONDON
AUGUSTINE PRESS
MCMLIV

" In Whom do you put your trust ? " He (*the Candidate*) *ought to be able and, may it be said, allowed to give an unprompted reply to that question. It lies at the root of the whole Masonic super-structure it is hoped to raise. And the correct answer given, what does it mean ? Grand Lodge has given it a very extensive meaning. Belief in God at all has been held to mean the sense of responsibility to a Supreme Entity and the Unity of God means the admission of one unalterable standard of right and wrong. At this time of day it is difficult to say what intelligent man, other than a professed atheist, would be excluded. The writer himself has initiated Jews, Mohammedans, Hindoos and Parsees and, at least, one Buddhist.*

The Rev. *J. T. Lawrence*, Freemasonry, its History, Principles and Objects.

FOREWORD

WHEN Mr. Hannah told me that he was writing a second volume on Freemasonry and asked me to contribute a Foreword, my first impulse was to decline. A great many devoted and sincere Church people, both clerical and lay, are practising Freemasons, and some of them I number among my own friends ; could it really be right, I wondered, to stir up again in the Church of England a controversy which, after a short but somewhat lively career, seemed to have sunk into oblivion ? On further reflection, however, I changed my mind. For, having read both the present book and its predecessor and having spent some time examining Mr. Hannah's copious collection of masonic rituals, it seemed to me that there were two questions which needed an answer and to which, so far as I knew, no answer had been given.

The first question is simply whether Mr. Hannah has transcribed the masonic rituals and described the masonic ceremonies with substantial correctness. If he has not, then any further discussion fails to arise. If he has travestied the masonic organisation, it should be perfectly possible for an authoritative statement to be issued to this effect. If masonic secrecy forbids precise correction of the errors, it surely cannot forbid a denial of the statements in which the errors occur. As far as Mr. Hannah's first book is concerned no such denial has been made, so far as I am aware. What has, however, manifested itself, as the present work points out, is a deliberate attempt to prevent investigation of the matter. This being so, I do not think non-masons can be blamed if they assume that Mr. Hannah's statements are in their essentials correct.

In that case, the second question is whether it is possible for a Churchman, whether clerical or lay, to take part in ceremonies such as Mr. Hannah describes, without falling into grave irreverence. No doubt familiarity breeds insensitivity, and it would be rash to suppose that those who participate in the rites invariably pay detailed attention to the precise meaning of the words which are being used. This is true of other forms of irreverence, but it is not normally held entirely to excuse them. It is important not to exaggerate here. No one, I imagine, suspects the Archbishop of Canterbury or the Bishop of Norwich of being engaged in a secret plot to overthrow the Christian Faith. No one would suppose that the many devoted priests of all schools of thought who belong to one or another of the degrees of Freemasonry are trying to propagate a rival religion to Christianity. None of them (except perhaps a few eccentric such as the late Canon Covey-Crump, who appears from his writings to have been some kind of gnostic) need be suspected of anything worse than having been led by a somewhat indiscriminating impulse of enthusiasm into joining a great organisation justly celebrated for its noble charitable activities, without examining in advance (if, indeed, masonic secrecy made any such examination possible) the precise meaning of the language and the rites to which he was committing himself. I can only record the impression which, as a complete outsider, I have received from Mr. Hannah's transcription of the rituals. Assuming that transcription to be correct (and this is an assumption which my own examination of the rituals, so far as it goes, confirms), I have been both amazed and shocked at the idea of a Christian, and above all of a Christian priest, taking part in some of the ceremonies which he describes.

When I have asked priests of my acquaintance who are freemasons how they justify their membership of the masonic fraternity, they have usually replied that it provides them with opportunities of pastoral contact which they could not otherwise achieve. Some have added that there are admittedly certain anti-Christian elements in Freemasonry, and that it is very important that Christians should be freemasons as well in order to prevent these from getting the upper hand. It has sometimes been suggested that there are influential laymen who, if they were forced to choose between the Craft and the Church, would choose the former and abandon the latter. Whether any of these reasons provide valid arguments for silence the reader must judge. But I should very much like an answer to my two questions, and they cannot be avoided simply by pointing to the unquestioned integrity and sincerity of many clerical freemasons. Trial by compurgation has long been extinct in English law. It is not a question of the probity of persons but of the rational compatibility of two systems of doctrine; and it is a regrettable but undeniable fact that perfectly honest people can be very confused in their thinking. Until the two questions to which I have drawn attention are answered frankly, and are not evaded by irrelevant references to personalities, I cannot help feeling that there will be many people like myself who, admitting with some astonishment that many devout Christians manage by some obscure mental process to be freemasons, will nevertheless continue to suspect that Freemasonry is logically incompatible with Christianity.

E. L. MASCALL.

He who will not reason is a bigot ; he who cannot is a fool ; and he who dares not is a slave.

Lord Byron, note on Childe Harold's Pilgrimage.

I STARTED to write this book in answer to the numerous critics of *Darkness Visible* who have alleged that I misunderstood the nature of Freemasonry, and in particular that I overlooked entirely the " Christian implicits " of the Craft and Royal Arch degrees, and practically ignored the higher degrees to which they prophetically lead, and which are alleged to be fully Christian. A few non-Masons also deplored the fact that I had made no attempt to give any historical background or to explain how Freemasonry came into existence at all.

This original purpose grew into a larger book than was first intended, and I have attempted to trace the relationship between Freemasonry and Christianity from the beginnings of the former to the present day. Although there are many books freely available to the non-Mason which deal with the exoteric history of the order from many points of view, I have nevertheless included a certain amount of history in this volume in order to trace the religious development of the Craft from the Catholicism of the middle ages through the Deism of the eighteenth century to the woolly sentimental syncretism of the twentieth. Only thus can a possible Christian interpretation today be assessed in its proper context and perspective. As the brief appendix devoted to the " higher degrees " in *Darkness Visible* was clearly inadequate in providing information for a balanced judgment, I have expanded it in the second part of this book, and reproduced the rituals of the alleged Christian degrees in full.

The whole issue of the Christianity of Freemasonry is befogged by the popular misuse of the word Christian. It has become confused with the ethical standards upheld by Christianity (in common with other reputable religions) to such an extent that any demonstration of kindness or decency is called a " thoroughly Christian act." Which of course in a sense it is, and this is certainly a compliment to the Christian religion whose high moral standards have survived as ideals even for those who have lapsed from the Christian faith. Yet it is an ironic fact that in England today the well-meaning agnostic and the kindly pagan who have no use for creeds and sacraments and who do not accept Christ as their saviour will still feel insulted if they are called " not Christian " because they feel that this term is a reflection on their morals or charity. As I have no wish to cause any offence through this confusion I must stress at the outset that wherever the word Christian or Christianity is used in this book it refers to faith in our Lord and Saviour Jesus Christ, the incarnate Second Person of the Holy Trinity, the faith once delivered to the saints and proclaimed by the Church, His mystical body. It means the faith of the New Testament, the creeds, and the Fathers of the Church. For when Masons talk about the Craft as " Christian in all but name " or even as " upholding the real principles of Christianity " they are using the word in a very loose sense. " Islam (or Buddhism) in all but name " would be equally applicable. Even in the realm of ethics they seem unable to distinguish between purely natural morality common to pagan beliefs and the supernatural grace that the Christian receives in baptism which is the foundation of Christian morality—but that is another story.

The objection has been urged by a theologian of distinction who was once a Mason that Freemasonry is such an unintellectual hotch-potch of pomposity and platitude that any intellectual approach or critique misses the mark completely. There is much in this point of view, and I do not wish to take it all too ponderously, and yet the very lack of intellectual content in Masonry is one of its potential dangers. This century despite its alleged scientific outlook has seen a remarkable growth of strange irrational sects and religious substitutes, Theosophy, Christian Science, British Israel, Spiritualism, and Jehovah's Witnesses. Sunday-paper astrology is popular, lucky mascots are booming, *episcopi vagantes* and charlatan faith-healers multiply. Many weird superstitions flourish. And their very irrationality is almost a source of strength to them, for they are too absurd and often too vaguely nebulous for reasoned criticism, and therefore they escape it. It is like exploring a country in an impenetrable fog, made up of a mist of vague occultism thickened by a persistent drizzle of sentimentality sometimes masquerading as Christian. (If the metaphor is confused, so is the subject). It would be unkind and grossly untrue to place Freemasonry directly under this cloud. But it is on the misty outer fringe of it.

Then there is the curious but not uncommon phenomenon of the man of brilliant intellect in one field of knowledge who loses his critical faculty altogether in another. There is the scientist or mathematician of world fame who is attracted for some emotional reason or other into the crude mysticism of a freak religion, and will accept evidence for its authority and authenticity that he would not consider for one moment in his own sphere of knowledge. This seems analogous to the rare cases of prominent clerical Freemasons with firsts in theology.

Although many Masons such as the Rev. J. Fort Newton and Sir John Cockburn have endeavoured to raise Freemasonry into the position of a super-religion, it must be admitted that it refrains from crude infallible dogmatism ; yet it has its affinities, not only with the ancient pagan and Gnostic mysteries which were similarly undogmatic but with many modern superstitions as well that are completely lacking in rationality.

" And if I am reminded of the large number of people who today run after...superstitions," writes Fr. Bede Frost in a singularly penetrating attack on some irrationalities of the age,[1] " I shall reply, What else do you expect when for half a century this professing Christian country has allowed its children to be brought up without any definite Christian teaching in its schools? For you may rest assured that what is called ' Bible teaching ' is more often than not anything but Christian." But whereas freak religions have a certain external nuisance-value to the Church, Freemasonry has an internal yet parasitic influence within it, weakening its distinctive witness to the supernatural Christian faith by its syncretistic universalism and natural religion.

Of course Masons scoff at this idea. " Take a thoroughly Rotarian gathering of men, dress them up in a spectrum of aprons and collars, let them express themselves in the recitation of their rather odd and pompous ritual, touch them for a good deal of their money for their exceedingly well-conducted charities, then march them out to the bar for sherry and into the hall for a good dinner with speeches and songs, and you've got something that might strike one as very childish, but not as an esoteric cult," a Mason once explained, and the picture is not inaccurate of many Lodges. Yet behind it all, and particularly in the Royal Arch and certainly in the Rose Croix, it remains true that this same " thoroughly Rotarian gathering of men " al-

1. *Some Modern Substitutes for Christianity* (Mowbrays, 1942), p. 97.

though not consciously indulging in a separate cult, find (perhaps quite subconsciously) a certain spiritual and mystical outlet in their " rather odd and pompous ritual " and are satisfying religious instincts in a way quite other than that ordained by God in His Holy Church. If the ritual is taken at all seriously, this is quite beyond dispute. If it is not taken seriously, there is serious trifling with holy things.

The anti-Mason is frequently criticized for condemning Masonry on the evidence of quotations from Masonic mystics and prophets who, it is said, are not representative and speak only for themselves. Ward, Wilmshurst, Fort Newton, and many others of their stamp provide inexhaustible ammunition, and have proved a real embarrassment to Christian members of the Craft. The fact that such books often run into edition after edition is even more embarrassing. The further fact that hardly a number of the *Freemasons' Magazine* or the *Freemasons' Chronicle* appears without some article or reference that places the mystical content of Masonry logically in rivalry with the Church appears to be ignored.

For instance, in the *Freemasons' Chronicle* for Jan. 2, 1954, there is an article from a Grand Chaplain containing the following :—" I love this institution because it is non-denominational, or rather supra-denominational, and would like to prophesy that Freemasonry will play a large part in the unification of the diverse elements in Protestantism. It has been argued at great length as to whether or not Freemasonry is a religion. I firmly believe that it is. The tests of any religion lie (1) in its belief in Almighty God and the obligation to serve Him ; (2) on the performance of duties to God and Man based on the divine law found in a divine revelation (the Bible) ; (3) *all religions comprehend a system of faith and worship. Freemasonry conforms to all of these,* and those who have met within its *sacred* precincts have experienced that inspiration which comes from being nearer to God. It may not be a complete religion since it does not attempt to minister to women and children, and because it is highly selective, *but it is nonetheless a religion.*" (Italics mine.)

This again may be an individual and unofficial opinion even though it comes from a Grand Chaplain who ought to know the mind of the Craft. The article, however, was so admired by the Brethren that the Editor of the *Freemasons' Chronicle* announced in the next issue that owing to widespread demand it was proposed to reprint it as a leaflet for Lodge officers to distribute to new initiates. The official attitude of minimizing or even denying the religious element in Freemasonry is therefore, in the face of this and of the considerable body of literature already mentioned, disingenuous. Clearly those who regard Masonry in a religious light are far more representative of the Craft than Grand Lodge or the Masonic bishops dare to admit.

In *Darkness Visible* I rested my case on the Masonic ritual itself, with a minimum of quotations from Masonic authors. In this present book, however, there must inevitably be some such citations, because I am setting out to disprove the validity of a Christian interpretation of the ritual ; hence those who have tried to prove it are clearly relevant to my case. For I maintain that if a Christian interpretation is even attempted it must inevitably lead to the Gnosticism of Wilmshurst or Waite, or to the vague sentimental caricature of historic Christianity presented by Fort Newton.

No book has ever been written, or in my opinion could be written, that explains the ritual in terms compatible with the full Christian faith. The argument always appears to run on these weary lines :—

" Freemasonry is capable of a perfectly orthodox interpretation. You mustn't judge it by individual mystics on the lunatic fringe who are not representative."

" Splendid. Could you give me some outline of that interpretation ? "

" I could of course, but my solemn obligation of secrecy prevents it."

" This oath, then, only applies to explaining Masonry in terms of orthodox Christianity. It doesn't in any way hamper the streams of books commended by Grand Lodge Officers which explain it in terms of an Egyptian mystery or a Gnostic cult. Did Wilmshurst or Sir John Cockburn never take this oath ? "

" Sorry, but I really must be going. We're not supposed to discuss these things with non-Masons, you know."

So the dilemma remains unresolved in the profound hush of dignified silence. Is the Church of England too mortally involved, too embarrassed, or too frightened to speak her mind ?

To: The Rev. W. Roy Foster, Vicar of St. Augustine's, Queen's Gate, London (and also to Miss Baucutt, the Vicarage Housekeeper), in sincere gratitude for great kindness, and for heroic patience displayed under fire of much nocturnal typing of the manuscript, this book is affectionately dedicated.

C O N T E N T S

PART I

He divided the brethren into four classes : the first consisted of those who took no active part in the concerns either of their lodge or of mankind, who devoted themselves exclusively to meditating on the mysteries of the order, and on the meaning of the Trinity ; to studying the three elements of sulphur, mercury, and salt, or the significance of the square and the other symbols of Solomon's Temple. These Peter could look up to ; they were the elders, including Bazdéiew himself ; still, he could not understand what pleasure they found in their studies, and did not feel in the least drawn towards the mystical side of freemasonry.

The second category, in which he ranked himself, was composed of adepts who, though waverers like himself, sought the right path ; and who, though they had not yet found it, did not despair of discovering it some day.

The third class, the majority, were those who saw nothing in the order beyond its external forms and ceremonies, and were satisfied with a strict observance of them without troubling themselves about their hidden meaning. Among these were Villarsky and the Worshipful Master himself.

The fourth and last were the men, at that time also very numerous, who, believing in nothing, and hoping for nothing, clung to the brotherhood simply for the sake of being intimate with rich people and getting some benefit out of the intimacy.

Leo Tolstoy, War and Peace (Book Six, Chap. VII).

I

EXIT CHRISTIANITY

They also are to be had accursed that presume to say, that every man shall be saved by the Law or Sect which he professeth, so that he be diligent to frame his life according to that Law, and the light of Nature. For holy Scripture doth set out unto us only the Name of Jesus Christ, whereby men must be saved.
              The Thirty-nine Articles (No. xviii).
Continue to listen to the voice of nature.
              Masonic Ritual, Ceremony of Raising to the Third Degree.

"THE might of the Father of Heaven with the wisdom of the glorious Son through the grace and goodness of the Holy Ghost, yet being three persons and one God be with us at our beginning, and give us grace so to govern us here in our living that we may come to His bliss that shall never have ending, Amen." So begin the ancient Masonic Constitutions, which continue in the first general Charge to instruct the Mason "That ye shall be true men to God and Holy Church, and you shall use no error nor heresy by your understanding ... "[1]

The Book of Constitutions with which the initiate into Freemasonry is presented today, however, has a sadly different preamble. The First Charge, " Concerning God and Religion," states " Let a man's religion or mode of worship be what it may, he is not excluded from the order, provided he believes in the glorious architect of heaven and earth, and practise the sacred duties of morality...they are taught to view the errors of mankind with compassion..." And later on, " we being only, as masons, of the universal religion above-mentioned."

Here, then, is the bald summary of the Masonic apostasy from Christ which I propose to deal with in this chapter. Although

1. There are over a hundred manuscripts of various dates which contain these Old Charges. They are listed in the Rev. Herbert Poole's *The Old Charges* (Masonic Record Ltd., 1924) and in *A Handlist of Masonic Documents* by Douglas Knoop and G. P. Jones (Manchester University Press, 1924), the latter book gives details as to where most of them may be found in reprints. Naturally the wording varies somewhat ; my quotation (with modernized spelling) is taken from *Grand Lodge No. 1 MS.*, 1583.

Masonic Bishops and Archdeacons may continue to maintain that the Craft is "profoundly Christian in all but name", and a "handmaid of the Church," it would seem that the partial concealment of the godly black apron of their office in the Church by a second apron of more lurid colours pertaining to the handmaid leads to a mental as well as sartorial concealment and confusion. For when the Grand Orient of France went one further and eliminated the Great Architect altogether from their formularies, Grand Lodge of England broke off fraternal relations with it. English Masons do not skate over the controversy by declaring that it may be still profoundly theistic in all but name. Ignoring the fact that a French Protestant minister was at that time Grand Master of the Orient,[1] they consider that by dropping the Name of God it has become atheist, and that no believer in the deity can attend a Lodge where His Name is not honoured. But to extend this logic to the Masonic apostasy in England, to argue similarly that no believer in Christ could attend a Lodge where His Name is excluded and not honoured would be far too embarrassing.[2] It is one of those many awkwardnesses that must be met with dignified silence.

But let us return to history, and try to see how it all came about.

The origins of Freemasonry are still wrapped in some mystery, due to the shortage of documentary evidence. The fantasiast has stepped in where the historian fears to tread, and the rank and file of the Brethren are still inclined to be over-credulous concerning the immemorial antiquity of the Craft. In this century, however, the "authentic" school is steadily gaining ground at the expense of the myth and legend, and although a *magnum opus* to bring Gould's history up to date still awaits to be written, a great deal of material towards it has been published and is readily available, and there are several excellent books of

---

1. The Rev. F. Desmons. The rupture occurred in 1877.
2. French Masons, with far greater clarity of logic, are not backward in pressing this point, which they consider sheer hypocrisy. See *Le Symbolisme* (Juin-Juillet, 1953) in which, ironically, *Darkness Visible* received an extremely favourable review (*L'Ombre qui Luit*, by Marius Lepage). The following article in the same issue, *À propos de la Bible*, continues in the same strain.

Masonic history.[1]

There are of course strong differences of opinion and interpretation in the field, but as far as possible I shall try to cite only such facts as are reasonably certain in tracing the religious development of Masonry from the middle ages to the present day.

The medieval stonemason laboured under conditions very different from those of other crafts. The weaver, the leatherworker, the silversmith or the potter could work at home, living and dying in the same community in which he was born. Their trade gilds, therefore, were more compact, stationary, and easily organized. But clearly a vast cathedral or castle requiring a very considerable skilled labour force could not be built by such stonemasons only as happened to live in the immediate district. They had to be a mobile profession, travelling from job to job. Hence in the middle ages there is less evidence than in other crafts of local stonemason's gilds—except in larger centres such as London itself, where there was presumably always enough building or repair work to keep a considerable number of local masons busy all their lives. The London Masons' Company indeed was an extremely important body which was to play a leading role in the history of the development of speculative Freemasonry.

The centre of activity was the Lodge—and the term is found in this connection as early as 1278. This was a temporary hut or shed put up near the site of the new building which served primarily as workshop, storehouse for tools, the Master's office, and so on. But it seems also to have served as a social centre. Masons living away from home would eat and possibly even sleep there ; meetings and discussions took place, and a certain fraternal intimacy and fellowship would be established not unlike the atmosphere among the crew on board a ship today, or in other circumstances where men find themselves thrown

1. For a general survey of the field the following books can be recommended. D. Knoop and G. P. Jones, *An Introduction to Freemasonry* (1937) and *A Short History of Freemasonry to 1730* (1940) Manchester University Press. Lionel Vibert, *Freemasonry Before the Existence of Grand Lodge*. G. W. Daynes, *The Birth and Growth of the Grand Lodge of England, 1717–1926*. Masonic Record Ltd., 1926. Bernard E. Jones, *The Freemasons' Guide and Compendium*, Harraps, 1950. Fred L. Pick and G. Norman Knight, *The Pocket History of Freemasonry*, Frederick Muller, 1953. For the European background, Eugen Lennhoff, *The Freemasons* (translated from the German) Methuen, 1934.

together and working together away from their homes and families for prolonged periods. It has even been suggested by some that these conditions would provide an auspicious breeding ground for the esoteric elements which were later to invade the Craft.

There is little evidence of any unity or central organization knitting together these local and transient lodges. Yet the peripatetic nature of the trade made for some degree of uniformity of custom, and the rules, customs, and traditions of the stonemasons are preserved for us in the series of Constitutions or Old Charges to which reference has already been made. These documents are of supreme importance to the Masonic historian, for they are his chief source of information.

There are numerous versions, regional groups, and " families " of these Charges, as might be expected, but the normal pattern of them opens with an invocation to the Holy Trinity, and contains a history of the building trade from the beginning of time. A great deal of legendary as well as Biblical stories are introduced ; the Tower of Babel is frequently mentioned, and of course King Solomon's Temple, but it is significant that the legend of the death and raising of Hiram the architect now attached to the third degree in the Masonic ritual is nowhere to be found in any of these Charges.[1] Nor, indeed, is Solomon's Temple given any special prominence at all.

Then follows the Constitutions proper, a series of rules and moral precepts which are to be binding on the mason, including an injunction to love God and the Church, sundry exhortations to keep the Charges, and a brief closing prayer.

There is hardly a trace of evidence here, or anywhere else, that the early stonemason had any esoteric interests or teaching as such, or that he attached any moral significance or spiritual symbolism to his trade or working tools in any way. Modern Freemasons are so accustomed to project backwards into time their " peculiar system of morality, veiled in allegory, and illustrated by symbols " based on the building trade that this legend is indeed a long time a-dying. And where, in these early Constitutions, there were obligations of secrecy, there is prac-

---

1. A very similar legend attached to Noah, however, with the same necromantic significance of trying to obtain a secret from a dead body, is found later in the *Graham MS*, 1726, which significantly includes reference to the Mason Word.

tically no reason to suppose, before the introduction of the Mason Word, that anything other than trade secrets and the confidences of their own business affairs were involved. The mason was enjoined to be a good Christian and loyal Churchman, in which he probably succeeded neither better nor worse than the members of any other worthy profession.

It seems likely, however, that these Charges did provide the germ of the Masonic ritual. They were probably read out to the assembled Brethren, including the traditional history, when a newcomer or apprentice was admitted to the Lodge and took his obligation, thus forming a rudimentary initiation rite not dissimilar to those still to be found in the City Livery Companies. Other crafts had somewhat similar ceremonies and customs.

The second factor which contributed to the development of Masonic ritual was the Mason Word. No one has yet produced a plausible theory of its origins, original meaning, or etymological derivation, and possibly no one ever will, so obscure is its early history. It has become hopelessly corrupted through centuries of verbal transmission. It has emerged in print in fairly recent times as Mahabyn, Maughbin, Matchpin, Mahabone, Macbenach, all of which are very recognizable ancestors of the Word as given in the Lodge today. It is of course a great deal older than its present context of the Hiramic legend, and the meaning which is now given to it referring to the death of the builder is probably quite arbitrary. All that, however, doesn't matter in the least. Even regarded as sheer mumbo-jumbo, this Word plays an extremely important part in Masonic history and ritual.

We have seen that Masonry differed from other crafts and professions in that craftsmen tended to be peripatetic rather than static. In, say, a clothweavers' gild in the average town every member of it would be known personally, and there would be no need for secret means of mutual recognition or identification. But a man seeking employment from afar in the building of a castle or cathedral might be quite unknown to the Master Mason or to any of the Brethren, and would have no other way, apart from his own skill if given a trial, of proving himself a properly qualified stonemason. The Mason Word, then, imparted only under oath of secrecy to the skilful and initiated craftsman, seems to have fulfilled some of the functions of the Trade Union card today. But it has been fairly well established that the Mason Word originated in Scotland, where it was established at least as early as 1550, and spread to England not before the seventeenth century.[1]

Certain ceremonies became attached to the imparting of the Word. There were certain test questions and answers connected with it which may have given rise to the Masonic catechisms or lectures of later years. It was only to be imparted in a certain bodily position of the giver and receiver known as the Five Points of Fellowship. Early versions of these vary somewhat in detail and order, but substantially they were the same as found in the Lodge today—hand to hand, foot to foot, knee to knee, breast to breast, and hand over back. In course of time, then, this Word with its accompanying forms and ceremonies became more than a mere means of recognition ; it was embodied in the rudiments of the ritual, where later an allegorical and even occult significance was ascribed to it. We begin to see the genesis of the speculative element of modern Freemasonry evolving from the usages and customs of the operative stonemason, though it remained on a Christian basis at least until 1723.

No very clear account has ever yet been given as to how, why, or exactly when operative stonemasons' lodges became purely speculative, and finally, except in the sphere of allegory and symbolism, divorced altogether from that trade. It is certain that gentlemen who had no connection with operative masonry became " accepted " members of Lodges. The earliest known instance is that of John Boswell, laird of Auchinlech, who in 1600 was a member of the Lodge of Edinburgh. Whether from motives of patronage, antiquarian or architectural interest, love of convivial company or sheer curiosity it is hard to say, but the fashion continued and grew. In Aberdeen the " acceptance " was in the majority by 1670, when of the forty-nine members of the Lodge only ten were operative masons.[2]

1. See *The Scottish Mason and the Mason Word,* by Douglas Knoop and G. P. Jones, (Manchester University Press, 1939). Exactly how or when the use of the Word spread southwards is not adequately explained. Few as the known facts are, no single theory altogether fits them.

2. *A Short History of Freemasonry to* 1730, by Knoop and Jones, p. 65. The facts are drawn from original Lodge records which date from that year.

In seventeenth-century England the "gentlemen Masons" tended to gather in separate Lodges of their own apart from the operatives, and this fact is a highly significant link in the chain between medieval Masonry and the Grand Lodge era of the eighteenth century and onwards. For in all probability it was in these Lodges of the Acceptance, free from all practical considerations connected with the building trade, that the speculative elements and particularly the ritual were developed.

At this point other theories of the origins of Freemasonry should perhaps be mentioned, one of which may probably have a substratum of truth at least as a contributory influence. We may dismiss out of hand the lunatic fringe of fantasiasts who profess to trace a direct historical continuity between the Craft today and King Solomon, or the Druids, the mysteries of ancient Egypt, of Eleusis, of Dionysius, or any other ancient system. If modern Masons like Sir John Cockburn have claimed that Freemasonry is the steward and guardian of the ancient mysteries of which it is the legitimate heir, all that can be conceded to them is that there are indeed striking parallels and resemblances even in the actual signs and symbols ;[1] symbolism, however, is an exceedingly vague subject on which to be dogmatic and precise, and as ancient mysteries and religions had many points in common even where no common ancestor can be traced, it is hardly remarkable that the Masonic mysteries today should also show similarities to them.

We may also dismiss, for want of evidence, but with a little more respect, the discarded historical hypotheses of Dionysian Artificers, the Roman *Collegia* or the Comacine Masons as forming the genesis of the Craft. Nor have advocates of the German *Steinmetzen* or the French *Compagnonage* substantiated their case. The Knights Templar transmission theory is intriguing, but rests upon supposition, legend, and a wholly spurious charter still preserved as an oddity in Mark Masons' Hall. No theory which postulates an arcane or esoteric tradition preserved by stonemasons through Saxon, Norman, or medieval history can be supported by any evidence which a critical historian could take seriously, though popular superstitions to the contrary die very hard.

1. See *Freemasonry and the Ancient Gods*, by J. S. M. Ward (1921).

We can see a little clearer, however (though the fog still remains thick), in considering the influence of Rosicrucianism.[1] The theory has been pushed to quite ridiculous extremes ; the Rev. F. de P. Castells even talks of " the plain, elementary fact that ' Freemasons ' is only another name for *Rosicrucians*," and that " Rosicrucians, that is, Christian Kabbalists...or as we should call them now, Speculative Freemasons...worked in England under the shelter of the Masons' Guilds."[2] This, of course is fantastic over-statement.

With the publication of *Fama Fraternitatis*, *Confessio Fraternitatis*, and the *Chemical Nuptials* in the early seventeenth century, Rosicrucianism enjoyed a certain revival in Germany which spread to England. Rosicrucianism was a form of " Christian " theosophy which derived to some extent from the Jewish Kabbala ; its mythical hero and founder was Christian Rosenkreutz or Rosy-Cross, and while it was indirectly interested—or some of its adepts were—in alchemy and in the elixir of life, it was in general more concerned at this time with symbolic alchemy, spiritual immortality and even reincarnation.

Whether or no Rosicrucianism was really an organized secret society or merely a general school of philosophy, it enjoyed a certain vogue in England just at the time when gentlemen, some of them of a philosophical turn of mind, were beginning to permeate the Masonic Lodges. There is no evidence whatsoever that either Robert Fludd or Thomas Vaughan, the most prominent of English Rosicrucians, had any connection with Freemasonry, but it is beyond dispute that Elias Ashmole, who if not actually a Rosicrucian, took a deeply learned interest in it, was initiated in the Lodge at Warrington in 1646. Secret societies were very much the fashion, even if only dabbled in and although the point has been strongly contested[3] it seems

1. See A. E. Waite's *The Brotherhood of the Rosy Cross* (Rider & Son, 1924) and *The Secret Tradition of Freemasonry* (1937) for well-documented accounts of Rosicrucianism and its alleged influence on Freemasonry.

2. *Our Ancient Brethren the Orignators of Freemasonry* (A. Lewis, 1932) pp. 96 and 281-2. The Proceedings of the Metropolitan Chapter of the Masonic *Societas Rosicruciana in Anglia*, particularly from Kenneth D. Mackenzie and Robert Wentworth Little, abound in absurd exaggerations and fabrications of this kind.

3. e.g. by Lionel Vibert, *The Early Freemasonry of England and Scotland*, in Vol. XXI of *Ars Quatuor Coronatorum*.

likely if not probable (I hesitate to put it more strongly with the shortage of documentary evidence), particularly in view of certain theosophical elements which emerged in the Masonic ritual, that Elias Ashmole was not the only accepted Mason of that period who was interested in Rosicrucianism, and that the Craft was to some extent influenced thereby.

The well-known lines from Adamson's *The Muses Threnodie* (1638) are quoted by almost every Masonic historian to prove something or other, so I may as well quote them too:—

" For what we do presage is not in grosse,
For we be brethren of the Rosie Crosse ;
We have the *Mason word* and second sight,
Things for to come we can foretell aright."

What exactly this means, and whether the " Rosie Crosse " refers to a specific Rosicrucian society, to the second degree of the Royal Order of Scotland, or to some other Rose Croix grade in Masonry, or to Craft Masonry in general, has never been established. But it appears to suggest some connection between Rosicrucian symbolism and occultism with the Mason Word, and hence with Masonry. Adamson, it has been pointed out, may have been an " accepted " member of the Lodge of Scone and Perth, No. 3.

It is even possible (but I think unlikely from the many dissimilarities) that the Hiramic legend was based on the story of the tomb of Christian Rosenkreutz as told in the *Fama Fraternitatis*. The discovery of the Vault in the Royal Arch, however, resembles the Rosicrucian legend more nearly, but in both these cases the Christian element is wanting in Masonry, leaving only the Gnosticism based on legends in a Jewish context. The nature of the connection between Rosicrucianism and the Rose Croix of Heredom degree will be discussed in its appropriate chapter.

To return to history on surer grounds ; in 1717 the " acceptance " at least in London had outnumbered, dominated, and largely dispossessed the operative element in the Lodges, and from now on we can drop the term " acceptance " and refer simply to Freemasons.[1]

1. Strict Emulation workings, which claim to be the oldest and the norm of Masonic ritual, to this day include an anachronistic reference to operative elements. In the Explanation of the Working Tools, it says " But as we are not *all* operative Masons, but rather free and accepted or speculative, we apply these tools to our morals." Some workings and revisions remove the anachronism by omitting the word " all ".

The year 1717 marks the birthday of modern Freemasonry. As we have seen, it was not something new invented out of nothing by the two clergymen, Dr. James Anderson, a Presbyterian minister, and Dr. John Theophilus Desaguliers, of French Hugenot family but who was in Anglican orders, or by any of the early associates of these leading figures. But at this period, when four speculative London Lodges came together and formed the first Grand Lodge, the movement was organized, profoundly modified,[1] and given fresh Constitutions. Other Lodges joined, new ones were formed, and Freemasonry spread and prospered.

It is by following the successive editions of the Constitutions that we may trace the religious development of Masonry. According to the Cooke MS. (ca. 1410) the operative Mason was informed that " hit behoveth hym fyrst princypally to (love) god and holy chyrche & alle halowis." In Elizabethan times the reference to the saints was dropped, and the first statement was expanded in the form quoted at the opening of this chapter, in conformity with post-Reformation Anglican orthodoxy. The first edition of Anderson's Constitutions (1723), however, in conformity with the tolerant spirit of the age of reason, influenced by the prevailing Deism and natural (as opposed to revealed) religion, eliminated almost all traces of Christianity from a previously Christian fraternity. The First Charge, " Concerning God and Religion," read as follows:—"A *Mason* is oblig'd by his Tenure, to obey the Moral Law ; and if he rightly understands the Art, he will never be a stupid Atheist nor an irreligious Libertine. But though in ancient Times Masons were charged in every Country to be of the Religion of that Country

1. Towards the end of the nineteenth century a curious theory was put forward for the first time that the old operatives, incensed at being swamped out by the speculatives, withdrew themselves and maintained a continuous and separate organization, preserving an ancient ritual, side by side with Grand Lodge up to the present day. A certain Clement E. Stretton professed to have these rituals, and endeavoured to revive the cult. The rituals which he produced, however, have not the slightest internal evidence of antiquity, nor is there a scrap of documentary evidence to substantiate his claims. The Channel Row (Westminster) Assemblage of Operative Masons, however, continues to meet and work these rituals in a much-edited form. For a sympathetic account of their claims (which are ignored by most serious historians as fantasy) see J. S. M. Ward's *Freemasonry and the Ancient Gods*, pp. 70–4, and a series of articles running through 1951 and 1952 by Miss M. C. Debenham in the co-Masonic journal *The Speculative Mason*.

or Nation, whatever it was, yet 'tis now thought more expedient only to oblige them to that Religion in which all Men agree, leaving their particular opinions to themselves ; that is, to be *good Men and true*, or Men of Honour and Honesty, by whatsoever Denominations or Persuasions they may be distinguished..."

The phrase " 'tis now thought more expedient " seems to indicate that a deliberate change was being consciously effected in the religious nature of the Craft, involving what no less an authority than the late J. Heron Lepper called " the abandonment of what was undoubtedly an Ancient Landmark."[1] The Rev. W. W. Covey-Crump, however, late Canon of Ely Cathedral and a considerable Masonic scholar, declared that " the intention of those who introduced the change in 1722 was not to alter the essentials of Masonry, but rather to modernize the expression of them...They were legislating to strengthen the philosophic (I am inclined to say ' Kabalistic ') outlook of a new party which had recently taken up an almost moribund Craft Guild ; and, by extending its aims and influence, was giving it a fresh lease of life among men of much higher social position."

Bro. Ivor Grantham contends that the " Religion in which all Men agree " is the fundamental faith of those who accept all that is implied in the conception of the fatherhood of God and the brotherhood of man "[2]...a sentiment not striking in its originality which is echoed *passim* in a great deal of Masonic literature today.

The historical preamble to these same Constitutions was re-written. The Augustan Age in its classical elegance looked down with condescension on the " native wood-notes wild " of

1. The phrase ' ancient landmark ' has a technical significance in Freemasonry, referring to fixed and unalterable principles of the Craft which must not be tampered with. Every Master on attaining the Chair of a Lodge vows to uphold and maintain them, and Grand Lodge itself is precluded by the Constitutions from even discussing their alteration. The loop-hole is, of course, that no one knows precisely what the Ancient Landmarks are. There have been many lists, but no official definition.
2. These three quotations are from *Ars Quatuor Coronatorum*, Vol. LVI Part 1. Article and discussion on *Freemasonry and the Idea of Natural Religion*, p. 38. The article was by Knoop and Jones, read by the former, as Mr. P. G. Jones is not a Freemason. See also *The Religion of Early Freemasonry* (Chicago University Press, 1939) by C. H. Lyttle, which takes the same line.

its predecessors, and rather despised all things medieval. In this spirit Dr. Anderson had a contempt for the ancient ' Gothic ' constitutions, and although his history is no more historical or less legendary than those which preceded it, it is written in an attempted approximation to Johnsonian English. In this history there is one reference only to Our Lord, and that in brackets. After a reference to the Emperor Augustus follows " in whose Reign was born God's Messiah, the great Architect of the Church. " That is all. After 1815 the historical preamble, which had been extensively revised, was dropped from the Constitutions, and the apostasy as far as these official formularies are concerned was complete. On the other hand, the conventional Christian endings to certain of the prayers in the ritual appear to have lingered on until the Union of 1813, and occasionally to the present day in Ireland.

In 1738 there was a further revision of the Constitutions, and the passage quoted was re-drafted to read : " In ancient Times the Christian Masons were charged to comply with the Christian usages of each Country where they travell'd : or work'd. But Masonry being found in all Nations even of divers Religions, they are now generally charged to adhere to that Religion in which all men agree (leaving each brother to his own particular Opinion) that is, to be good men and true, men of Honour and Honesty, by whatever Names, Religions, or Perswasions [sic] they may be distinguished." The further revision of 1756, however, harked back to the earlier statement that in ancient times Masons were enjoined to be of the religion of any country in which they might happen to reside, whether Christian or not.

During the eighteenth century another Masonic body arose in opposition, or at least in rivalry, to the new Grand Lodge. The history of this period is intricate and obscure and it need not concern us in detail ; this body, however, became known as the " Ancients ", or Atholl Masons (due to the long tenure of the Grand Mastership by the Dukes of Atholl), and the original Grand Lodge (which they accused of innovations) as the " Moderns. " It used to be thought that the Ancients were actually a schism or break-away from the parent body, but more recently the view has gained ground that, although certain individual Lodges and individual Masons may have changed allegiance from one to the other, the Ancients grew up quite independently, enjoying strong support from Ireland, incorporating Lodges that had never come within the orbit of the Grand Lodge of London. To complicate things still further, there seems to have been a third body, not very closely defined, whom J. Heron Lepper calls " Traditioners, " who were nominally in obedience to the Moderns, but strongly in sympathy with the Ancients.[1]

Bitterness, strife, and rivalry increased between the two bodies. Bernard E. Jones tabulates the innovations with which the Moderns were charged ;[2] many of these were concerned solely with matters of ritual, the office of Deacon, the preparation of Candidates, and so on. An important difference was the position of the higher degrees which were coming into favour, the Royal Arch in particular. The Moderns tended to set their face against them. From the religious point of view, however, it appears that the Ancients objected to the de-Christianizing policy of the Moderns, both in the Constitutions and in the ritual. They accused the Moderns of omitting prayers altogether (which was probably unfounded) and of neglecting Saints' Days, particularly the feasts of St. John the Baptist and St. John the Evangelist, the two Patrons of Freemasonry.

As regards ritual details, Ancient and Modern, the historian is very much in the dark, for most of our information comes from spurious disclosures which may or may not be accurate.[3] The semi-authentic printed ritual published as an aide-memoire to the Masons themselves did not begin to appear until well on in the nineteenth century.

1. Yet another body was the short-lived " Grand Lodge of England South of the River Trent ", which lasted from 1779–1889. This was founded on a personal quarrel, and had little importance. There is also some rather scrappy evidence for the existence of an independent Grand Lodge of York, possibly founded some years before 1717, and continuing until the close of the eighteenth century.
2. *Freemasons' Guide and Compendium*, pp. 201–2. This book gives the clearest account of the whole complicated dispute that I have yet come across.
3. The most important of these is Prichard's *Masonry Dissected* (1730). From internal evidence, and from the consternation which it caused Grand Lodge, as shown in the minutes, most Masonic historians to-day regard it as substantially reflecting the ritual of its time, and cite it as evidence. There is still a slight coyness in admitting this too publicly, and when the Leicester Lodge of Research reproduced it in facsimile, the more secret portions were significantly omitted! This in itself seems an admission.

The Constitutions of the Ancients, however, are informative, and fully substantiate the fact that Christianity though perhaps watered down, was still maintained. Bearing the exotic title of *Ahiman Rezon : or, A Help to a Brother*,[1] these Constitutions are the work of an indefatigable Irishman Laurence Dermott, for many years Grand Secretary to the Ancients. Dermott borrows plentifully from Anderson where it suits him to do so, and yet, from the second edition onwards, the note of rivalry and even hostility creeps in. The ponderous fatuity of Dr. Anderson's excursions into history are deliciously satirized in a foreword ; the claim that Adam was a Freemason, for instance, must clearly be improved upon, so Dermott tells us that " having tried my Pen...I began to flourish away in a most admirable Manner, and in a few Days wrote the first Volume of the History of Freemasonry, wherein was a full Account of the Transactions of the first Grand Lodge, particularly the excluding of the unruly members, as related by Mr. *Milton*. " But alas ! this history never saw the light of day, for a neighbour's puppy broke in and ate most of the work which he had expected " would outlast the teeth of time. " The Constitutions, therefore, with many apologies, were not to be prefaced by a history.

Dermott in a more serious vein declares later, " A Mason is obliged by his Tenure to believe firmly in the true Worship of the eternal God, as well as in all those sacred Records which the Dignitaries and Fathers of the Church have compiled and published for the Use of all good Men ; So that no one who rightly understands the Art, can possibly tread in the irreligious paths of the unhappy Libertine, or be induced to follow the arrogant Professors of Atheism or Deism..." He allows for Jews in spite of this, yet apparently avoided the charge of indifferentism by drawing a definite line between Jewish and Christian Lodges. Certainly prayers are provided for each ; the Christian prayer for the initiate concludes " Endue him with a Competency of thy divine Wisdom, that he may, with the Secrets of Freemasonry be able to unfold the Mysteries of Godliness and Christianity. This we most humbly beg, in the Name, and for the sake of Jesus Christ our Lord and Saviour.

1. First Edition, 1756. My own copy, from which I quote, is the fourth edition, printed in Dublin, 1780.

Amen. " The Irish Constitutions, which contain a certain amount of ritual matter, continue to this day to include a Christian prayer for permissive use in the third degree ceremonies.

By the end of the eighteenth century a reconciliation was in the air. Both sides seem to have tired of the long quarrel with its mutual recriminations and bickerings, and in 1813 amidst scenes of general relief and rejoicings the two Grand Lodges, with the Duke of Kent as Grand Master of the Ancients and his brother the Duke of Sussex of the Moderns met together in a Lodge of Reconciliation. Certain Articles of Union, drawn up by a previous Lodge of Promulgation,[1] were read and approved, and the United Grand Lodge of England came into being with the Duke of Sussex as its first Grand Master.

There was compromise on both sides. The Moderns gave way on the Royal Arch, which was accepted by them in a face-saving expedient which defined it as not a separate degree, but as the completion and fulfilment of the third. The Ancients gave way on the other " higher degrees, " which were jettisoned. Some carried on independently and for a while precariously ; many eventually found a home under the hospitable roof of Mark Masons' Hall. But it was declared definitely in Article 11 that " pure Ancient Masonry consists of three degrees, and no more : viz. those of the Entered Apprentice, the Fellow Craft, and the Master Mason, including the Supreme Order of the Holy Royal Arch."[2] The second part of the same Article, however, not being in the present book of Constitutions, is less well known. It runs:— " But this article is not intended to prevent any Lodge or Chapter from holding a Meeting in any of the Degrees of the Orders of Chivalry, according to the Constitutions of the said Orders." This seems to allow a loophole for the Knights Templar. Grand Lodge and Grand Chapter, however, make no claims of jurisdiction over these Orders, and they are given in this article no more than a quasi-recognition. A few Lodges

1. These Articles of Union may be found in the posthumous editions (fourteenth and after) of Preston's *Illustrations of Masonry*, which was edited and brought up to date by Dr. Oliver: also in *The Craft and the Royal Arch*, by W. H. Topley: and in any Masonic Encyclopædia.

2. The Royal Arch is not actually controlled by Grand Lodge but by Grand Chapter. For an account of the close relationship between these bodies, see note p. 74.

and Chapters may have continued for a while to work Templar degrees, but these Orders soon withdrew into jurisdictions of their own, and the clause became a dead letter.

There was compromise all round. Instead of the Festivals of the two Sts. John to which the Ancients were devoted there was substituted St. George's Day, a good patriotic observance having no particular connection either with Freemasonry or (in practice) with religion.[1] The Moderns sacrificed several ritual and ceremonial points which were deemed innovations, and in general the ritual of the Ancients was adopted. Each body had its own version of the Mason Word, and both of them were used. But the Ancients sacrificed their Christianity. Looking at English Masonry as a whole. it may be said that 1813 rather than 1717 or 1723 was really the date on which the final apostasy became complete. The Grand Master, the Duke of Sussex, was both an autocrat and a convinced Deist, and the spirit of Anderson and his associates triumphed. Non-Christian Universalism and natural religion were established. Only such prayers were offered to the Great Architect as could not prove a stumbling-block to the Jew nor foolishness to the Greeks by being offered in Christ's name. The first of the Charges in the new Constitutions, already quoted, excluded only the stupid atheist and irreligious libertine from that body which has since been described as " more than a Church...not *a* religion but is Religion, a worship in which all good men may unite that each may share the faith of all." [2] Such is the position today.

---

1. The original Articles of Union, it is true, stipulated that the Annual Festival should take place on or soon after the feast of St. John the Evangelist, but this was very soon altered. The Constitution now reads " The Wednesday next following St. George's Day."
2. The Rev. J. Fort Newton, *The Builders* (7th edition, 1949) p. 180.

II

THE GROWTH OF UNIVERSALISM

" It is absolutely useless for a Frenchman to try to understand English Masonry unless he realizes that the Crown, the Anglican Church, and the United Grand Lodge of England are one God in three persons."

Marius Lepage, in Le Symbolisme, Oct. 1953.

THE few small shreds of specific Christian symbolism which survived the Union of 1813, more by accident than by design and divorced from any Christian context, in the ritual set forth by the Lodge of Reconciliation will be considered in the following chapter. In the meantime, let us trace the religious development of Freemasonry from the Grand Lodge era to the present day as reflected by contemporary literature apart from the constitutions, charges, and ritual. What sort of men were they, and what part did Masonry play in their lives ?

Although in the seventeenth century there was probably some influx among the Acceptance of gentlemen philosophers interested in Rosicrucianism and occultism, it would be hazardous indeed to maintain that this element dominated the Craft, even though they probably influenced it. The membership in general seems to have been largely artisan, with still a sprinkling of operative masons. Very little is known of Masonic activity in the Lodge in the seventeenth century, but the establishment of Grand Lodge raised both the prestige of Freemasonry and the social status of its membership in the eighteenth. Membership increased noticeably when in 1721 the Duke of Montague became the first noble Grand Master, and this lesson has been thoroughly taken to heart by the Craft. It is now in the Constitutions that the Grand Master must be of the nobility, and Royalty when willing is welcomed with even more profound gratification. The Ancients, not to be outdone, cast about feverishly for a nobleman before they found one in the Earl of Blessington in 1756. And incidentally in Ireland the present Grand Master, Raymond F. Brooke, is the first untitled person to occupy the throne since its foundation in 1725, but this may be in deference to republican Eire. Snobbery is a very general human failing not altogether absent even in Freemasonry.[1]

Of the four Lodges which came together to form the first Grand Lodge, three seem to have been mainly artisan, while the fourth, the *Rummer and Grapes* (named, as was the early custom, after the tavern in which it met) had as its Master the Duke of Richmond, and among its members such notabilities as Payne and Desaguliers (both of whom became Grand Masters) and Anderson. As membership increased and fresh Lodges were warranted the proportion of gentlemen (I use the word for convenience in the sense which the eighteenth century applied to it) rose ; Freemasonry enjoyed a vogue in the fashionable world when clubs were becoming popular, and the secrecy and conviviality of the Craft made a wider appeal in that latitudinarian and unspiritual age than its moral or arcane teachings. Contemporary Lodge minutes and accounts, as well as many pamphlets and articles in attack and in defence which appeared at this time, certainly suggest this.[2] The rituals, as far as one can tell, were briefer than today, and consisted largely of rehearsals of the lectures or catechisms. At times initiates would be pushed through the three degrees in the same evening and the actual ceremonies or " makings " had not yet acquired the prosy platitudinous moralizings that accrued in the following century, when Masonry became thoroughly bourgeois in outlook. The banquets with their multitudinous and deeply-drunk toastings and boisterous Masonic songs were drawn out,[3] William Hogarth's celebrated picture " Night, " which shows the inebriated Master of a Lodge with apron and jewel, drenched with the contents of a chamber-pot emptied over him from an upstairs window, being escorted from a tavern which has been identified as the *Rummer and Grapes* by his Tyler with sword and key, has been

1. It is usually a by-law of Naval and Military Lodges that no sailor below the rank of Petty Officer, or no soldier below the rank of Sergeant, is eligible for initiation in this universal Brotherhood.

2. Originals of these eighteenth-century pamphlets are scarce and treasured collectors' pieces, but most have been reprinted or reproduced in the transactions of the various Research Lodges (see *A Handlist of Masonic Documents* cited p. 17 which gives details). Two of the exposures, *Three Distinct Knocks* and *Jachin and Boaz* are still available in cheap modern editions (William Reeves Ltd.)

3. See article *An Apollinaric Summons* in *Ars Quatuor Coronatorum*, XXV, p. 31.

denounced as almost treacherous anti-Masonry. This, however, is to judge the eighteenth century by the standards of the twentieth. Certainly Hogarth was himself a Freemason, but he satirized his Brethren with no more severity than he satirized other sections of society. I think the eighteenth century would no more have called Hogarth anti-Masonic than we would call *Punch* anti-clerical today for printing occasional jokes about pale curates. It was a rougher age, and satire was accordingly more crude.

There is little evidence, indeed, to suggest that the spiritual side of Freemasonry was taken very seriously, but on the other hand there is no reason to think that in their social junketings they were either better or worse than the spirit of the age. The interest taken in Masonic charities was far less intense than today, and indeed even proportionately they were on a smaller scale, but here they were somewhat in advance of an unhumanitarian century. Freemasonry aroused considerable publicity, and was attacked and exposed in a veritable spate of pamphlets. Some merely pandered to curiosity, like Samuel Prichard's celebrated *Masonry Dissected* in 1730, but it seems likely that they were also used as *aides-mémoire* by Masons themselves. Others satirized, poking fun at the Masonic apron (always good for a laugh), ceremonies, public processions, and absurd claims to historical grandeur and antiquity. Some, like Prof. Robison at the close of the century in *Proofs of a Conspiracy* attacked Masonry as the hidden hand of revolution and conspiracy, and although he concentrated on Continental Lodges and secret societies, English Masonry was besmirched by it. Some brought charges of licentiousness and profanity. Some merely attacked.

The fact that there were fewer attacks on Masonry from the religious point of view corroborates the impression that the social and convivial aspects of Masonry predominated. But in these early days of the Grand Lodge era, the Lodge was not as popular with the higher clergy as it is today,[1] and in any case Hanoverian clerics tended to be latitudinarian and even worldly. As early as 1726 the anonymous author of *The Free-*

1. The first Freemason to be Archbishop of Canterbury appears to have been Dr. Howley, from 1828–48, a latitudinarian who opposed the Oxford Movement. The second, Dr. Geoffrey Fisher.

Masons Accusation and Defence[1] wrote :—" But, say you, there are Men of Quality, Dignitaries of the Church, and many others of Consideration, *Free Masons*. To which I answer, that there is no Act of Parliament yet in force to oblige every Man of Quality to be a Man of Sense...I should be very sorry to hear that any Clergyman whatever should so far degrade his sacred Function as to contaminate it with the wretched Fooleries of *Baccanalian* Riots. I hope the *Apron*, which is one of the Symbols of your Order, was never put on by any Man on whom the Bishop had laid his Hands, and endued the Robe of Righteousness. If any Person has so done, it has consequently made his Ordination of none Effect ; and were I a Prelate in Power, I would severely punish such Wretches who should put over or under that sacred Habit, the Trappings of the Devil ..."

Yet even in the early eighteenth century there were occasional Masons who made pretentious religious claims for the Craft, and therefore opponents who stigmatized it as a Gnostic mystery-cult. Among the former was Edward Oakley, Provincial Senior Grand Warden in Carmarthen, who in 1728 addressed his Brethren in the following terms. After referring to Masonry as a " sacred mystery " he said :—" Inasmuch as it hath pleased the Almighty One, Eternal, Unalterable God, to send out his Light, and his Truth, and his vivifying Spirit, whereby the Brother-hood begins to revive again in this our Isle, and Princes seek to be of this sacred Society, which hath been from the Beginning and always shall be : the Gates of Hell shall never prevail against it...for since God, my dearest Brethren, is for us, who can be against us ? Ye are living Stones, built up a spiritual House, who believe and rely on the chief *Lapis Angularis*, which the refractory and disobedient Builders disallowed ; you are call'd from Darkness to Light ; you are a chosen Generation, a royal Priesthood." [2]

Among those who attacked Masonry on religious grounds was a certain " Verus Commodus " who wrote in a letter to a friend[3]

---

1. Reprinted in the *Leicester Masonic Reprints*, 1920, and in *Early Masonic Pamphlets*, by Douglas Knoop, G. P. Jones, and Douglas Hamer, 1945.
2. *Early Masonic Pamphlets*. p. 214.
3. This letter was appended to the second edition of *The Grand Mystery of Free Masons Discover'd*, 1725. It has been reprinted in *Early Masonic Pamphlets*, pp. 136–140.

"...it is observable, That the Creed of St. Anthanasius is treated very scurvily and opprobriously amongst divers of their Principals ; and the Divinity (nay even the Divine Accomplishments of our Saviour) are handled by some of those Wretches, with a most shameful buffoonry and Contempt...But now, Sir, to draw a Conclusion ; and to give my Opinion seriously, concerning these prodigious Virtuosi ; my Belief is, That if they fall under any denomination at all, or belong to any Sect of Men, which has hitherto appear'd in the World, they may be ranked among the GNOSTICS ; who took their Original from Simon Magus ; These were a Sect of Men, which ridicul'd not only Christianity, but even Rational Morality ; teaching, That they should be sav'd by their capacious Knowledge and Understanding of no Mortal Man could tell what. They babbled of an amazing Intelligence they had, from nobody knows whence ; They amus'd and puzzled the harebrain'd, unwary crowd, that follow'd 'em, with superstitious Interpretations, of extravagant Talismanic Characters, and abstruse Significations, of uncommon Kabalistick Words ; which exactly agrees with the Proceedings of our Modern Free Masons...I must take the Freedom to say, That there are Schisms and Fractions, more than enough already, in our most Excellent Religion."

Other passages could be quoted, but in the main the eighteenth century attacks on the Craft were centred on its puerilities and insobriety. The publication of William Preston's *Illustrations of Masonry* in 1772, and more particularly of *The Spirit of Masonry* by William Hutchinson in 1775, with the official sanction of Grand Lodge, did a great deal to raise Freemasonry from a convivial association to the school of religious and moral philosophy which it has since become to so many of its members. Both books were received with great enthusiasm, and set the tone for the philosophical Masonic writings of the following century. Hutchinson's interpretation of the third degree as symbolizing the new law of Christ rising from the death and corruption of the old law of Judaism will be considered in another chapter in the context of the Hiramic legend. In 1814 Jonathan Ashe's *Masonic Manual* appeared, which followed Hutchinson's theme closely, and had little to add to it. Although the theory of an exclusively Christian interpretation of Masonry became progressively untenable as the Craft developed in universality, it survived what might have been considered an official death-blow in 1813 and was continued by some writers even in the nineteenth century. But even Hutchinson is far from consistent, and his followers became less so.

The most prolific Masonic writer of the nineteenth, or indeed of any century, was an Anglican vicar, the Rev. George Oliver, who produced dozens of books between 1823 and 1875. Each book, credulous and historically worthless, seems to produce a new theory and a new interpretation. His main thesis, however, is that Freemasonry was revealed in all its ancient undenomina-tional purity to Adam by God Himself, and was transmitted through the patriarchs, surviving the flood, reaching its climax in the days of King Solomon, and eventually passing into the Christian tradition, of which Hiram is a type. The heathen mysteries of Egypt and Babylon, of Greece and Rome, are not, therefore, the ancestors of Freemasonry, but corrupt and spurious offshoots from it. But just as the religion of the Old Testament patriarchs was a pure undogmatic theism, so Masonry today is open to all believers in a one true God, though at the same time it is thoroughly Christian. Poor Dr. Oliver ! He wrote too much and too often. No one today takes his version of Masonic history seriously, but his legacy of woolly confusion between Christianity and universalism still hangs over the confused utterances of many a Masonic Anglican priest and prelate to this day.

Two people in the nineteenth century saw this insoluble dilemma and attempted, each in his own way, to face it squarely and logically. Neither of them received the attention which the subject merited, nor left any lasting impression on Masonic thought. The first was a Devon Mason, M. C. Trevilian, a name almost unknown to modern Freemasons. His misgivings on the compatibility of Freemasonry with Christianity were brought to a head, apparently, by a completely non-Christian Masonic funeral service for a certain John Rippon in Exeter in 1838, a ceremony which excited a good deal of local controversy. Trevilian (a layman) left the Order as a result, and in 1849 he published over his own name *A Letter on the Antichristian Character of Freemasonry to the Rev. Wm. Carwithin, D.D., Deputy Provincial Grand Master for the County of Devon,* which, with a lengthy appendix, gave logical and devastating arguments against the Christian becoming a Freemason. Christ, he claimed, had been cast aside, and a purely natural religion substituted for Him. In the Lodge " the Bible", he says, " is mentioned as the record, not of the great work achieved *for* us of Salvation, but of holy precepts wherewith to achieve our own," and he cites among other passages the prayer said over each initiate that he may achieve true godliness, not through Christ, but " by the secrets of our Masonic art. " " The faith described," he declares, "is pure Deism ; it may be very pious and sincere ; but it is not the faith of the Christian but of the genuine Deist."

In dealing with the apostasy of omitting all Christian endings to Masonic prayers so that non-Christians may be spared offence, he faces the argument heard then as now, that to the Christian the very mention of God tacitly includes Christ. " I was corrected, " says Trevilian, " by the observation of a Rev. Gentleman, ' Can any Trinitarian address prayer to God, without in that term acknowledging Christ as an integral part of the Deity addressed ? ' I would wish to ask him now whether, having obsequiously put aside the *name* of Christ, we are at liberty likewise (through the same regard for the feelings of others) to put aside absolutely His *work and mediation ;* and to consider these to be intrinsically as needless as the mention of the Name ?...No, there is no room for any such quibbling subterfuge. " The same Rev. Gentleman, however, we are told, later on also seceded from the order on conscientious grounds.

Trevilian develops at length the comparison between the apostasy of the Christian Mason and the denial of Peter. At our Lord's betrayal and passion, he points out, there was a mixed crowd consisting of both enemies and friends. " And what was the most bitter ingredient in the cup of sorrow which this Man of sorrows was presented with on that eventful night ? Was it the ill-treatment and buffetings of his persecutors ? No ; this he took voluntarily upon Him...it was the desertion of his friends, and particularly the anti-Christian declaration of Peter ; this moved His gentle spirit, and was grief to his soul...The crime of the Christian Freemason is that, in a similar assembly, i.e., in an assembly where the name of Christ is by many held in contempt, and His mediation refused, he also does not stand by his Master,

but in complaisance to his fellow-Masons suppresses his knowledge of Him, a silent act which, speaking as loudly as words,
may be regarded as equivalent to an open denial...As to the
wrong done, the denying on the one hand, and the suppression
on the other, Christ being in each case disowned, surely no
one will say that there is any great difference between them.
Peter denies that Christ is his Lord and Master ; the Christian
Freemason suppresses or suspends the pretensions of Christ
to be his necessary Mediator and Intercessor in prayer...*dis-
owning Christ for the time being ;* and both answering to the
prophecy (Psalm VI, 12) that it should be the ' friends ' of
Christ who should ' bring reproach upon Him '...Let us make
the addition of *motive* to each. The parallel will then stand thus.
Peter disowned Christ *through fear ;* the Christian Freemason
disowns Him *through complaisance*...to disown Christ on such an
account is nothing less than to betray Him...to ' crucify Him
afresh, and to put Him to an open shame.' Indifference is the
basest quality of the mind. " And these words of Trevilian ring
as true, as apposite and as unanswered today as when they
were written.

The second writer to face the dilemma saw it from a more
practical and less theological angle ; although considerably
disturbed by it he never left the Craft. This was H. J. Whymper,
who had the rank of Past Deputy District Grand Master for
Punjab. He was active in Freemasonry in India at a time of
expansion when many non-Christians, mainly Moslem and
Hindu, were being initiated into the Lodges, and the anomaly
of different faiths joining in the same religious ceremonies
startled him into writing *The Religion of Freemasonry* in 1888.
This book started at a disadvantage. The great Masonic scholar
W. J. Hughan, far better versed than Whymper in Masonic
history, had promised to write an introduction before he saw
the manuscript ; when he came to read it he found himself in
disagreement at every turn with Whymper's main thesis, but the
only solution he himself suggests is that unless the various
religions " are prepared to practise as well as expect toleration
by thus maintaining the actual and obligatory foundations of
the Society, the continuity and identity of the Institution cannot
be permanently and uniformly preserved...by thus extending
the scope of our Ancient and Honourable Society, we are adding

immensely to its beneficial influence and practical usefulness, especially abroad."

Whymper starts, of course, with the assumption that Freemasonry is a religious fraternity. " We can have no concern, neither can we at all sympathize with a brother who can read or repeat our ritual and yet attach no religious meaning to it, " he writes. " We maintain that the upholders of the belief that no connection exists between Freemasonry and religion, depend entirely on their own individual assertions, all the weight of evidence being on our side."

On less sure grounds he continues to argue that the religion of Freemasonry is still Christianity, despite the excision of all specific references to it in the Charges, constitutions, and ritual. He cites here and there from Dr. Oliver's *Discrepancies of Freemasonry* to justify his point. Briefly, his main argument is that Freemasonry prior to the Grand Lodge era was Christian, that its Christianity was an unalterable landmark, that no minute is preserved expressing a deliberate intention of removing that landmark, therefore it has never been removed. Hughan's introduction rightly demolishes this argument, and points out, particularly from the changed wording of the Charges, that Masonry at that period tended away from Christianity to " cosmopolitanism and religious universality."

But Whymper is unanswered and unanswerable when he points out the inconsistency and insincerity of the position of the " Volume of the Sacred Law " in Masonic ceremonies. In English-speaking countries and where the membership of the Lodge is predominantly Christian in background, this volume was (and is) the Bible, containing both Old and New Testaments. Indeed it is doubtful whether the use of any other volume was ever envisaged in the early days of Grand Lodge. But particularly in India the Koran and the Vedas came to be substituted for it, especially for the oaths, and it became established by authority that the V.S.L. need not necessarily be the Bible at all. Yet the ritual remained more or less constant for Lodges of all faiths. Hence the unresolved absurdity, if not blasphemy, of passages in the ritual referring to it as " the unerring standard of truth and justice," or " the sacred writings to govern our faith," or " the record of God's revealed will " when different and quite contradictory " revelations " are referred to. How can such a medley be " unerring ? " So Whymper will not have it that the V.S.L. can be other than the Bible. " The ties which should exist between a brother and that which he esteems to be the Word of God have been, and are being, relaxed, and will soon be entirely severed by the light and careless feeling necessarily engendered by the doctrine that *any* book is good enough to be esteemed the Volume of the Sacred Law. A Christian cannot view this state of things with satisfaction. In the words of a well-known writer, ' he feels that to reduce our blessed Lord into the category of human seers is practically to dethrone Him. Christianity will tolerate no rival. They who wish to raise a tabernacle for some other Master, be it even for the greatest worthies of the old economy—a Moses or Elias—must be warned that Christ, and Christ alone, is to be worshipped. ' "

Universality, therefore, is preposterous. " Has this effort to suppress Christian allusions and connections been attended by any good ? " asks Whymper, in words strongly reminiscent of Trevilian, Penney Hunt, and other anti-Masons. " Has it even helped to make a more consistent universal system ?... On the one hand the Christian has stifled his feelings, he has cancelled and done away with Christian allusions, so as not to cause offence to others, and to obtain universality...on the one side the Christian refrains from speaking of Christ as his Saviour, and on the other hand our Hindoo brethren openly assert that Jesus Christ's position is on a mere level with Zoroaster, Mahomed, Khrishna, Rama, and others...the Christian alone has abandoned his religion, whilst the brethren of all other beliefs have asserted theirs."[1]

Whymper suggests the solution that Lodges of different religions displaying different sacred books should be grouped under separate Masonic jurisdictions, with the ritual modified if necessary in each, yet retaining rights of mutual visitation. This suggestion has of course never been adopted or even seriously considered. Hughan stated in his introduction that it would " weaken the unsectarian character of the Institution," and the spirit of universalism was far too strong for Whymper even to obtain a serious hearing. The Bible is still only optionally the Volume of the Sacred Law. So to this day his dilemma remains unresolved and Christian Masons continue to be vague and

1. Op. cit. p. 205.

myopic on these fundamental issues.[1]

The twentieth century has seen a certain social change in Freemasonry. Although nobility and even Royalty have never been lacking to assume the Grand Mastership, Freemasonry was predominantly *petit bourgeois* in membership, consisting mainly (of course there are many exceptions) of small traders, artisans, and shopkeepers. An effort to spread its membership among intellectuals resulted in the formation of Old School and University Lodges on a larger scale ;[2] this raised the proportion of the professional classes, the social prestige of the Craft, and to a startling extent the number of Anglican clergy. That this movement has coincided with the growth of liberalism, pan-protestantism, and the decay of dogmatic faith in the Church of England is clearly an historical fact ; to hazard a guess as to the identity of a cart or a horse in this coincidence must, I think, be left to future historians. Suffice it to say that the two go together, and that there are clerical Masons who proudly proclaim a direct harnessing between them, and that the pattern is already established. The Rev. J. Fort Newton, for instance, wrote : " The various sects...are moving towards the Masonic position, and when they arrive, Masonry will witness a scene which she has prophesied for ages...our little dogmas will have their day and cease to be, lost in the vision of a truth so great that all men are one in their littleness."[3] The ultimate

1. " Freemasonry being embracing all religions, the V.S.L. is for each candidate the Book of his Faith by which is pledged his promise, as proves the well-known fact that in the Far East, not one but several such volumes may be found in use within the same Lodge, and even the same day's ceremonies, each in turn as the one binding on he who pledges himself upon it. Being thus undenominational in character, as it has become since the Union of 1813. there can be no right cause for the Master to read any passage of the Book of one particular faith to a gathering comprising adherents to others, and it could be regarded as a breach of the understanding.

   " The Sacred Volume in Freemasonry is in fact a *Symbol,* just as are the Square and the Compasses, and displayed to the Lodge as the *Three Great Lights.* "

   Freemasons' Chronicle, Dec. 19, 1953.

   This most recent statement (of which I have not presumed to alter the grammar) clearly makes nonsense of the oft-repeated claim that " Freemasonry is founded on the Bible."

2. A few, of course, were already in existence. At Oxford the Apollo University Lodge was chartered in 1818, and the earliest Cambridge Lodge dates from 1754.

3. The Rev. J. Fort Newton, *The Builders* (7th edition, 1949) p. 183. I forbear quoting from the even more startlingly frank utterances

(continued on foot of page 44)

super-religion, it seems, is not Christianity but Freemasonry.

The higher percentage of intellectuals in the Craft, however, has certainly raised the standards of Masonic scholarship. The early decades of the century indeed were marked by a fresh outcrop of mystical fantasies—the blasphemies of Wilmshurst, the anthropological credulities of J. S. M. Ward sponsored by Sir John Cockburn, the scholastic occultism of A. E. Waite (and among the Theosophical co-Masons not recognized by Grand Lodge, the sheer lunacy of Bishop Leadbeater)—but at the same time the sober scholastic tradition established by Gould, Sadler, Murray-Lyon, and Findel gained ground and flourished. Such historians as Lionel Vibert, G. W. Daynes, J. Heron Lepper, Douglas Knoop, Ivor Grantham, Bernard E. Jones, H. Hiram Hallett, the Rev. Herbert Poole, and Fred L. Pick (to mention a few) have vastly raised the intellectual stature of the Craft, which indeed has never stood higher.

Not one of these Masonic scholars, however, has attempted seriously to tackle Freemasonry on its philosophical and religious aspects, particularly its relationship to Christianity, and hence this field has been left wide open to the ravings of the lunatic fringe. The reason for this is threefold. First, the Masonic scholar is seldom interested in the religious question. Secondly, there is the absolute ban on religious discussion in the Lodge for fear of disturbing the fraternal harmony through controversy. This extends even to the scholarly atmosphere of Research Lodges such as the famous *Quatuor Coronati*, whose published proceedings are a mine of historical information, but show a cautious disinclination to discuss other aspects of the Craft. Thirdly, it seems clear that Masonry and Christianity in its dogmatic and exclusive sense are incompatible if both are taken seriously, hence no Masonic scholar or Christian theologian has dared risk his reputation in either camp by attempting a reconciliation. Either the religious side of Masonry is played down or denied (very difficult in the third degree of the Craft, and quite impossible in the Royal Arch) or Christianity is reduced to mere morality and a sentimental affection for the Sermon on the Mount.

The truly astonishing touchiness and irritability of the Frater-
of *Light Invisible* on the undermining effects of Masonry upon Christianity because the clergyman-mason ("Vindex") who wrote it continues to remain anonymous.

nity when this dilemma is raised by non-Masons, their anxiety to stifle all outside criticism and kill it with silence (extending even to pressure on booksellers and libraries) is in itself a cogent witness not only to the insecurity of their ground, but to their awareness of it.[1] Twice in this century has Freemasonry been criticized from without from the point of view of Christian orthodoxy. In 1926 the Rev. C. Penney Hunt, a Methodist minister, wrote and published *The Menace of Freemasonry to the Christian Faith*, a cogent and stinging criticism which made considerably publicity. " Grand Lodge, " the author says in an appendix to the second and subsequent editions, " actually issued a warning to deter men even from printing the book— and exerted pressure on editors not to review and on booksellers not to sell. "[2] What other body (other than totalitarian dictatorships) would dream of stifling criticism by such methods, or even feel the need to do so ? The result of the stir, however, was that yet another Christian body was added to the list of those who have formally condemned Masonry on theological grounds. The General Methodist Conference at Bradford in 1927 warned its members against initiation. This has never been repealed, but on the other hand it never became effective.

With the second occasion I am myself, with Dr. H. S. Box,[3] more personally concerned, and the events are too recent (indeed still current) to assess, nor is it for me to do so. Through a series of unforeseen chances, however, there has been more publicity in the 1950's than Penney Hunt received in the 1920's and the reactions both public and private have been more violent in the attempt (paradoxically) to maintain the traditional " dignified silence. " A preliminary article *Should a Christian be a Freemason ?* in the January 1951 edition of *Theology* touched off a storm, which led to Dr. Box and others raising the issue in the Canterbury Convocation. Due largely to the persuasive intervention of the Masonic Bishop of Reading (Dr. A. Groom Parham) this was never debated. Controversy continued in the religious

1. The Society for the Promotion of Christian Knowledge, for instance, of which the Archbishop of Canterbury is President, issued a directive to their bookshops that *Darkness Visible* must not be stocked. They have also banned any advertisement of it in their organs, *View Review* and *Theology*.
2. Eighth edition, p. 77.
3. Author of *The Nature of Freemasonry*.

press, however, and a full-scale debate was staged in the Church Assembly in the following June. This body was not in any case competent to deal with the theological issues but lay Masonic support could be relied on ; critics of Masonry were frankly out-manœuvred by the unexpectedness and speed with which Masons themselves with little warning arranged the debate and placed it on a supplementary agenda, and the result was an appeal to sentimentality, to the social and ecclesiastical eminence of Masons, moral irrelevance, even including personal abuse, in which the theological issue was again completely side-stepped. Even a Kelham Father rose to defend the Craft.[1] The motion for an enquiry, moved by a Mason, was overwhelmingly rejected, to the declared delight of the mover. The Assembly was then congratulated by its Masonic Chairman. The *Church Times*,[2] which drew caustic attention to " the patent manœuvres behind the scenes by which discussion has been stifled in Convocation and side-tracked in the Assembly " declared that " There is sheer lack of logic in saying : ' We have absolutely nothing to fear from an enquiry. Therefore there must on no account be an enquiry. ' "

The publication of *Darkness Visible* followed almost exactly a year later. *Reynold's News* and other papers took it up ; the most unexpected publicity, however, came from the *Daily Mirror* who in one of their publish-and-be-damned moods devoted an illustrated feature article to it entitled *Secret Signs of a Million Men* which not only sold out the paper in London by mid-morning, and was the sensation of Fleet Street taverns, but instantly rocketed *Darkness Visible* into a best-seller. Quite unconcerned with the religious issue, with my motives in writing the book, or indeed with anything beyond sensationalism and curiosity, Fleet Street unwittingly re-launched a theological controversy still unresolved and unanswered. Evasiveness, irritation, and irrelevance coupled with the traditional policy of hushing it up is so far the usual Masonic response.[3] A bad-

1. Fr. D. H. N. Allenby, S.S.M.
2. June 29, 1951.
3. When, apparently, rumours were current that such a book was about to appear, I received an anonymous phone call to meet an unknown gentleman in the foyer of the Savoy Hotel. I kept the appointment, and was offered £1,000 in banknotes in return for a written undertaking not to publish the book, or any further attacks on Masonry. Who he was I still have not the slightest idea.

tempered anonymous reply, *Light Invisible* was written by an Anglican clergyman with a Unitarian theology, but this strange book freely admits the incompatibility of Masonry with orthodox Christianity.

The existence of the dilemma seems embarrassing both to Grand Lodge and to the Church. The former, obsessed with its respectability and social status, greatly values the ecclesiastical support of Archbishops and Bishops among the clergy who enjoy the rank of Grand Chaplain, just as local Lodges usually welcome the presence of the Vicar. Any withdrawal would be an intolerable and humiliating affront. The Church, on the other hand, dares not offend or provoke thousands of influential and often financially substantial laymen by enquiring into the religious implications of their Freemasonry, even if the mutual solidarity of the episcopate were ever to allow such an enquiry. There is fear on both sides, hence the search for truth is stifled, and the religious bigamy continues. Only Rome can afford to smile at the situation, and continue to win converts.

III

CHRISTIAN REMAINDERS

If we just go on being brotherly to one another it doesn't matter what we believe about God. . . . " Take away theology and give us some nice religion " has been a popular slogan for so long that we are apt to accept it, without inquiring whether religion without theology has any meaning. And however unpopular I may make myself, I shall and will affirm that the reason why the Churches are discredited today is not that they are too bigoted about theology, but that they have run away from theology.

Dorothy L. Sayers, Creed or Chaos ?

IN *Darkness Visible* I wrote that the only clear and specific Christian allusions which survived in the Craft ritual after 1723 appeared to be the Christian symbols of faith, hope, and charity (the cross, anchor, and chalice) which appear on Jacob's Ladder in the tracing-board of the first degree, and the " bright morning star, whose rising brings peace and salvation to the faithful and obedient of the human race " in the ritual of the third degree. The Lectures, however (I do not mean the charges or the tracing-board lectures, but the " Emulation lectures " or " sections " in catechetical form which give a commentary on the ritual) provide another instance in quoting words of our Lord, but without mentioning His name.

In the First Lecture, Second Section, there is the following passage on the admission of an initiate into the Lodge :—

Q. How did you gain admission ?

A. By three distinct knocks.

Q. To what do those three distinct knocks allude ?

A. An ancient and venerable exhortation, Seek, and ye shall find ; ask, and ye shall have ; knock, and it shall be opened unto you.

Q. How did you apply that exhortation to your then situation ?

A. Having sought in my mind, I asked of my friend, he knocked, and the door of Freemasonry became open to me.

Although our Lord's words are quoted, they are given an entirely different context. The Mason asks, not of his Heavenly Father, but of a friend, his sponsor in Masonry. The door is the door to the Lodge, whereas Christ said, " I am the door : by me if any man enter in, he shall be saved."[1]

Yet another Christian survival from pre-Union days is to be found in a ritual issued under the authority of William Harvey, Provincial Grand Master of Forfarshire from 1934–36. The printed version has run into some twelve editions, and is in fairly popular use particularly in the west of Scotland. This preserves, among other pre-Union archaisms, a reference in the first degree obligation to the Lodge " dedicated to the memory of Holy St. John." Most American rituals also preserve this dedication, usually and more correctly in the plural, " Saints John," for both St. John the Baptist and St. John the Evangelist were regarded as patrons (and by the fanciful, as members), of the Order. In England, as we have seen, this dedication does not appear to have survived the Union of the Ancients and Moderns in 1813. The first lecture, fifth section, however, used to conclude with the following reasons for the Johanine dedication :—

Q. Why were the Lodges dedicated to St. John the Baptist ?

A. Because he was the forerunner of our Saviour, and by preaching repentance and humiliation, drew the first parallel of the Gospel.

Q. Had St. John the Baptist any equal ?

A. He had ; St. John the Evangelist.

Q. Why is he said to be equal to the Baptist ?

A. Because he finished by his learning what the other began by his zeal, and thus drew a second line parallel to the former ; ever since which time Freemasons' Lodges, in all Christian countries, have been dedicated to the one or the other, or both, of these worthy and worshipful men.

It is not certain who was responsible for the omission of this passage ; both Mackey and Oliver ascribe it to Dr. Hemming, but the name of Peter Gilkes, Preceptor of the Emulation Lodge of Improvement, has also been suggested. A hint of it still remains in present-day versions of the lectures, in this rubric :— " There is sometimes given a supplement to the Fifth Section, but it is not orthodox." Webb's and Sickert's Monitors in America, however, continue to depict as a Masonic symbol the two parallels, representing these two saints, tangent to a circle between.

There is another old lecture adopted by Preston which further

1. John, X, 9.

developed on more fanciful lines the reasons for the Johanine dedication, and explained the parallels :—

" From the building of the first Temple at Jerusalem to the Babylonish captivity, Freemasons' Lodges were dedicated to King Solomon ; from thence to the coming of the Messiah, they were dedicated to Zerubbabel, the builder of the second Temple ; and from that time to the final destruction of the Temple by Titus, in the reign of Vespasian, they were dedicated to St. John the Baptist ; but owing to the many massacres and disorders which attended that memorable event, Freemasonry sunk very much into decay ; many Lodges were entirely broken up, and but few could meet in sufficient numbers to constitute their legality ; and at a general meeting of the Craft, held in the city of Benjamin, it was observed that the principal reason for the decline of Masonry was the want of a Grand Master to patronize it. They therefore deputed seven of their most eminent members to wait upon St. John the Evangelist, who was at that time Bishop of Ephesus, requesting him to take the office of Grand Master. He returned for answer, that though well stricken in years, being upwards of ninety, yet having been initiated into Masonry in the early part of his life, he would take upon himself the office. He thereby completed by his learning what the other St. John effected by his zeal, and thus drew what Freemasons term a *line parallel* ; ever since which time Freemasons' Lodges, in all Christian countries, have been dedicated both to St. John the Baptist and St. John the Evangelist."[1]

The feasts of these Saints which used to be observed as Masonic festivals have extremely significant dates ; St. John the Evangelist falls on Dec. 27, St. John the Baptist on June 24, approximately corresponding respectively to the winter and summer solstices of the sun, which plays a great part in Masonic symbolism. It is difficult to escape the inference that this was the original reason for the double dedication, and indeed Mackey's *Revised Encyclopædia of Freemasonry* (an American publication) in making this very point, informs us that " In dedicating our Lodges to them (the two Sts. John) we do not so much declare our belief that they

1. An even fuller explanation, accompanied by rather fantastic scholarship, is given in the Rev. George Oliver's *A Mirror for the Johannite Masons,* 1848, which deplores the excision of this dedication.

were eminent members of the Order, as demonstrate our reverence for the Great Architect of the Universe in the symbol of His most splendid creation, the great light of day."[1]

In England today, however, the dedication is all but extinct, if not completely so. The form of Consecration of a new Lodge has no reference to it, and even in Scotland and America where it lingers, it seems purely nominal, and certainly does not exclude the Moslem and other non-Christian. It is quite possible for a Jew to live in Los Angeles without being particularly conscious of the patronage of St. Mary of the Angels, or at St. Helen's without showing any devotion to the Mother of Constantine.

The " bright morning star " in the third degree seems a clear reference to Revelation XXII, 16, and a survival of Christianity. *The Revised Ritual of Craft Freemasonry*, first produced by Franklin Thomas in 1888 and at one time popular in certain Indian Lodges, though never much used in England, faces this anomaly boldly, and alters the passage to "...lift our eyes to Him in Whose Hands alone are the issues of life and death, and in whose mercy we trust for the fulfilment of His gracious promise of peace and salvation to the faithful and obedient of the human race." To this is added a footnote, explaining that the original version, " if it have any meaning, can only allude to the Founder of the Christian Faith...the sentence in question would be quite consistent with the Christian degrees (Knight Templar, Rose Croix, etc.) but it is not in accordance with Craft Masonry which embraces men of every creed." This is perhaps logical, but I have seen no other ritual which follows it,[2] and the excision or alteration of a favourite purple passage in the Masonic ritual would doubtless be bitterly resisted.

Modern Masonic commentators vary in their interpretation of this symbol. E. H. Cartwright calls it frankly a Christian allusion which " apparently escaped the notice of the revisers at the Union, when the Christian references generally were excised."[3] And this is by far the most probable explanation. Others, however, are at pains to give a non-Christian interpretation ; and relate it to the " Blazing Star " of the first degree, or

1. Vol. 1, p. 268.
2. Not even a privately-printed one in my possession which appears to have been issued especially for a Lodge of Jewish faith.
3. *A Commentary on the Freemasonic Ritual*, p. 192.

to the " Sacred Symbol " (the letter G in an irradiated triangle) of the second.

Major Meredith Sanderson, however, says " This is a figurative allusion to Sirius or *Sothias*, the dog-star, which by its rising at dawn brought tidings of the approaching inundation, and so brought Peace and Salvation to Egypt."[1]

The Rev. F. de Castells writes that " the Christian interpretation has been given up, although it remains a beautiful illustration...Any star, and for that matter, any object shining over our heads would have been equally suitable...the author of Revelation borrowed it, as we have done, from the classic writers of Greece...for ages, and almost all the world over, the name was a popular and generally accepted cognomen for the planet Venus. Whenever the Greeks spoke of ' the Light Bringer ' (Phosphoros) they were referring to Venus, in which they saw the Herald of the Dawn." He therefore concludes that, to the Mason, the Bright Morning Star refers to the " Ineffable Essence in whom we have discovered the ultimate Source of Light, physical, intellectual, and divine."[2]

J. S. M. Ward follows Sanderson's interpretation, yet allowing also for a Christian interpretation.[3] A. E. Waite, too, allows a varied interpretation, including a reference to Osiris :— " We remember this, and other speaking connotations, when our eyes are lifted to a certain bright and Morning Star, whose rising brings peace and salvation. We remember, it may be, the Sign of Osiris slain, the Sign of the Mourning of Isis, the Sign of Typhon and Apophis, and the Sign of Osiris risen. We remember the rending of Iacchos and his symbolical restoration...we remember greater things... of the Great Master of all, concerning whom it is said : *passus et sepultus est* ; but thereafter : *tertia die resurrexit*."[4] In a later passage he interprets the same allusion as a prophecy of Christian Masonry in the Templar grades :— " Templar grades issued from unknown preceptories, witnessing of secret things learned by St. John as he leant on the Master's breast, of Him Who is the Bright and Morning Star, prefigured

1. *An examination of the Masonic Ritual*, p. 51.
2. *The Apocalypse of Freemasonry*, pp. 160–1.
3. *The M(aster) M(ason's) Handbook*, pp. 49–51.
4. *The Secret Tradition in Freemasonry*, pp. 37–8.

in the speaking darkness of the Third Degree."[1]

Christian Masons at pains to justify their adherence to non-Christian Craft Masonry are particularly prone to light on this interpretation, arguing from it that as " Masonry is a progressive science"[2] the Craft is but the Old Testament of Masonry, foreshadowing the New in the alleged Christian degrees. Although it must be admitted, and indeed stressed, that there is no official interpretation of Masonic symbolism, and that each Mason is perfectly entitled to interpret as he pleases, we shall see later that this analogy is false, and from the point of view of Christian orthodoxy, untenable.

As for the Christian symbols commonly found in the traditional design of the first degree tracing-board, it may perhaps be pointed out that these representations are not absolutely standardized ; considerable liberty is granted to the artist where a Lodge has the imagination or the funds to depart from stock Masonic-outfitter goods, and in many cases the Latin cross, the anchor, and the chalice (or sometimes heart) are replaced by the initials F., H., and C. This variableness does not really matter or even score a debating point, for it is beyond dispute that the faith, hope, and charity which are symbolized derive from the three Christian " Theological Virtues," but they are not identical with them. The tracing-board lecture explains them as follows :—

"...Jacob's ladder...is composed of many staves or rounds, which point out as many moral virtues, but three principal ones, which are Faith, Hope, and Charity : Faith in the Great Architect of the Universe, Hope in salvation, and to be in Charity with all men. It reaches to the Heavens, and rests upon the Volume of the Sacred Law, because, by the doctrines contained in that Holy Book, we are taught to believe in the dispensations of Divine Providence, which belief strengthens our faith, and enables us to ascend the first step ; this Faith naturally creates in us a Hope of becoming partakers in the blessed promises therein recorded, which Hope enables us to ascend the second step ; but the third and last, being Charity,

1. Ibid, p. 178. Waite's Christianity, however, was Gnostic. He looked on the Sacraments of the Roman and Eastern Orthodox churches (he had a profound contempt for Anglicanism) only as gateways of initiation to inner occult mysteries for the few.
2. *Ceremony of Passing.* See *Darkness Visible,* p. 124.

comprehends the whole, and the Mason who is possessed of this virtue in its most ample sense may justly be deemed to have attained the summit of his profession ; figuratively speaking, an Ethereal Mansion, veiled from mortal eyes by the starry firmament..."

Bearing in mind that Masonry is not committed to the inspiration of the Bible, that the " Volume of the Sacred Law " is not the Christian Bible, but the sacred scriptures of any faith according to the religion of the Mason, and therefore only incidentally the Bible in Christian countries, it will be seen that Masonic faith and hope are not *per se* faith and hope *in Christ*, and that Masonic charity is not *Christian* charity. Indeed in most rituals it is not St. Paul who is quoted on this virtue, but Portia, from the *Merchant of Venice*,[1] and it is constanly stressed. that Masonic charity is to be exercised " without detriment to oneself or one's connections."

In this same tracing-board, early commentators have equated the irradiated star at the top of the ladder with the Star of Bethlehem. William Hutchinson's *The Spirit of Masonry*, (1775) has in the sixth section of the Entered Apprentice lecture the following explanation of the star :—

" We may apply this emblem to a still more religious import : it represents the star which led the wise men to Bethlehem ; proclaimed to mankind the nativity of the Son of God ; and *here* conducting our spiritual progress to the Author of our redemption."

This Christian interpretation, however, seems entirely ruled out today, and is seldom if ever put forward. The tracing-board lecture in its present form specifically states that " The Blazing Star, or Glory in the centre, refers us to the Sun, which enlightens the earth, and by its benign influence dispenses its blessings to mankind in general."

Such, then, is the tiny catalogue of specific or alleged Christian symbols and references remaining in the Craft, which have survived the disappearance of their Christian context. It seems incredible that any case for the Christianity of Freemasonry could be based on such slender evidence. The Koran, unlike the

---

1. " Suffice it to say (charity) has the approbation of Heaven and earth, and, like its sister, mercy, blesses him who gives as well as him who receives." *Ceremony of Initiation*. (See *Darkness Visible*. p. 105.)

Masonic ritual, even contains polite references to Our Lord Himself and His Mother, but that does not make it a Christian book. Yet this type of reasoning continues to be produced by Christian Masons today.

IV

THE HIRAMIC LEGEND AS A
CHRISTIAN ALLEGORY

Types and shadows have their ending,
For the newer rite is here.
                    St. Thomas Aquinas, Pange lingua gloriosi.

Idolatry consists in worshipping God under any other conception of Him
than that which is set before us in the Gospels. . . . Idolatry is indeed a deadly
thing.
                    Archbishop William Temple, Personal Religion and the
                    Life of Fellowship.

"ALL right, then," a certain type of Mason will argue. "So the Masonic ritual *isn't* Christian at all, on the surface. But beneath the surface you will find an allegorical meaning which is Christian even though Masons of other religions can also see in it an allegory of their faiths."

Allegorizers and symbolists can find anything in everything if they try hard enough, and Freemasonry provides a happy hunting ground for their efforts. On the assumption that three of anything symbolizes the Holy Trinity, Masonic mystics have produced an impressive series of triads in their workings to prove how Christian they are, on the analogy that a tricycle is a more Trinitarian means of transport than a car or a bicycle and therefore more acceptable to God. There is the trinity of the Master of the Lodge and his two Wardens. There are three Greater Lights and three lesser, three degrees, three rosettes on the apron, three " regular steps," even three assassins in the third degree. An enterprising Mason by the name of C. E. Ferry once compiled a list of seventy such triads from the ritual to demonstrate the Trinitarian orthodoxy of the Fraternity.[1] But of course the Hindu could ponder this list with an equal satisfaction.

Crosses, too, are in plentiful supply. The poniard which is applied to the naked left breast of the Candidate on his entry to

1. This manuscript, called *The Triad*, is in the library of Lodge Quatuor Coronati.

the Lodge is a cross of sorts ; Masonic symbolists have therefore made this piece of ritual an emblem of our Lord's passion. A tau cross is made with the feet when the " regular steps " are taken, and the Candidate for the third degree crosses his feet before he is " slain." The Tyler who guards the Lodge from without is emblematic of St. Peter with the keys of Heaven. The blue with which the apron is trimmed is the traditional colour of the Blessed Virgin. In more mystic vein it has been pointed out by Masons (and by the non-Masonic Venerable Bede centuries before) that the two pillars Boaz and Jachin at the porch of King Solomon's Temple (which form the secret words of the first and second degrees respectively) represent the founder of the House of Jesse and the Father of the Blessed Virgin, the first and the last of the male ancestors of our Lord, and are therefore prophetic of the Saviour.

Another fruitful source of allegory is the comparison between the stages of Masonic advancement and the sacraments of the Church. Thus initiation represents Baptism ; passing to the second degree, confirmation ; raising to the third degree, Communion with the Crucified Lord ; installation to the Master's chair, Holy Orders, and so on, always suggesting that Masonry has extra spiritual gifts not to be found in the Church.

" An attempt has been made, " writes W. H. Topley in concluding his book *The Craft and the Royal Arch*,[1] which sets out these parallels in a diagram, " to outline the salient features of the Masonic Sacramental System as the writer sees it, a System which portrays in terms of allegory and symbolism, the path of man's pilgrimage from his entrance to this world to his departure therefrom, and even dares to peer into that unknown futurity, beyond the realm of time and space when this mortal shall have put on immortality. If beneath its social structure and outer coverings, Freemasonry is not something like this, then it is hardly worthy of the serious consideration of thoughtful men."

All these lesser allegories and symbols, however, revolve round, and are dependent upon the core of the allegory in Craft workings, that Hiram Abiff is a type of our Lord, from which it follows that the legend of the third degree is therefore an allegorical re-enactment of the drama of our redemption.

1. p. 92.

For the benefit of the non-Mason, here is the Hiramic legend, quoted except for the portions in brackets from the words of the Masonic ritual itself.

" He (Hiram Abiff) was slain just before the completion of King Solomon's Temple, of which he was the principal architect. The manner of his death was as follows. Fifteen Fellow Crafts of that superior class appointed to preside over the rest, finding that the work was nearly completed and that they were not in possession of the secrets of the third degree, conspired to obtain them by any means, even to have recourse to violence. At the moment, however, of carrying their conspiracy into execution, twelve of the fifteen recanted, but three, of a more determined and atrocious character than the rest, persisted in their impious design, in the prosecution of which they planted themselves respectively at the east, north, and south entrances of the Temple, whither Hiram had retired to pay his adoration to the Most High, as was his wonted custom at the hour of high twelve. Having finished his devotions, he attempted to return by the south entrance, where he was opposed by the first of those ruffians, who for want of other weapon, had armed himself with a heavy plumb rule, and in a threatening manner demanded the secrets of a Master Mason, warning him that death would be the consequence of a refusal. Hiram, true to his obligation, answered that those secrets were known to but three in the world (Solomon, Hiram King of Tyre, and himself, the three Grand Masters) and that without the consent and co-operation of the other two he neither could nor would divulge them, but intimated that he had no doubt patience and industry would, in due time, entitle the worthy Mason to a participation of them, but that, for his own part, he would rather suffer death than betray the sacred trust reposed in him.

" This answer not proving satisfactory, the ruffian aimed a violent blow at the Master's head, but being startled by the firmness of his demeanour, it missed his forehead and only glanced on his right temple, but with such force as to cause him to reel and sink on his left knee. Recovering from the shock he made for the north entrance, where he was accosted by the second of these ruffians, to whom he gave a similar answer with undiminished firmness, when the ruffian, who was armed with a level, struck him a violent blow on the left temple which brought

him to the ground on his right knee. Finding his retreat cut off
at both these points, he staggered faint and bleeding to the east
entrance, where the third ruffian was posted, who received a
similar answer to his insolent demand, for even at this trying
moment our Hiram remained firm and unshaken, when the
villain, who was armed with a heavy maul, struck him a violent
blow on his forehead which laid him lifeless at his feet. The
villains bore the body away, and hastily buried it outside the
city.

"A loss so important as that of the principal architect could
not fail of being generally and severely felt. The want of those
plans and designs which had hitherto been regularly supplied to
the different classes of workmen was the first indication that
some very heavy calamity had befallen him. The Menatschin or
prefects, or more familiarly speaking, the overseers, deputized
some of the most eminent of their number to acquaint King
Solomon with the utter confusion into which the absence of
Hiram had plunged them, and to express their apprehension
that to some fatal catastrophe must be attributed his sudden
and mysterious disappearance. King Solomon immediately
ordered a general muster of the workmen throughout the
different departments, when three of the same class of overseers
could not be found. On the same day the twelve Craftsmen who
had originally joined in the conspiracy came before the King,
and made a voluntary confession of all they knew, down to the
time of withdrawing themselves from the number of conspirators.
This naturally increased the fears of King Solomon for the
safety of his chief artist. He therefore selected fifteen trusty
Fellow-Crafts, and ordered them to make diligent search after
the person of Hiram, to ascertain if he were yet alive, or
had suffered death in the attempt to extort from him the secret
of his exalted degree.

" Accordingly, a stated day having been appointed for their
return to Jerusalem, they formed themselves into three Fellow
Craft Lodges, and departed from the three entrances of the
Temple. Many days were spent in fruitless search ; indeed one
class returned without having made any discovery of importance. A second, however, were more fortunate, for on the
.evening of a certain day, after having suffered the greatest
privations and personal fatigues, one of the Brethren, who had

rested himself in a reclining posture, to assist his rising caught hold of a shrub that grew near, which to his surprise came easily out of the ground. On a closer examination he found that the earth had been recently disturbed. He therefore hailed his companions and with their united endeavours re-opened the ground, and there found the body of Hiram very indecently interred. They covered it again with all respect and reverence, and to distinguish the spot, stuck a sprig of acacia at the head of the grave.

" They then hastened to Jerusalem to impart the afflicting intelligence to King Solomon. He, when the first emotions of grief had subsided, ordered them to return and raise Hiram to such a sepulture as became his rank and exalted talents, at the same time informing them that by his untimely death the secrets of a Master Mason were lost. He therefore charged them to be particularly careful in observing whatever casual sign, token, or word might occur whilst paying this last sad tribute of respect to departed merit.

" They performed their task with the utmost fidelity, and on re-opening the ground one of the Brethren looking round observed some of his companions with their heads turned over their right shoulder, their hands raised with the backs to their faces, struck with horror at the dreadful and afflicting sight, while others viewing the ghastly wound still visible on his forehead, smote their own in sympathy with his sufferings. Two of the Brethren then descended into the grave and endeavoured to raise him by the Entered Apprentice grip, which proved a slip. Then they tried the Fellow Craft's, which proved a slip likewise. Having both failed in their attempts, a zealous and expert Brother took a more firm hold on the sinews of the hand, and with their assistance raised him on the Five Points of Fellowship (hand to hand, foot to foot, knee to knee, breast to breast, and left hand over back) ; while others, more animated, exclaimed *Machaben* or *Machbinna*, both words having a nearly similar import, one signifying the death of the builder, the other, the builder is smitten.

" King Solomon therefore ordered that those casual signs, and that that grip and word, should designate all Master Masons throughout the universe, until time or circumstances should restore the genuine.

" It only remains to account for the third class, who had pursued their searches in the direction of Joppa, and were meditating their return to Jerusalem, when, accidentally passing the mouth of a cavern, they heard sounds of deep lamentation and regret. (In American and some Scottish workings, these cries of regret gave rise to the penalties of the three degrees. The first exclaimed ' O that my throat were cut across, and my tongue torn out by the root, rather than that I should have been accessory to the death of our good Master.' The second exclaimed ' O that my breast had been torn open rather than I should have assisted in the death of our innocent Master. ' And then the third most lamentably exclaimed ' O that my body had been severed in two, rather than I should have smitten and killed our sublime Master '). On entering the cave they found three men answering the description of those missing, who, on being charged with the murder, and finding all chance of escape cut off, made a full confession of their guilt. They were then bound and led to Jerusalem, when King Solomon sentenced them to that death the heinousness of their crime so amply merited.

" The Master was ordered to be re-interred as near to the Sanctum Sanctorum as the Israelitish law would permit ; there in a grave, from the centre three feet east and three feet west, three feet between north and south, and five feet or more perpendicular. He was not buried in the Sanctum Sanctorum because nothing common or unclean was allowed to enter there ; not even the High Priest, but once a year ; nor then until after many washings and purifications against the great day of expiation for sins ; for by the Israelitish law, all flesh was deemed unclean. The same fifteen trusty Fellow Crafts were ordered to attend the funeral, clothed in white aprons and gloves as emblems of their innocence."

This is the legend which is dramatically performed in the ritual of the third degree. The Candidate impersonates Hiram, and is " slain " during the recitation by the two Wardens and by the Master. Later he is " raised " by these same three officers. The darkened Lodge is illuminated solely by the light of a single candle in front of the Master's pedestal.

" It is thus," the Candidate is told, " all Master Masons are raised from a figurative death to a reunion with the former companions of their toils. Let me now beg you to observe that the light of a Master Mason is darkness visible, serving only to express that gloom which rests on the prospect of futurity. It is that mysterious veil which the eye of human reason cannot penetrate unless assisted by that light which is from above. Yet even by this glimmering ray, you may perceive that you stand on the very brink of the grave into which you have just figuratively descended, and which, when this transitory life shall have passed away, will again receive you into its cold bosom. Let the emblems of mortality which lie before you lead you to contemplate on your inevitable destiny, and guide your reflections to that most interesting of all human studies, the knowledge of yourself. Be careful to perform your allotted task while it is yet day ; continue to listen to the voice of Nature, which bears witness, that even in this perishable frame resides a vital and immortal principle, which inspires a holy confidence that the Lord of Life will enable us to trample the King of Terrors beneath our feet, and lift our eyes to that bright Morning Star, whose rising brings peace and salvation to the faithful and obedient of the human race."

Before considering this legend as a Christian allegory, there is one vital difference that will be readily noted. Hiram is raised only in his dead body, for the purpose of a more honourable burial, though the " genuine secrets " which died with him are raised, as it were, in the Royal Arch degree. The Candidate, on the other hand, is raised from a figurative death to a new life, from a " dead level," as an old lecture expresses it, " to a living perpendicular."

Another difference, not so much of form and matter as of intention, so to speak, is that Hiram died in order to *preserve* a secret truth, a secret moreover which we learn in the Royal Arch is concerned with the name and nature of God. Our Lord, on the other hand, was put to death for his fearless *proclaiming* of the true secret, because that truth was profoundly uncomfortable and had therefore to be destroyed by the civil and religious authorities.

Superficially indeed the differences appear greatly to outweigh the resemblances. The recurring number of fifteen in the Hiramic legend, the points of the compass at which Hiram was attacked, the instruments with which he was slain, the secrecy of his burial (though both were buried hastily), with no soldiers to guard, or government seal to protect the body, and every detail concerning the quest and finding of the body, have no Christian parallels. If one must seek an anti-type for Hiram, there are many myths and characters which fit far more aptly, and which are indeed more likely. Canon Covey-Crump, in *The Hiramic Tradition*, lists not only Osiris, Persephone, Hecate, Orpheus, Bacchus, Adonis, Tammuz and Mithra, but also such historical characters as Thomas à Becket (where there are striking resemblances of detail),[1] Jacques de Molay (the last General of the Knights Templar) and Charles I. A possible interpretation, too, is that the Hiramic legend incorporates the persistent myth (and sometimes historical fact) of the architect of some particular masterpiece being slain in order to prevent his ever again equalling the achievement. Coupled with this is the idea of the foundation-sacrifice.

If, however, Hiram represents Christ, we are faced at once with the fact that this degree teaches a Gnostic heresy rather than Christian orthodoxy. The death of Hiram in itself, even though symbolizing the death of Christ, avails nothing ; it is not an objective propitiatory sacrifice wrought *for* the Candidate, but rather a type of the experience which the Candidate himself, representing Hiram, must undergo by his own efforts in his quest for light. This is precisely how the Gnostics, roundly condemned by the Church, regarded the crucifixion. Apart from the superficial blasphemy, then, the allegorical identification of Hiram with Christ in this context is extremely dangerous in that it lays Freemasonry wide open to the charge of being a revival of the old Gnostic heresies and mystery-religions. Yet this identification is at least a century and a half old.

As far as is known for certain, the Hiramic legend only entered Masonry in the early eighteenth century, after the Craft was substantially de-Christianized, 1725 or thereabouts is the commonly accepted date, when the trigradal system became established. True, it may have derived, as explained in Chapter I, from a similar and earlier legend on the death of Noah, which had the same original necromantic significance of

---

1. See Hugh Ross Williamson, *The Arrow and the Sword*. The resemblance is all the more striking, as the author is not a Mason and was not acquainted with the details of the third degree when he wrote this book.

attempting to wrest a secret from a corpse. Few Masonic scholars of repute, however, have ever maintained that the Hiramic legend was actually devised and inserted as an allegory of our Lord. Of this there is not a shred of evidence, internal or external ; all that can be considered is the attempt to read a Christian allegorical meaning into a clearly non-Christian legend of unknown source.

There are certain higher degrees—these are worth studying in more detail—which have as their " secret " the fact that Hiram really is Christ, wrapped up in an allegory for the benefit of the Craft which is not yet ready to receive the inner truth. As without exception these degrees are some years later than the introduction of Hiram into the Craft, and arose mainly in France and Germany, there is an element of *post hoc ergo propter hoc* in this position, and it would appear that these degrees were formulated partly in reaction against the non-Christian universalism of Craft Masonry. The Christian interpretation then filtered down unofficially from these higher degrees, and was accepted by some writers as a permissive allegory for the craft.

This hypothesis is certainly supported by the chronology of references to Hiram as an anti-type of our Lord. R. F. Gould cites Prof. J. G. Buhle (1804) for the information that " Hiram was understood by the older Freemasons as an anagram H.I.R.A.M. —Homo Jesus Redemptor AnimaruM ; others made it Homo Jesus Rex Altissimus Mundi ; whilst a few, by way of simplifying matters, added a C to the Hiram, in order to make it CHristus Jesus, etc."[1]

Who exactly these " older Freemasons " are is not specified ; A. E. Waite, however, quotes chapter and verse for the appearance of this celebrated anagram in the Degree of Perfect Master of St. Andrew, as promulgated at the General Convocation of Wilhelmsbad in 1728.[2] This degree had as its tracing-board a representation of Hiram in the likeness of the Lord of Glory.

Again Waite (who had studied the original rituals) tells us that " In the Grade of Perfect Architect it is affirmed that the

1. *The History of Freemasonry,* Vol. II, p. 114, quoting from J. G. Buhle, *Ueber den Ursprung und die Vornehmsten Schicksale des Ordens der Rosenkreuzer und Friemaurer,* 1804.
2. *Emblematic Freemasonry,* p. 158.

Mysteries of Masonry are none other than those of Religion ;
but this fact was kept a profound secret. It was revealed to those
only whose discretion had been tried and proved. To others
Symbolical Secrets were transmitted apart from all explanation
...The Passion of Christ is the true explanation of the whole
Hiramic mystery. The three blows suffered by the Master
Builder are emblematic of the three judgments pronounced on
the Divine Man by Pilate, Annas, and Caiaphas (also to the
buffetings before Caiaphas and Pilate, the scourging, and the
death on Calvary). The death of Hiram answers to the death of
Christ. When the Candidate is extended upon the Master's
tomb—according to French procedure—the Brethren by
whom he is surrounded symbolize the Disciples weeping about
the Cross. The Lost Word is in analogy with the words uttered
on the Tree of Calvary : the *Eloi, Eloi, Lama Sabachthani.*
The true significance of the Substituted Words is said to be :
The Son of the Widow is dead. The grave in which Hiram
was laid hurriedly by his murderers typifies the Rock-Hewn
Sepulchre...the Masons who sought and found the Master
in his grave answer to those disciples who came to embalm the
body of the Son of God. The Raising of Hiram is the resurrection. The Twelve Elect Masons who received the Secrets of
the Order from King Solomon as a reward of fidelity,[1] and then
scattered in the four quarters, correspond to the Twelve
Apostles who went forth to preach the Gospel, after receiving
His Holy Spirit from the Great Architect of the Universe."[2]

This degree, Waite tells us, provides a summary of the Christo-
logical tradition drawn from various sources and other degrees.
In the Ancient and Accepted Rite, as revised by Albert Pike
in America in the middle of the nineteenth century, the 26th
degree known as Prince of Mercy (not worked in England)
also regards Hiram as a type of Christ in His death and resurrection, presented " in language known only to the Initiate."
Before recapitulating the allegorical teaching of the first three
degrees, however, the Prince of Mercy informs the Initiate
to the 26th degree: " Certain explanations have been given, by
Christian Masons, of some of the ceremonies of the first three

1. This number of twelve does not appear in present-day Craft workings
   in England, though it does in Ireland. Details, however, vary considerably in different ritual versions of the legend.
2. *The Secret Tradition in Freemasonry*, pp. 173-4.

degrees, which, whatever your faith, may not be uninteresting to you, since you are in no wise required to receive them as correct." After the explanation comes brief expositions of the symbolism for the Hebrew, Mohammedan, and " to the Mason of every faith."[1]

The Templar tradition gives another slant on this allegory, and the Allied Degree of Knights of St. John the Evangelist, which is still worked in England today, contains the following teaching to the Candidate :—

" It is now my duty to explain to you the origin of Masonic rites as now practised. It is said that the Crusaders, finding themselves unable to expel the Saracens from the Holy Land, agreed with Godfrey de Bouillon to veil the mysteries of religion under emblems, by which they would be enabled to maintain their devotions in secret...The model which they selected was Solomon's Temple, which emblematically represents the Christian Church. Hence it follows that the mysteries of the Craft are in reality the mysteries of religion. The knights were, however, careful not to entrust this important secret to any whose fidelity and discretion had not been fully proved. They therefore invented different degrees to test their candidates, and gave them only symbolical secrets, without explanation, to prevent treachery, and solely to enable them to make themselves known to each other...It was, however, only in the Master Masons' degree that our Knightly brethren began to unfold the true mystery by narrating the assassination of H(iram) A(biff) at the hands of false brethren. The symbolic mystery of H(iram)'s death represents to us that of the Messiah, for instance, the three attacks that were made on the Master Builder at the three gates of the Temple, allude to the three points of condemnation against Christ at the tribunals of Caiaphas the High Priest, Herod the King, and Pilate the Roman Governor...The three blows...are also symbolic of the buffet on the cheek, the flagellation and the cruel crown of thorns. The brethren assembled around the tomb of H(iram) represent the disciples lamenting the death of Christ on the cross. The Master's word which is said to be lost, since the death of H(iram) A(biff), is the same that the Messiah pronounced on the cross, and which

1. *Liturgy of the Ancient and Accepted Scottish Rite of Freemasonry for the Southern Jurisdiction of the United States*, Part IV, 1944, pp. 129–49.

the Jews did not comprehend. (Eloi, Eloi, Lama Sabachthani). Instead of these words in the third degree, our ancient brethren substituted (Mahabone) which in Arabic signifies ' The son of the widow is dead '...The sprig of acacia is the figure of the cross which was made of wood from an acacia tree. The Royal Arch, referring to the captivity of the Jews, shows us the persecution of the Christians under the Roman Emperors, and their liberty under Constantine the Great."[1]

Although historically this hypothesis comes well within the lunatic fringe of fantasy, and although in England this degree does not ante-date the nineteenth century, the extraordinary similarity even of phraseology between this Lecture and Waite's quotations already given from earlier Continental degrees suggests an earlier derivation for it, possibly stretching back as far as Baron von Hund's Strict Observance in the mid-eighteenth century, the hey-day of the higher degrees.

Towards the end of the eighteenth century (but not, as far as I am aware, before), we find references to the Christ-Hiram in writers for Craft Masonry, not as inner secret teaching, but as a possible allegory for Christian Freemasons. William Hutchinson wrote in 1775 :—" The acquisition of the doctrine of redemption, is expressed in the typical character of *Huramen* (inveni) and by the application of that name with Masons, it is implied, that we have discovered the knowledge of God and his salvation, and have been redeemed from the death of sin, and the sepulchre of pollution and unrighteousness. Thus the Master Mason represents a man under the Christian doctrine, saved from the grave of iniquity, and raised to the faith of salvation."[2] This, however, does not prevent him from saying in the same book " (Masonry) directs us to divest ourselves of confined and bigoted notions, and teaches us that humanity is the soul of religion...As Masons, we only pursue the universal religion, the *religion of nature*. Worshippers of the God of Mercy, we believe that in every nation, he that feareth him and worketh righteousness is accepted of him. All Masons, therefore, whether *Christians, Jews, Mahomedans*, who violate not the rule of right, written by the ALMIGHTY upon the tables of the

1. *Ritual of the Knights of the Holy Sepulchre and Novice and Knight of St. John the Evangelist, As Authorized by the Patriarchal Council, 1949.*
2. *The Spirit of Masonry*, 2nd edition, p. 100.

heart ; who *do* fear him, and *work* righteousness, *we* are to acknowledge as brethren ; and, though we take different roads...we mean to travel to the same place...how lovely is an institution fraught with sentiments like these."[1]

A few nineteenth-century writers who follow Hutchinson in this identification of Christ and Hiram may be cited in passing. The voluminous and historically worthless output of the Rev. George Oliver has already been considered in a preceding chapter ; he manages to assume the identity of Christ and Hiram without at the same time impairing the universalism of Craft Freemasonry. The Rev. Moses Margoliouth pointed out that of the three tools with which Hiram was slain, the level and the plumb-rule when placed one upon the other form a cross, and that the mallet was a necessary tool for fastening anything to the cross. He continues " I do not know how so important a portion of Christian doctrine could be better illustrated by symbols. Taking this view of the third degree, we have not only the picture of our Grand Master's death, but also a graphic portrait of the murderous conspiracy of Caiaphas, Herod, and Pontius Pilate."[2] Again Whymper, in the significant book already referred to, simply takes the identification for granted. " We are not here raising any theory as to Hiram being a type of Christ," he declares. " If any other than the English Constitution can receive Hiram as typifying someone else, well and good, it is nothing to us. If another Constitution can differently apply all the symbols which, when introduced into our system, were intended to have a Christian significance, so be it ; but any applicability which may be discovered concerns us not."[3]

The present century, with its greater emphasis on the universality of Freemasonry, has seen the abandonment of this historically untenable claim that the Hiramic legend was originally intended as a Christian allegory. Few would maintain that this is *the* interpretation and key of the mystery, but merely that it is a valid and permissive one. Let us examine a few popular writers on the subject.

J. S. M. Ward was a *soi-disant* Bishop, but in no sense a

1. Ibid, p. 151.
2. *Genuine Freemasonry Indissoluby Connected with Revelation*, 1852.
3. *The Religion of Freemasonry*, 1888, p. 102.

theologian.[1] He had, however, along with an overdose of
irresponsible fantasy, some considerable learning in archaeology
and folk-lore. He wrote a bulky book in an endeavour to prove
that the true anti-type of Hiram was Osiris or Tammuz,[2] yet
elsewhere he admits that " we are not entitled to say one
meaning is right and another is wrong. Both may be right...
the student is perfectly entitled to consider that both the
Christian and the pre-Christian interpretation of these symbols
are equally deserving of respect."[3] However, Ward develops the
Christian allegory on fantastic lines. In the same book[4] he
writes " The title H(iram) AB(iff) is taken direct from the
Hebrew of 2 Chron., Chapter 4, Verse 16, and means ' H(iram)
His Father '...it is of interest to note that *abib* in Hebrew means
' Ears of corn ', or ' Green fruits '...if the word *abib* is the
correct rendering for the second half of the name in question,
we get a clear reference to the Sacramental bread." (Is it to be
hoped, then, that some future Masonic Pope will re-cast the
Divine Praises at Benediction to include " Blessed be Hiram in
the most Holy Sacrament of the Altar?")

When W. L. Wilmshurst identifies Hiram with Christ, he
makes it quite clear that he fully understands and accepts the
position that the interpretation must inevitably be Gnostic and
not orthodox, as I have already pointed out. Here at least he is
logical. Christ is for him, not in any unique sense the incarnate
Son of God, but a master-hierophant and super-initiate of occult
mysteries. The Church on earth, he maintains, which follows
the exoteric aspects of His ministry but ignores the esoteric, has
failed to do more than lead the questing soul to the portals of
the inner mystery. " The Gospels," he writes, " became a
manual of Initiation-instruction to the whole world according
to the measure of the individual capacity to receive it...The
recurrent cycle of the Church's year...is a true chart of the path

1. See T. R. Brandreth, *Episcopi Vagantes and the Church of England*, p. 43,
   for Ward's episcopal credentials.
2. *Who was Hiram Abiff?* 1925.
3. *The M(aster) M(ason's) Book*, 1929, p. 107. Cf. *Light Invisible*, which
   states that " Hiram . . . is not a rival to Christ, or to Mahomet, nor to
   Vishnu, but is a type and symbol of them all. . . .   Here indeed in
   the legend of Hiram is a mystery . . . which is the anti-type and symbol
   of every death-and-resurrection *motif* of every religion, Christianity
   included." (p. 47–8).
4. pp. 75, 77.

to be followed by those who themselves seek initiation under the mastership of the Great Hierophant and Exemplar of regenerative science ; while in the Sacrament of the Altar is portrayed albeit under different symbolism, the actual process of Initiation and the same transmutative changes in the body and mind of the recipient as are emblematized to the Masonic Candidate in the Craft Degrees." He concedes, therefore, that " Religion will not die…nor will ' the Church ' in some form cease to exist and to fulfil a certain ministry. But today a supplementary form of ministry is required and Masonry can provide it."[1]

It is against this background that Wilmshurst, in a purple passage of apocalyptic hyperbole, allegorizes to the point of blasphemy. Transported in the spirit to the Grand Lodge Above, he describes his celestial initiation, of which the earthly Masonic ceremonies are a type. As the Masonic apron is made of lamb-skin, it is therefore to Wilmshurst the sacramental Body of Christ, the Lamb of God. " The Great Benignity, the Hierophant… drew a garment as it were of pure white lambskin from the substance of His own person, in which garment and flesh were one, and girded it about my loins as an apron, saying ' This is my body, given for you, that your body may be given for me.' And again waves of coloured sound poured over me from the choired voices singing ' *Ecce Agnus Dei, qui tollit peccata mundi !* ' And a great strength passed into me, so that all weakness fled and I stood erect before Him, an accepted Apprentice Mason in the Grand Lodge Above." But as the Candidate in the third degree dies the death of Hiram, so is Wilmshurst in his Gnostic apocalypse himself crucified in a manner following the death of Him of whom he claims Hiram to be the type. " I hung suspended from that invisible Life-Tree ; myself a cross ; myself the crucified upon that cross…And my Craftsman's apron, at once a weight and a support to my straining loins, felt growing into me, to be becoming of my very flesh and substance. I knew now why, traditionally depicted as a loin-cloth, this garment alone was worn upon the Cross by the King of the Jews, the Supreme Chief of all Initiates…Nothing of me still was, save the labouring spirit that strove to be born but could not."

Eventually, however, came his joyful raising, and " my good

1. *The Masonic Initiation*, (1924) pp. 216–7.

Brother gripped me as a Master Mason. We drew together in an embrace of fellowship so fervent that we seemed to coalesce beyond the possibility of further separateness."[1]

I quote these disgusting blasphemies only because, apart perhaps from the revolting details of the apron, Wilmshurst does at least show logically the direction in which an even symbolical identification of Hiram with Christ must inevitably lead. How else, if Hiram is Christ, can the third degree be interpreted except through the Candidate's own initiation through his own mystical crucifixion ? The Christian indeed dies unto sin with Christ in his baptism, but it is the most satanic of all heresies to believe that the Christian can achieve his own salvation by being crucified independently of Christ, by repeating in himself the one sacrifice once offered by the only One who could possibly offer it.

Not unnaturally Christian Masons are inclined to disown altogether the mystical rubbish of Ward and Wilmshurst, and find it highly embarrassing. Yet the fact remains that both these authors have enjoyed enormous sales for their books, which certainly suggests a considerable interest in them, and wide sympathy, if not agreement, with their point of view. Many of Ward's books, including the one from which I quote, are prefaced in highly commendatory terms by Sir John Cockburn, once Grand Deacon of England, and Deputy Grand Master of Australia. Wilmshurst, whose works are still commended in the Masonic press, was rewarded for his services in lecturing to Lodges on the meaning of Masonry by the conferment on him of Provincial Grand Rank by the late Earl of Harewood in person in October, 1926. Masons should certainly consider these points before writing off these and similar authors as individual fantasiasts without any authority, influence, or standing in the Craft. However offensive and blasphemous their sentiments may be, Christian Masons *as Masons* have never made any effective protest against these books. As Christians they only do so in evasive terms when such literature is quoted against them by non-Masons.

So when Canon Covey-Crump in *The Hiramic Tradition* included our Lord among the gallery of possible originals for

1. Op. cit. These quotations are all from the chapter *Apocalypsis*, pp. 146–182.

71

Hiram, although he wrote in the more sober tradition of Hutchinson and Oliver in listing merely the external similarities without following them to their logical conclusions, he was not only treading on very dangerous ground, but doing so in very dangerous company. And this is the inevitable position of all those well-meaning Masons who adopt, probably in all innocence, this interpretation.

Not that the alternatives are very much better. If the ritual is followed with sincerity it clearly partakes of the nature of an alien mystery-cult of some sort, whoever Hiram was. It claims to confer an esoteric light which leads to immortality, and if Hiram be not Christ, it opens the door to the Grand Lodge Above by a short cut which completely by-passes Calvary. In either case it is substituting or supplementing the divinely-ordained rites of the Church which Christ founded by others secretly practised behind locked doors.

If the hearty businessman Mason, or the hearty Anglican Vicar, can laugh the whole thing off as a bit of moral allegory or even harmless mummery (which of course is the attitude of the majority), they can only work the ritual at the expense of some sacrifice of spiritual sincerity and integrity, for all is performed most solemnly and prayerfully before the open Word of God, and in His Holy Name.

If Masonry is not religion, it is certainly playing at religion.

V

THE HOLY ROYAL ARCH

For consider, O all ye who are busy with such inventions :—Whereas He alone is called God the Father, Who really is so, whom ye call Artificer ; whereas the Scriptures also know Him only as God ; whereas again the Lord acknowledges Him only as His own Father, and knows no other.

St. Irenaeus (A.D. 203) Against Heresies.

" Again there is sprung up
An heretic, an arch one."

Shakespeare, King Henry VIII.

THE early history of the Royal Arch degree is baffling and obscure. There are those who claim for it an antiquity equal to the rest of Craft Masonry of which, they say, it has always formed an integral part. Others maintain that, although some of the esoteric teaching and symbols now found in the Royal Arch are traceable in embryo to the early decades of the eighteenth century it was not until the 1740's and 1750's that it arose as a separate degree.[1] Those preferring to base conclusions on established facts rather than starting with a theory and finding or twisting facts to fit it tend to take the latter view.

It has been suggested that the core, at least, of the Royal Arch legend was at one time included in Craft workings as the " Master's Part," that is, in the ceremony of installation of the Worshipful Master to the chair of the Lodge. The Rev. George Oliver thought it originated with the Chevalier Ramsay in France. Others find evidence for an Irish origin. All that is known with certainty is that by the middle of the eighteenth century Royal Arch Masonry had taken root in England and steadily increased in popularity, particularly among the

1. See Knoop and Jones, *The Genesis of Freemasonry*, Chapter XIII ; Bernard E. Jones, *Freemasons' Guide and Compendium*, Chapter XXXIV ; and John Stokes, *Royal Arch Masonry* for recent historical scholarship in this degree. Notable contributions in the nineteenth century are Gould, *History of Freemasonry*, Vol. 11, p. 457 *et seq.* ; W. J. Hughan, *Origin of the English Rite of Freemasonry*, p. 79 *et seq.* ; and Henry Sadler, *Masonic Facts and Fictions*, p. 165.

Ancients. Not only did it provide a happy ending to the tragedy of the third degree, a discovery which made good the loss, and genuine secrets to replace the substituted secrets with which the Craft must be content, but it also had a stronger element of mysticism, probably with a more elaborate ritual, which made its appeal to some at a time when the official religion of the Established Church was at its lowest and driest ebb.

The well-worn formula with which the Articles of Union in 1813 accepted the Royal Arch, that " Pure Antient Masonry consists of three degrees and no more ; viz. those of the Entered Apprentice, the Fellow Craft, and the Master Mason (including the Supreme Order of the Holy Royal Arch) " and the declaration to the newly-exalted in that order that he has not taken a fourth degree, but has merely completed the third, are not so much historical statements of fact as articles of compromise. The Moderns would not allow more than three degrees. In the eighteenth century the Royal Arch was in practice a separate degree. So it is to all intents and purposes today, under the separate (though of course overlapping) control of Grand Chapter, not of Grand Lodge.[1]

Ritually the Royal Arch is not so much a fulfilment and completion of the third degree as a sequel to it, based on a legend separated by nearly half a millenium from the death of Hiram.[2]

As I have already given the Royal Arch ritual in full in

1. Both bodies are administered from Freemasons' Hall in London. The Earl of Scarbrough is Grand Master of the Craft, and also First Grand Principal of Supreme Grand Chapter. His deputy the Earl of Derby is second Grand Principal. Indeed it is laid down that these offices in Grand Chapter, together with the Grand Scribe (secretary), Treasurer and Registrar devolve upon those holding the corresponding positions in Grand Lodge, if they are qualified by having taken the Royal Arch degree. In about two-thirds of the Provinces there is the same identity of Provincial Grand Master of the Craft and Superintendent of the Chapter. Local or " Private " Chapters must be attached to Lodges, and bear the same number, and in most cases the same name. There is no separate Board of Benevolence and no separate charities. Hence it may be said that the distinction between Grand Lodge and Grand Chapter is administratively purely departmental.

2. There is a series known as the Cryptic Degrees, still worked, which fill in this gap to a certain extent, to the fall of Jerusalem, and give some account of the building of the vault and Hiram's prophecy that at his death the secrets would be safely concealed. These degrees are Most Excellent Master, Royal Master, Select Master, and Super-Excellent Master. The rituals (latest issue, 1934) are published from Mark Masons' Hall.

Darkness Visible a very brief recapitulation of the legend is all that is required here.[1] The scene is Jerusalem in the days of Zerubbabel after the Decree of Cyrus which ended the Babylonian captivity. Work has already started on clearing the ground of the ruins of King Solomon's Temple preparatory to rebuilding it. Three Sojourners arrive from Babylon and request the Sanhedrin (which the Royal Arch Chapter represents) to be allowed to take part in this undertaking. Zerubbabel, Joshua, and Haggai who preside question them, and finally put them to work clearing away the ruins, instructing them to report immediately if they make any discovery they deem of importance. In the course of their labours they discover the top of a dome. They remove three keystones, and one of the Sojourners is lowered into the vault beneath, where he finds a scroll (the long-lost Pentateuch), and an altar in the form of a double cube ; on the front are the initials of the original three Grand Masters ; Solomon King of Israel, Hiram King of Tyre, and Hiram Abiff. On the top of the altar is a " plate of gold " with a triangle within a circle. On the circle is inscribed the name JEHOVAH, and on the three sides of the triangle JAH BUL ON. These discoveries are reported to the Sanhedrin, which declares that the long-lost secrets have been discovered ; the Sojourners are rewarded by being invested with the insignia and secrets of the Royal Arch, and three lectures, historical, symbolical, and mystical, are delivered to them explaining further the teachings of this supreme degree.

It has been alleged that in the eighteenth century this degree had specifically Christian elements as worked by the Ancients. No rituals actually survive to prove or disprove this, and it must be largely a matter of conjecture. But there can be no disputing the position now. As J. S. M. Ward has said, " The R.A. today is not Christian, and particular care has been taken to eliminate anything which would indicate a Christian meaning. ...This fact is important and enables men to enter our order

---

1. There is no " authorized " or official ritual for the Royal Arch, any more than in the Craft. Several workings have been published by A. Lewis, including Aldersgate, Sussex, Metropolitan, Complete, Oxford, and Perfect. Geo. Kenning & Son publish Hornsey and Cornwallis workings. Many others (my own collection has over thirty) have been privately printed ; that of M. M. Taylor enjoying considerable popularity. Quotations in the text, unless otherwise specified, are from Aldersgate, which in practice serves as a norm.

who are not Christians in the strict sense of the word."[1]
From which it would appear to follow that only those " who are
not Christians in the strict sense of the word " can logically
enter the Royal Arch at all. Despite the existence of considerable
numbers of Royal Arch clergy and even bishops which might
seem to disprove this contention, certain facts are abundantly
clear and have never been answered or disproved.

It is very often pointed out that the Royal Arch Chapter is
opened with the Collect for Purity (" Almighty God, unto whom
all hearts are open...") with which the Order of Holy Communion in the Book of Common Prayer begins. Royal Arch
masons unfamiliar with this rite will occasionally go so far as to
imply that Cranmer and his successors were paying Freemasonry
a delicate compliment by including this Masonic prayer in the
liturgy of the Church.[2] " Many Masons listening on the radio
to the inspiringly solemn Coronation Service in the Abbey,"
reported the *Freemasons' Chronicle* of June 20th, 1953, " must
have been struck to hear recited in its entirety by the Archbishop
of Canterbury in the course of the Dedication rites, the Prayer
in use in the Royal Arch at the Opening of the Chapter."
In the Anglican liturgy, of course, this prayer is offered in
Christ's name, and is a Christian prayer. In the Royal Arch
the closing words " through Christ our Lord " are most pointedly
omitted, and therefore it ceases to be a Christian prayer. It
could be offered to almost any God. In the Masonic context it
precedes the triangular invocations of Jehovah Jah-Bul-On.

Nobody who knows what religion means could claim that the
Royal Arch is not " religious." Even those who maintain that
Craft Masonry is just harmless playing at Old Testament games
and moral allegory would find it impossible to say the same of
this degree. It breathes religion from beginning to end, and
claims to teach about the name and nature of God Himself.
The following facts are simply indisputable. All quotations are
from the ritual itself.

The title is the *Holy* Royal Arch, and holy means set apart
for a sacred use.

1. *An Explanation of the Royal Arch Degree*, p. 13.
2. Actually this collect does not appear to have been introduced into
   Royal Arch workings before the revision of the Rev. Adam Brown,
   about 1834. It is not to be found in most Scottish rituals, where
   borrowing from the Prayer Book would be less popular.

The pass-word to it is *Ammi Ruhamah*, or, " My people have found mercy."

The prayer over the Candidate asks God to " grant that the Brother who now seeks to participate in the *light of our mysteries* " may be endued with a portion of the divine Spirit.

The Candidate is bidden to " advance toward the *Sacred Shrine* in which they (the mysteries) are deposited, by seven steps, halting and bowing at the third, fifth, and seventh, for at each step you will approach nearer to the Sacred and Mysterious Name of the True and Living God Most High."

This name, veiled on the Altar, is JEHOVAH JAH-BUL-ON.

The Three Greater Lights of the degree are the " creative, preservative and annihilative powers of the Deity " a correspondence to Brahma, Vishnu, and Shiva.

The three Principals at their installation are given as their own " secret " words three titles of God, *Jah* for Zerubbabel, *El Shaddai* for Haggai, and *El Elohe* for Joshua.

The five signs of the Royal Arch " mark in a peculiar manner the relation we bear to the Most High as creatures offending against His mighty will and power, yet still the adopted children of His mercy." They are even referred to as " Sacred Signs."

The third lecture deals with the " mystical portion of this Degree," and declares that it " inspires its members with the most exalted ideas of God, it leads to the exercise of the purest and most devout piety."

The name of Christ is completely omitted throughout.

Anyone but a Freemason who drew up a new ritual incorporating all these points and submitted it to his Bishop to ask permission to use it for meetings of Boy Scouts or a Men's Guild would be assured of a monumental snub. He would even be told that, as a Christian, he was dabbling in dangerous things. If he protested that such a ritual was not religious at all, he would be laughed at. Freemasonry, however, has been described even by Bishops as a handmaid of the Church. But Mother Church has never asked for her handmaid's references.

Clearly some pretty drastic allegorizing must be resorted to !

Those who draw parallels between the first three degrees of the Craft and the birth, life, and death of Our Lord consider that the Royal Arch represents His resurrection, or even His ascension, and the beatific vision. " When the sprig of acacia blooms at the head of his soul's sepulchre," Wilmshurst writes of the newly-exalted Mason, " he will understand at one and the same moment the mystery of Golgotha, the mystery of the death of Hiram, and the meaning of the Royal Arch ceremony of exaltation.... It is then that the mystery is consummated. The Great Light breaks. The Vital and Immortal Principle comes to self-consciousness in him. The Glory of the Lord is revealed to him and in him, and all his flesh sees it.... The condition attained by the illumined Candidate is the equivalent of what in Christian theology is known as the Beatific Vision and in the East as *Samadhi*." But as we have seen, the identification of Hiram with Christ, and of the Candidate with Hiram, in the third degree, must inevitably lead to Gnosticism; even more true is this in the Royal Arch. " He is able to discern that it was himself who was at first ' without form and void ' and who in virtue of that *Fiat Lux* has at last become transformed from chaos and unconsciousness into a form so perfect and lucid as to become a co-conscious vehicle of the Divine Wisdom itself."[1]

Those wishing to see a Christian meaning in the Royal Arch will sometimes point out a similarity between the discovery of the long-hidden word in the vault and the *logos* doctrine of the prologue to St. John's Gospel. There is some Masonic authority for this identification. Until nearly the middle of the nineteenth century the first verse at least, " In the beginning was the word, and the word was with God, and the word was God," commonly appeared in the ritual. It does to this day in the United States, where the rituals in many respects follow early forms now largely discarded in England. An early manuscript ritual (about 1797) of the Chapter of Hope, No. 49, at Deptford contains the instruction that if the Candidate was a Christian, the first chapter of St. John's Gospel was to be read to him, but if a Jew, the fortieth chapter of Isaiah, " Comfort ye, comfort ye, my people," etc.

But any identification of the " word " in Freemasonry with the " word " (*logos*) in St. John's Gospel will result in near blasphemy. The *logos* of St. John does not refer to the name of God, the incomprehensible Jehovah, nor to the Law, nor to the Scriptures, but to the creative and healing power of God ; the

1. *The Meaning of Masonry* (10th Edition, 1951) Chapter IV, *The Holy Royal Arch.*

word of God in the sense that God spake the word, and the heavens and the earth were created. The climax of St. John's prologue is " the word was made flesh, and dwelt among us " in the incarnation of our Lord and Saviour. Would any Mason dare to say of the metal letters of which his word is composed surrounded by six lighted candles that " the word was made brass, and dwelt among us?" That of course is the symbolical inference of the Royal Arch ritual, which declares that three of those lighted candles which surround the words on the altar " represent the Sacred Word itself, and are emblematical of the creative, preservative and annihilative powers of the Deity."

The word is only verbally communicated, almost as an incantation, in the Chapter, a syllable each at a time by groups of three people standing together so as to form a series of triangles with their feet and hands. " In times of antiquity names of God and symbols of divinity were always enclosed in triangles; in the days of Pythagoras the triangle was considered the most sacred of emblems " explains the Mystical lecture of this degree. The whole process suggests the primitive idea of a talismanic and occult significance given to a mystic and secret divine name and to its correct pronunciation. There is nothing Christian about this whatsoever, and nothing could be further from the meaning of the *logos* of St. John. As to the nature of the word itself, the priests and prophets of the Old Testament would have been horrified at its blasphemy and its syncretism. If good Christian folk, including our Anglican clergy, really enjoy this kind of thing, it is a pity that the name of God should be the subject of it.

The triad-mongers who would believe that the Holy Trinity is represented by any group of three have rich material in the Royal Arch. Apart from externals such as the three Principals, three Sojourners, three keystones to the arch, three greater and three lesser lights and so on, there are two distinct trinities of divine names or attributes specifically introduced. The Christian Royal Arch Mason, then (along with the Hindu), may indeed claim with justification that this degree is " definitely trinitarian."

The first of these trinities is the word itself, the " Sacred and Mysterious Name " made up of Jah, Bul, and On. It is hard to find any Masonic commentator of any faith who does not agree that Bul is a version of Baal. There is less unanimity about On, the majority equating him with Osiris, but others with the city of On (or Heliopolis) identified with sun-worship. The Oxford Royal Arch ritual adds in explanation of the word that " Joseph in Egypt married the daughter of Potiphera, Priest of On."[1]

Albert Pike was one of the greatest figures of Masonry in America. The Ancient and Accepted Rite, of which he was Grand Commander, is in its present form largely the work of his hands, and the rituals are still based on his revision. No name stands higher in America, and he is venerated in this country as well by those in the higher degrees. His words therefore cannot be brushed aside as a mere unofficial and individual private opinion. But even if he could be so disowned, it would be difficult to find fault with his declaration on the Royal Arch word, which even without his authority has its own weight of truth and logic. In a now rare book which very naturally is practically unknown to Masons today,[2] he wrote:—

" I think it is high time that Royal Arch Masons began to look seriously at this matter. If there is anything *real* in our professions, if our Royal Arch Masonry is not a hideous and detestably hypocritical farce, it is almost a religion. We inscribe on the mitre of the High Priest, *Kadosh-l 'Yehuah—Holiness to the Lord !* We forbid taking his name in vain ; and we claim to be the lineal descendants of those Israelites to whom every Baal was a destestable thing, an unclean abomination ; to associate whose name with that of the Lord God of Israel would have been an unpardonable sacrilege. And we find Royal Arch Masons pretending to bring up into the *Sanctuary*, from the place where it was deposited by Solomon, the Holy Ark of the Covenant of the Lord, on which once were the cherubim, and where the Shekinah, the very God, cohabitant, spoke to Israel the oracles of truth ; and written on this, by the side of the name of God, *and forming part of the same Triad*, the unclean name of

1. From Genesis XLI, 50.

2. *The Holy Triad—A Reply to the Grand Chaplain and Grand High Priest of the Grand Royal Arch Chapter of Massachusetts.* (Washington, 1873) pp. 24 *et seq.*

Baal...[1]

" When they so accept Baal as a name of the true and Supreme God, and as put upon the Ark as such by Solomon, they accept it with all its surnames. It is Baal-Zebub, Baal-Amun, Baal-Tsaphun, and Baal-Paar or Peor......

" The whole question...is whether Baal was *to the Hebrews of the time of Solomon* the name of an evil and malignant being, at enmity with Jehovah, accursed and detested. If it was, it has no business on the Ark, and infinitely less in a word of Triads... The name of Baal *cannot* form one of those Triads ; because Baal *is not* a member of the divine trinity. To make it so is sacrilege, is blasphemy, is an insult offered to God with whose name the abomination is thus coupled...No man or body of men can make me accept as a sacred word, as a symbol of the Infinite and Eternal Godhead, a mongrel word, in part composed of the name of an accursed and beastly heathen god, whose name has been for more than two thousand years an appellation of the devil...No word has any business in the Royal Arch degree that makes the name of a heathen deity one of the names of the true God."

So said a prominent and authoritative Mason ; hence the allegation that it is only the anti-Mason who can interpret the word so is groundless.

What answer, then, can be made to this crushing indictment of blasphemy ? Our good Anglican Bishops to whom we look for spiritual guidance can only reply that it is all very symbolic, and that they don't *really* mean Baal when " we three do meet and agree in love and unity the Sacred Word to keep and never to divulge the same...." But Albert Pike was surely aware of that. It was even the symbolical use of the word that he objected to.

Here is the explanation as it is actually given to the Candidate in the Mystical Lecture :—

" It is a compound word, and the combination forms the word Jah-Bul-On. It is in four languages...Chaldee, Hebrew, Syriac, and Egyptian. Jah is the Chaldee name of God, signifying ' His essence and majesty incomprehensible '. It is also a

1. In American Royal Arch workings the Ark of the Covenant is discovered in the vault. Inscribed on it is the same " sacred and mysterious name " as on the Altar in English workings, with slight variations in spelling.

Hebrew word, signifying ' I am and shall be ', thereby expressing the actual, future, and eternal existence of the Most High.
Bul is a Syriac word denoting Lord, or Powerful ; it is in itself a
compound word, being formed from the preposition Beth, in or
on, and Ul, Heaven, or on high ; therefore the meaning of the
word is Lord in Heaven, or on high. On is an Egyptian word,
signifying Father of All, thereby expressing the omnipotence of
the Father of All, as in that well-known prayer ' Our Father,
which art in Heaven '. The various significations of the words
may be thus collected : I am and shall be ; Lord in Heaven or
on High ;

> ' Father of All ! in every age
> In every clime adored
> By saint, by savage, and by sage,
> Jehovah, Jove, or Lord ' ".

The explanation may sound innocent enough, though the
inclusion of Pope's Universal Prayer is a clear admission of an
anti-Christian syncretism. Surely, says the Christian Mason,
there is nothing unorthodox in teaching that God is Lord in
Heaven, and Father of All, even though the Royal Arch (as
a priestly Mason of many degrees admitted), " presents for the
adoration of its initiates an idea of God which is derived from
the pagan religions of antiquity."[1]

Why any Christian should adore an " idea of God," pagan or
otherwise, presented to him by any body other than the Church
has never been explained ; clearly the Christian revelation appears to them in need or capable of supplementing. But the
plain answer is that an innocuous dressing-up of one whom
Bro. Pike called an unclean abomination makes the name no
more Christian than that of Lucifer who, the Bible tells us, is
equally deceptive in presenting himself as an angel of light.

At the risk of becoming repetitious this point must be brought
home. It would be quite as easy, and masonically quite as
legitimate, and certainly no less Christian, to devise a symbolical
trinity such as Jah-Lucifer-Pan. The Mystical Lecture could
explain the last two items thus :—" Lucifer is a Latin word
meaning Bearer of Light.... Pan is a Greek word signifying

---

1. The Rev. J. L. C. Dart, *Christianity and Freemasonry*, in *Theology*,
April, 1951.

Love...the various significations of the words may be thus collected ; I am and shall be ; Bearer of Light ; God of Love." How harmless it sounds ! And however silly, this analogy is perfectly valid. It is only two centuries of Masonic usage and muddled thinking that has made their trinity seem respectable to them.

In the second trinity of the Royal Arch ritual the verbal approximation to Father, Son, and Holy Ghost is much closer. This is made up of the three Hebrew characters Aleph, Beth, and Lamed which appear at the points of the triangle on the Altar. With an exegesis that would horrify even the most ignorant Rabbi, these letters are explained thus :—

" The characters at the angles of the triangle are of exceeding importance, though it is immaterial where the combination is commenced, as each has reference to the Deity, or some Divine attribute. They are the Aleph, the Beth, and the Lamed of the Hebrew, corresponding with the A, B, and L of the English alphabet. Take the Aleph and the Beth, they form AB, which is Father ; take the Beth, the Aleph, and the Lamed, they form BAL, which is Lord ; take the Aleph and the Lamed, they form AL, which means Word ; take the Lamed, the Aleph, and the Beth, they form LAB, which signifies Heart or Spirit. Take each combination with the whole, and it will read thus: AB BAL, Father, Lord ; AL BAL, Word, Lord ; LAB BAL, Spirit, Lord."

But this again is Baal masquerading with an even closer resemblance to an angel of light. Moloch also could be taken to mean Lord or Powerful, and this trinity is as anti-Christian as Father, Moloch ; Word, Moloch ; Spirit, Moloch.

Any attempt, therefore, to read Christian symbolism or allegory into the Royal Arch leads to blasphemies even greater than in the Craft. Such an attempt is a confusion of superficial verbal similarities, based on even greater confusion of thinking.

VI

MARK AND ARK

The man presumed the stone to be ancient, much as he represented it to have been rudely carved by himself in an idle mood, and to display letters intended to bear neither more nor less than the simple construction of BILL STUMPS HIS MARK. . . .The Pickwick Club (as might have been expected from so enlightened an institution) received this statement with the contempt it deserved, expelled the presumptuous and ill-conditioned Blotton, and voted Mr. Pickwick a pair of gold spectacles. . . .

Charles Dickens, The Pickwick Papers.

TRADITIONALLY the Mark degree in Masonry was regarded as an off-shoot from the second, or Fellow Craft degree. As usual, there is much confusion and doubt over its early history and nature[1] and only the briefest survey is appropriate here,

The practice among medieval Masons of marking their work for purposes of identification with a distinctive character or device, analogous to the hall-marks of the goldsmith and silversmith, is well known, and these masons' marks are a distinctive feature of many an ancient cathedral and church all over Europe. In Scotland the practice seems to have been especially widespread and organized ; the celebrated Rosslyn chapel in particular abounds with these marks. William Schaw, Master of Works to James VI of Scotland ordered, in the famous Schaw Statutes of 1598, that the marks of all masons should be duly registered and inserted in their work. The practice is not quite extinct in stone quarries and masonry yards even today. This system of masons' marks, however, was purely ' operative ' and

---

1. Books dealing specifically with this degree are fewer than books about the Craft or Royal Arch. There are, however, the following : J. A. Grantham, *An Introduction to Mark Masonry* (privately published, 1934) Bernard H. Springett, *The Mark Degree* (A. Lewis, 1946). Bernard E. Jones, *Freemasons' Guide and Compendium* (Harrap, 1950), Chapter XXXV on Mark Masonry. Kenneth R. H. Mackenzie, *The Mark Work* (originally published 1884, reprinted, revised by the Rev. J. T. Lawrence, by A. Lewis, 1944). This little book is mainly concerned with the conduct of the ritual, but it also deals briefly with the symbolism and history of the degree. There are also articles in the various Masonic Encyclopædias.

practical. Not until the eighteenth century, as far as is known, did its symbolism enter the sphere of speculative Freemasonry.

The degree system in the eighteenth century was, compared with today, extremely fluid. There were no separate Mark Lodges as now, and private Lodges, particularly among the " Ancients," conferred such degrees as were traditional with them. Grand Lodge in its earlier days was more a federation of Lodges than a controlling body over them, and it was not until the Union in 1813 that Masonry was regimented and codified, and extraneous degrees, other than the Royal Arch, were literally dislodged. Some of the material now in the Mark degree may at one time have been included in the Fellow Craft, hence isolated references to distinctively Mark symbolism do not necessarily imply that a separate degree was worked. To make things even more complicated, the Mark was at one time two successive degrees, Mark Man for the Fellow Crafts, and Mark Master exclusively for Master Masons ; the present single degree now incorporates the substance of both. And in addition a number of extraneous Mark titles hovered around to embroider the motif, the Link and Wrestle, Link and Chain, Mark and Link, Passing the Bridge, the Fugitive Mark, Christian Mark, Cain's Mark, Travelling Mark, Black Mark, and so on. As separate degrees, if indeed they ever really were so, they are now extinct, yet some of their symbolism is said to survive in local workings of North Country Mark Lodges. Passing the Bridge is a theme that still appears in some American Chapters as a preliminary to the Royal Arch (for which the Mark degree is there a prerequisite) and in Britain it emerges in two of the higher degrees, the first or Harodim degree of the Royal Order of Scotland, and the rather similar Red Cross of Babylon in the Allied group. There are hints of it, too, in the fifteenth degree of the Ancient and Accepted Rite known as the Knight of the Sword. This is not worked in Great Britain, except occasionally as a museum piece.

The main sources of information on the confused early history of the Mark are the minute-books and records of early Lodges. The first reference seems to be in the by-laws of Lodge Doric Kilwinning, of Port Glasgow, which stipulated in 1758 that the fee for being made Mark Master was to be 1s. 1½d. The greatest name associated with the introduction of Mark Masonry into the south of England was Thomas Dunckerley (an illegitimate son of George II as Prince of Wales), who, as Provincial Grand Master of Hampshire visited the Chapter of Friendship in Portsmouth, " and having lately rec'd the ' Mark ' he made the Bre'n 'Mark Masons' and 'Mark Masters,' and each chose their Mark." The Marquis of Granby Lodge in Durham was conferring the degrees by 1773, St. Thomas's Lodge, London, in 1777. From then on to the Union of 1813 Mark Masonry seems to have spread fairly rapidly.

The Union, however, dealt the Mark a crippling blow by refusing to recognize it as part of " pure and antient masonry." Yet their ceremonies went on, and some Lodges where the tradition was well established continued to work the degree without any authority. In 1851 Mark Masonry started its independent existence in London with the foundation of the Bon Accord Lodge, which received its charter from the Chapter of that name in Aberdeen. In Scotland the Mark was fully recognized, but there was much long-drawn-out wrangling in both countries over the legality of this charter and the right of Bon Accord Aberdeen to confer it ; in spite of this, however, the new Mark Lodge flourished in London, and by 1856 it had achieved a membership of some hundred and twenty.

An effort was made in this year to secure Grand Lodge recognition for the degree, and a resolution was actually passed by that body authorizing its sanction. But at the next meeting Grand Lodge refused to confirm the minute on the ground that it was not empowered to make such an innovation. This was a final and decisive blow ; all hopes of recognition disappeared, and the two bodies have ever since lead their own independent lives.

The Bon Accord Lodge accepted the inevitable and leagued with three others to bring into being the first Mark Grand Lodge. Again there was opposition and strife, for some Mark Lodges regarded this new body as self-constituted and spurious, and preferred to receive their charters from the Supreme Grand Chapter of Scotland, which made for strained relationships. It was not until 1878 that peace and harmony were finally restored, and the old Mark Grand Lodge became the present Grand Lodge of Mark Master Masons of England and Wales and Dominions and Dependencies of the British Crown.

The present position is in some respects anomalous, but it

works, because the English love anomalies and take pride in making them work. Although official recognition is still lacking, relations are extremely cordial and co-operative at every turn between the two bodies, and there are many who attain high rank in both. The Mark Grand Lodge, operating from cramped and temporary quarters in Kingsway, use Freemasons' Hall in Gt. Queen Street for their Quarterly Communications and other large assemblies. They have their own Fund of Benevolence for the relief of Mark Masons and their families in need, and for educational grants, but they liberally support the hospital and the schools of the main Masonic body. For after all, every Mark Mason must first also be a Master Mason in the Craft—there is of course no such thing as initiation *ab initio* into the Mark, or into any other of the higher or side degrees. The lack of official recognition has in practice become the merest technicality.

The Mark ritual is of interest from the religious point of view because it contains certain elements claimed to be Messianic, and in England at least (unlike the Craft rituals) it contains a significant quotation from the New Testament.[1] Its general character and drama are more " operative," and this has been adduced as an argument for its greater antiquity, but the historical evidence for this is extremely obscure.

Let us examine this degree in greater detail

The Candidate for advancement, as it is called, wears his Master Masons' apron ; customs vary, but the usual form of preparation is to remove the coat and roll up the shirt sleeves. He is announced as one " who has served his time as an Entered Apprentice, worked in the quarries as a Fellow Craft, and is now desirous of becoming a Mark Master Mason to qualify him to preside over a Lodge of Operative Masons." The password

1. The earliest printed Mark workings are in the irregualr disclosure, Carlile's *Manual of Freemasonry*, pp. 190–9. The two degrees of Mark Man and Mark Master are preserved, but the material is very dissimilar to the ritual today. It has been suggested that Carlile's sources were spurious, but Bernard E. Jones (*Freemasons' Guide and Compendium*, pp. 537–8) assumes that they give a substantially accurate picture of the workings of that time.

Modern authentic rituals are published from the Mark Masons' Hall " published under the Authority of the General Board " and the copy I follow in this chapter is dated 1946. A. Lewis & Co. (Masonic Publishers) also publish Mark rituals. Scottish versions will be found in Wm. Harvey's *Complete Manual of Freemasonry* (Dundee, 1950), *Scottish Craft Rituals* (Kenning & Son), *The Scottish Ritual of Craft Freemasonry* (John Bethune, Edinburgh) and others.

(Joppa) and the pass grip (given by locking the fingers as one would do in pulling another up a steep place, and bringing the tips of the thumbs together), are given for him by the Inner Guard. He is admitted on the chisel, which is applied to his left breast and tapped with the mallet.

The Candidate proves himself a Mason by perambulating the Lodge, and giving the Craft signs to the officers, and then kneels while this prayer is offered :—" May the Great Overseer of the Universe pour down on this convocation the continual dew of His blessing, and whether we be stationed on the plains of Zaradatha or in the forests of Lebanon ; whether employed on the rough Ashlar or in putting in the keystone of a Mystic Arch, may He be with His faithful workmen ; and when called off from our labours here, may we be found worthy to receive the wages promised to those who work diligently in His Holy Temple. So mote it be."

He is then told that in accordance with ancient custom he must choose his own distinctive mark, any device not already in use by a member of the Lodge, and this is duly recorded. He is designated a Mark Man, his device on a card is surrounded by the equilateral triangle (the mark of the Worshipful Master) as a sign of approval, and holding this with his thumb in the palm of his hand he presents it at the wicket in front of the Senior Warden, and receives his " wages."[1]

Having been thus admitted a Mark Man, he is now advanced to the degree of Mark Master. He proceeds to the pedestal in the east by nine steps, the first five as if ascending a winding staircase as in the Fellow Craft degree, followed by two steps long and slow, and another two short and quick. Kneeling on both knees, with both hands on the Volume of the Sacred Law, he takes his Obligation. In addition to vowing secrecy, he swears that " I will not unjustly use any Brother's mark, but will receive it when presented to me, and grant his request, if just, and within my power, the same not being detrimental to myself or my connections, but I shall not feel myself bound again to relieve him until he shall have redeemed his mark from his former obligation."

The penalty which he swears to accept if unfaithful is a relatively mild one ; the removal of his right ear and right hand.

1. The wage is usually a token about the size of a penny, bearing various symbols of this degree.

It shares with the somewhat similar penalty of the Installed Master in the Craft the distinction of being not completely lethal, however vexatious its infliction. As a pledge of his fidelity the Candidate seals the oath by kissing the Sacred Volume four times.

After the obligation the Candidate is sent symbolically back to work in the quarries, actually out of the Lodge to the ante-room. He is divested of his Masonic apron, and with the two Deacons who have withdrawn with him, puts on a larger working apron. They re-enter the Lodge, announced as " workmen from the quarries with materials for the building of the Holy Temple which they are anxious to submit for approval." The Junior Deacon carries a model of an oblong ashlar stone, the Senior Deacon a square one, and the Candidate a model of a keystone. These are in turn submitted to the Junior Overseer to be approved ; the first two are tested with the square, rapped with the mallet, and declared to be " fair work and square, such as is required for the building," and the Junior Overseer whispers the password. But when the Candidate follows the Deacons and produces his keystone, it is summarily rejected. " This is a curiously wrought stone," says the Junior Overseer, " neither square nor oblong. I cannot receive it." He refuses, therefore, to give the Candidate the password, as the work is not in accordance with his plans.

The three then proceed to the Senior Overseer where the process is repeated ; the Deacons present their work and give the password, the Candidate's keystone is again rejected, and he has not the password to give. Yet the Senior Deacon is impressed. " Although it is not in accordance with my plans, yet from the masterly skill displayed in its execution I am unwilling to reject it on my own responsibility," he explains. He gives the Candidate the option of returning to the quarries to try again, or of submitting the keystone at his own risk and without the password to the Master Overseer. The Candidate adopts the latter course, and not only is his work again decisively rejected, but he is sternly rebuked for his presumption. The Senior and Junior Overseers, too, are rebuked for allowing the Candidate to proceed thus far, and the Master Overseer orders the keystone to be " heaved over among the rubbish."

The drama of the rejected keystone is temporarily interrupted at this point by the announcement of the Senior Warden that it is time for the Craftsmen to receive their wages. Accordingly the Deacons marshall up the Brethren in line to march to the Senior Warden's wicket. The Mark Anthem, or part of it, which goes to the tune of " God Save the Queen," may optionally be sung while this is going on :—

Mark Masters, all appear
Before the Chief Overseer—
In concert move ;
Let him your work inspect,
For the Chief Architect,
If there be no defect,
    He will approve.

You who have passed the square,
For your reward prepare—
Join heart and hand ;
Each with his mark in view,
March with the just and true ;
Wages to you are due,
    At your command.

Hiram, the widow's son,
Sent unto Solomon
Our great keystone ;
On it appears the name
Which raises high the fame
Of all to whom the same
    Is truly known.

Now to the westward move,
Where, full of strength and love,
Hiram doth stand ;
But if imposters are
Mix'd with the worthy there,
Caution them to beware
    Of their right hand.

Now to the praise of those
Who triumph'd o'er their foes ;
Well played their parts :
To the praiseworthy three

Who founded this degree,
May all their virtues be
Deep in our hearts.[1]

The Brethren in turn approach the wicket, and each thrusts his hand through the hole in it to receive his wages. The Candidate who is last in line, has no way of seeing that the hand must be presented in a certain position, which is with the thumb, first and second fingers extended, the fourth and fifth fingers clasped to the palm, which is the recognized sign. In all innocence he simply pushes through his hand. The Senior Warden illustrates the meaning of the second half of the fourth verse of the Mark Anthem by seizing his hand and exclaiming " An imposter ! an imposter ! Off with his hand ! "

" Spare him ! Spare him ! " says the Senior Deacon. " He is not an imposter. I vouch for him as a Mark Man, having worked with him in the quarries."

" I denounce him," insists the Senior Warden, " as an imposter, having attempted to obtain the wages of a Mark Master without giving the token. The usual penalty must be inflicted."

Saner counsels prevail, however, after some argument, and the matter is taken to the Worshipful Master for judgment. The little crisis is all smoothed out. The Candidate proves himself as a Mark Man, and although the Worshipful Master cannot too strongly express his indignation that he should have attempted to obtain the wages of a Mark Master without being justly entitled to them, he recognizes that the fault was of ignorance and not of wilful intention to defraud. Accordingly he is again sent back to the quarries to knock out rectangular stones ; in other words, he sits down quietly in a corner of the Lodge.

After a brief spell of complete silence, the Senior Warden announces that the work is at a standstill.

" On what account ? " asked the Worshipful Master.

" For want of a Keystone for the Sacred Arch of King Solomon's Temple," replies the Senior Warden.

" I well remember issuing the designs for such a stone," expostulates the Master as he searches through his papers on the pedestal. " Here is a copy. Brother Junior Overseer, have you

1. This almost parody of a Christian doxology in these last lines is an ascription, not of course to the Holy Trinity but to Hiram King of Tyre, Solomon, and Hiram Abiff.

seen such a stone ? "

" Such a stone was brought to me for examination, but not being in accordance with my plans, I passed it to the Senior Overseer."

" Brother Senior Overseer," asks the Master, " What did you do with it ? "

" It not being in accordance with my plans," explains that officer, " nor with the instructions I had received, but possessing considerable beauty of workmanship, I passed it on to the Master Overseer for final approval or rejection."

" Brother Master Overseer, do you remember such a stone being submitted to you ? "

As there can be no further shelving the responsibility, the Master Overseer faces the music.

" I do, Worshipful Master, but seeing it was neither square nor oblong, nor in any way answering to my plans, nor to the instructions I had received, I ordered it to be heaved over among the rubbish, which was accordingly done."

" Let diligent search be made for it," says the Worshipful Master. " It is the most important stone in the building. Richly rewarded shall be he who succeeds in finding it."

The Brethren start searching, and it is, of course, the Candidate who finds it, guided by the Deacons.

" Worshipful Master," exclaims the Senior Deacon, " The stone is found ! "

" By whom ? "

" By the skilful Craftsman who prepared it."

" Let me see it." The Deacons bring up the Candidate, who presents the keystone to the Worshipful Master. He compares it with his plan. " It is indeed the very stone ! Brother Craftsman, I congratulate you not only on the skill displayed in having prepared this stone, but also upon your good fortune in being the bearer of it uninjured after it had been rejected by the Overseers, and to mark my deep sense of your merit and ability shall now proceed to entrust you with the secrets of the Mark Master Masons' degree."

It may be mentioned at this point (although in the ritual it is only explained later in the lecture) that the Overseers had lost the plans for the keystone, but the " ingenious and intelligent Fellow Craftsman, either having seen the perfect plan or forming a good idea of it from the nature of the work " carved it out on his own.

The conferring of the secrets follows. The Chaplain reads 2 Chron. II, 11-16, in which Hiram (or Huram) King of Tyre sends the other Hiram (Abiff) to King Solomon, and promises materials for the Temple. The last verse is the significant one for the pass grip and password Joppa, which so far the Deacon has given on the Candidate's behalf :—

" *And we will cut wood out of Lebanon, as much as thou shalt need : and we will bring it to thee in flotes by sea to Joppa : and thou shalt carry it up to Jerusalem.*"

The signs are given. The first one basically is the position of the fingers of the right hand when receiving the wages ; it is raised in the hailing sign, the normal salute used in entering or leaving the Lodge or addressing the Worshipful Master, and the penal sign chops the right hand off with the left. Then there is the Heave Over sign, a swinging movement inspired by the rejection of the keystone. At this point the 22nd verse of Psalm CXVIII is either read or chanted :—

" *The stone which the Builders refused is become the head stone of the corner.*" (Authorized Version)

Then there is the sign of Distress, accompanied by the words " Alas ! Alas ! My labour is lost ! " and lastly the sign of Thanksgiving, with clasped hands and uplifted countenance, with the exclamation " Thanks be to God, I have marked well."

The grip is imparted ; like the pass grip it is an elaborate handclasp which is far too conspicuous for recognition purposes outside the Lodge. It is given by linking the little fingers, closing the other fingers with their backs to each other each to each, and the thumbs touching as in the pass grip.

Next the Chaplain reads from Ezekiel, Chapter XLIV, verses 1, 2, 3 and 5. Again the last is the significant one :—

" *And the Lord said unto me, Son of Man, mark well, and behold with thine eyes, and hear with thine ears, all that I say unto thee concerning all the ordinances of the house of the Lord, and all the laws thereof ; and mark well the entering in of the house, with every going forth of the sanctuary.*"

This verse gives the word. The ancient word is *Keb Raioth* or sometimes *Kyrock*, " alluding to the people and signifying Companion of the Mark, but in most Lodges where the English language is spoken the words *Mark Well* are substituted."

Investiture with the apron follows, and Revelation II, 17, is read or sung :—

" *To him that overcometh will I give to eat of the hidden manna and I will give him a white stone and in the stone a new name written which no man knoweth saving he that receiveth it.*"

The jewel of the order is presented. This is a small model of the keystone ; on one side are certain Hebrew characters, and on the other, around a circle, are the letters H.T.W.S. S.T.K.S., standing for Hiram Tyrian Widow's Son, Sent to King Solomon. This is alleged to be the translation of the Hebrew characters. Later the Candidate has his mark engraved within the circle.

The ceremony concludes with the presentation of the working tools, the mallet and the chisel by which " we are reminded of the moral advantages of discipline and education, and are led to entertain a firm but humble hope that by the correction of irregularities and the subjugation of our passions, we may hereafter be found worthy to receive the approving mark of the Great Overseer of the Universe, as fitted to form part of that spiritual edifice, ' that house not made with hands, eternal in the heavens.' "

In the Mark degree, as in the Craft and Royal Arch, the triad-enthusiasts who assume that three of anything must symbolize the Holy Trinity have a happy hunting-ground. " One great one," says Bernard H. Springett in his popular little booklet[1] " is ever being impressed upon our minds, that of Body, Soul, and Spirit typified in turn by the W(orshipful) M(aster), S(enior) W(arden) and J(unior) W(arden) ; the Deacons and the Candidate ; the three Stones ; and at a later stage by the Candidate, the S(enior) W(arden) and the W(orshipful) M(aster)." Those interested can doubtless find many more.

A. E. Waite[2] says of this degree that " it takes us back to that earlier state of Masonry, the ante-Grand Lodge period, when rituals—such as they were—were not memorials of Judaistic Deism. There is none which bears comparison with it for the

1. *The Mark Degree* (A. Lewis, 1946) p. 62.
2. *A New Encyclopædia of Freemasonry*, Vol. II, p. 35.

wealth and significance of its Christian allusions and implicits."
Although Waite exaggerates, I think, both the pre-Grand Lodge
antiquity of the Mark degree and the extent of its Christian
implicits, it is perfectly true that the Mark was more popular
among the Ancients, with their rather stronger Christian tradition, than with the Moderns ; also that, as it was rejected at the
Union of 1813 its ritual was not subjected to the final de-
Christianizing policy of the United Grand Lodge.

In the sense that Our Lord is nowhere mentioned specifically
by name in the ritual, lectures, or prayers, the Mark degree is
no more Christian than the Craft. And incidentally the keystone
legend is no more scriptural than the rest of the Hiramic legend.
The morality of it seems a little confused.[1] Clearly the loss of the
designs for the keystone reflects no credit on the Overseers, and
in some versions of the ritual they are sternly rebuked, stripped
of all their privileges, and sent back to the quarries. The Craftsman represented by the Candidate is guilty of presumption and
of disobedience in turning out a stone which his private judgment tells him will one day be needed instead of turning out the
squared ashlar according to instructions. He is rebuked for this,
just as he is rebuked for claiming wages to which he is not
entitled, but is later honoured and rewarded when the stone is
urgently required to finish the Temple. In the altogether laud-
able context of commending private enterprise and initiative
against assembly-line monotony and bureaucracy in the quarries
the Craftsman's action is praiseworthy, and not un-Christian.
Yet the fact that the Craftsman has himself wrought the keystone, and has himself marked it with his own mark militates
against the validity of the symbolism so often urged, that this

1. An interesting and even less moral tradition which links the keystone
   with Jacob's Pillar, the Stone of Scone or Stone of Destiny in Westminster Abbey was to be found in the Early Grand Rite which once
   controlled some forty-seven miscellaneous and mainly extinct degrees
   in the south-west of Scotland. According to this legend, King Solomon,
   before the arrival of Hiram, had appointed a kinsman named Cavelum
   to be in charge of building the Temple, Hiram was jealous of him,
   and placed this Stone of Destiny so precariously over the north gate
   of the Temple that it fell on Cavelum and killed him. Solomon in his
   distress ordered the north gate to be for ever walled up ; hence Hiram
   paid the price of the murder in his own death, for he was denied the
   escape from his assassins that this fourth exit would have given him.
   Perhaps some future degree-monger will ascribe to this incident
   the crack in the stone which led to its being broken when it was removed
   from the Abbey by Scots Nationalists in 1951 !

" stone which the builders rejected " represents Christ, unless again the alleged " Christianity " of this degree is Gnostic rather than orthodox, with the Candidate himself, or in his works, representing Christ, and becoming *himself* the " head stone of the corner."[1]

For when A. E. Waite talks about " Christian implicits," and when others go even further and refer to the Mark as an essentially Christian degree, it is this rejection motif of the *lapis reprobatus* becoming the *caput anguli* which is mainly referred to. Officially of course the Mark degree falls into the same category as the Craft and Royal Arch in that all believers in a Higher Being are welcomed. " All masons know that no special religious tenet should be upheld in the Lodges—Mark or Craft— or referred to in any way."[2] But just as Craft Masons are free privately to interpret the Hiramic legend as a Christian allegory, so are Mark Masons to regard their workings as Christian prophecy, and in this latter case the purely superficial resemblances seem more obvious.

Although Masons profess to be devoted to the Bible, an extremely elementary scripture lesson seems to be necessary. There are two references to a foundation stone in the Old Testament. One is that which is quoted in the ritual, the 22nd verse of Psalm CXVIII : " The stone which the builders refused is become the head stone of the corner." We may pass over the not very important fact that the head of the corner does not mean the top but the extremity, not a keystone but a cornerstone. The stone, however, refers to Zion, in which is summed up the Kingdom of God. The other passage, Isaiah XXVIII, verse 16, makes this clear :—" Therefore thus saith the Lord God, Behold, I lay in Zion for a foundation a stone, a tried stone, a precious corner stone, a sure foundation."[3] This refers to the Kingdom of God, the divine protection of Jehovah, if not

1. Bernard Springett (*op. cit.* p. 50) describes an old ritual from Blackburn which avoids this difficulty by having the Candidate find the keystone in the quarry, but he has not wrought it himself. This, however, is exceptional and not in accordance with the authorized ritual put out by Mark Grand Lodge, nor with any of the twenty or so printed and manuscript rituals of this degree from England and Scotland in my possession.

2. *The Mark Work* (A. Lewis, 1944) p. 51.

3. Cf. also Genesis XLIX, verse 24 : ". .the hands of the mighty God of Jacob ; (from thence is the shepherd, the stone of Israel)."

to Jehovah Himself.

The Messianic application in the Bible is due to the fact that the person of the Messiah bears the same relation to a kingdom of living persons that Zion, the capital of the kingdom, does to the Kingdom. There is the further fulfilment of the verse from Psalm CXVIII in the rejection of Christ. Hence our Lord applies this prophecy to Himself.[1] St. Peter preaches of Jesus Christ of Nazareth that " this is the stone which was set at nought of you builders, which is become the head of the corner. Neither is there salvation in any other : for there is none other name given among men, whereby we must be saved."[2] He again teaches the same in his first Epistle General.[3]

For the Mark Mason to appropriate to a stone which he has himself fashioned for King Solomon's Temple a verse of scripture referring to a stone which God has fashioned and laid in Zion seems presumptuous, to say the least of it. But to claim his own handiwork as a prototype of Christ is blasphemous. The symbolism of a spiritual temple made up of living stones is clear enough, and the Mark Mason would be wise to leave it at that. For when they interpret their own Masonic version of this symbolism in a Christian sense, they are merely being led astray by similarities of phraseology, illogically forgetting or ignoring the fact that no work of human hands can be the True Christian Cornerstone, nor can salvation be found in it.

This same inherent vagueness of thinking is exemplified in the second " messianic " passage found in the Mark workings. When the Candidate is given his jewel, a small white replica of the keystone bearing his own mark, and the name of Hiram in mystic letters, the 17th verse of the second chapter of the Book of Revelation is sung or recited, as we have seen. " To him that overcometh will I give to eat of the hidden manna, and will give him a white stone, and in the stone a new name written, which no man knoweth saving he that receiveth it."

Although this passage occurs in the authorized English Mark ritual and in many of the local variants, it is not found in some of the older rituals, nor in any of the Scottish workings, ancient or modern, as far as I am aware. On the other hand, it does

1. Matthew XXI, 42. Mark XII, 10 and Luke XX, 17.
2. Acts IV, 11-12.
3. I Peter II, 7.

appear in many American Mark rituals, which often follow more primitive originals. But on the whole it seems probable that the verse was inserted because it appeared apt, rather than that the jewel was originally devised to conform with this apocalyptic imagery. In any case, it is a little unfortunate.

The keystone contains the name of Hiram as well as the Candidate's own mark, and (for what it is worth) the Mark Anthem in the ritual stresses in its third verse that Hiram, not Christ, is " our great keystone " and that it is his " name which raises high the fame of all to whom the same is truly known." The " new name written, which no man knoweth saving he that receiveth it," however, appears to be applied to the Candidate's own mark, despite the superficial inaptness that this mark is not given him, but is chosen by the Candidate himself, and approved on the keystone by the addition of the Worshipful Master's Mark. In the address on the working tools, the Candidate is " led to entertain the hope that by the correction of irregularities and the subjugation of our passions, we may hereafter be found worthy to receive the approving mark of the Great Overseer of the Universe, as fitted to form part of that spiritual edifice, ' that house not made with hands, eternal in the heavens.' " The quotation from Revelation appears to give the impression that it is Christ Himself who will thus stamp our work with His approval, even though His Name and mediation are nowhere invoked in that work.

Commentators have differed over the exact meaning and origin of the white stone referred to by St. John. The most generally received explanation, however, is that it referred to the common superstition of the belief in talismanic stones bearing a magical name. Magic in all its forms entered largely into the life of the great cities of Asia, and particularly at Ephesus.[1] Adopting this imagery, St. John implies that the true, the divine " magic " inscribes on the human character and life the Name of Christ, the new Name with all its freshness and eternal youth, which can only be understood by those who have been redeemed in that Name, in contrast with the poor imitations that enthralled (and continue to enthral, it seems) pagan society. As a " Christian implicit " then, the introduction of this text proves nothing. It sounds well, and it has doubtless comforted the heart of many

1. see King, *Engraved Gems*, the chapter *Gnostics and their Remains*, p. 97 *et seq.*

a Christian Mark Mason to feel that his little talisman is an apocalyptic symbol of his approbation in Christ. Yet as usual the symbolism is muddled and illogical.

The Mark degree is no more Christian than the Craft. It can be allegorized in a Christian direction only by misunderstanding the exclusive character of Christianity, the uniqueness of our redemption in Christ, and the true meaning of faith.

A little light relief may be afforded to the reader at this point by a brief consideration of the Ark Mariner degree.[1]

The history of this triviality need not detain us in detail. Earliest references to it come from Bath, in the year 1790, and the famous Baldwyn Chapter at Bristol appears to have worked it a few years later. In 1794 the " Diluvian Order, or Royal Ark and Mark Mariners " appears to have combined with the Knights Templars with Thomas Dunckerley as Grand Commander. The degree had a greater vogue among the Ancients, however, and shared the fate of so many others of being excluded at the Union of 1813. It continued a precarious existence until it was taken over in 1871 by the Mark Masons, and the " Grand Master's Royal Ark Council " was set up.

Ark Mariner Lodges today are attached or " moored " to the Mark Lodges in the same way that Royal Arch Chapters are attached to Craft Lodges, and the Mark degree is, therefore, an essential prerequisite for " elevation ". There is no continuity of legend, however. For the Ark Mariner, as its name suggests, removes us from the purlieus of King Solomon's Temple and plunges us backwards into the waters of the Flood.

Worshipful Commander Noah rules the Lodge, assisted by Shem and Japhet as Wardens. The other ceremonial officers are the Senior and Junior Deacons, the Director of Ceremonies, the Guardian, or inner guard, and the Warden or outer guard. God is saluted in this nautical degree as the Supreme Commander of the Universe. Ham is not respectable enough to be repre-

---

1. An authorized ritual is published from Mark Masons' Hall, latest edition, 1950, which is the one I follow in this description. A. Lewis also published an edition together with the Mark ritual in 1936. There is not a great deal of separate literature on this degree apart from articles in Masonic encyclopædias etc., and papers published on the *History of the Ark Mariners' Degree* which appeared in the Transactions of the Manchester Association for Masonic Research (Vol. 10, 1919–20), read by the Rev. W. W. Covey-Crump. This same clergyman also privately published a pamphlet (undated) *The Symbolism in the Ark Mariners' Degree.*

sented at all ; he is omitted with execrations, presumably for his unfilial conduct in stripping off his father's Masonic apron and revealing his nakedness. The fact that his descendants became slaves of dark complexion, and therefore, generally speaking, ineligible for regular Masonry, contributes to his disfavour ; as the lecture explains Ham has " no place amongst us on account of the curse pronounced on his posterity."

The Candidate presents himself under the name of Noachida, and enters the Lodge on the point of a triangle presented to his breast. Prayer is offered to the Great Commander : " .... In Thy name we meet this evening to elevate a Brother, who with us may continue to commemorate so wonderful a deliverance as that of Noah and his family from the Deluge. Grant that he may prove a true Brother, able to unfold the mysteries of Ark Masonry.... May we so conduct ourselves in the Ark here, that when we are called hence by the Supreme Commander of the Universe, we may find a blessed Sanctuary in the mansions of everlasting rest."

He is led around an equilateral triangle the three points of which are marked by the three officers, and represent Beauty, Strength, and Wisdom. The obligation is taken, not on any sacred writings (which were not then in existence, it is explained) but on the Porphyry Stone, an emblem not found in Genesis but which according to Masonic tradition served as a pillow on which " the good old Patriarch Noah reposed, when he daily returned from his pious labour in building the Ark." It was placed in the centre of the Ark when finished, was used as an anchor to moor it to Ararat when the floods subsided, and later as an altar stone for Noah's first sacrifice of thanksgiving on dry land. The penalty of the obligation is to have the ribs broken, and to be overwhelmed by the waters and swept off the face of the earth.

The Candidate then advances to the east by nine steps. The first three are round the triangle, representing Wisdom, Strength and Beauty, the fourth is to the middle of the triangle. The last five are forward to the east, and represent " those five cardinal virtues peculiarly characteristic of Masonry—Watchfulness, Discretion, Brotherly Love, Truth, and Charity."

There are seven signs, representing such matters as swimming, the equilateral traingle, the rainbow, the stretching out the hand to welcome home the dove, accompanied by the words " Lo, she cometh." The grip represents climbing trees and mountains, symbolizing the unregenerate antediluvians trying to escape the rising waters. Words are given, such as Jared, Methuselah, and Lamech. The apron, adorned with triangles and rainbow ribbon, is " an emblem of love and virtue, and, as such more valuable than any gift an Emperor or King can bestow." The working tools are the axe, the saw, and the auger or borer. " The axe felled the trees, and they, being cut down, were emblematic of the fall of the old world. The saw dividing the timber into planks is emblematic of the separation of Noah and his family from the rest of mankind by the Lord. The auger making holes in the planks teaches the use of affliction in producing self-abasement and searchings of heart. As the Ark was built by these tools, we are shown that by perseverance in Faith, Hope, and Love, we may be shut into an Ark of safety, when the elements shall melt with fervent heat, and the whole Earth shall be dissolved."

Canon Covey-Crump, in a privately printed pamphlet, declares that the Porphyry Stone is the same as the keystone, the " stone which the builders rejected " in the Mark degree, and therefore the Porphyry Stone, too, represents Christ, and is the " cherished palladium of those who fully appreciate its value... encarnadined with the Blood of Atonement and Mercy." This, however, is far-fetched and not generally accepted. There is no hint of it in the ritual.

Certainly both in the Bible and in the writings of the Fathers the Ark is mystically interpreted as a prototype of Christ, the Ark of our salvation. Hence there are Masons who claim that this degree, too, although open to all religions, is implicitly Christian. Perhaps so. Children playing at Noah's Ark in the nursery, or youths singing the well-known ditty " The animals went in two by two, Hurrah ! Hurrah ! " are doubtless also prophesying their redemption in Christ, as well as satisfying their adolescent need for a bit of fun. Even Canon Covey-Crump wrote a little apologetically of the Ark Mariner that he hoped his remarks would " exonerate this degree from any stigma of inanity."[1] J. S. M. Ward, whose enthusiasm for higher grades of all sorts was usually ardent, described it as " quite a

1. *The Symbolism in the Ark Mariners' Degree* (undated) p. 5–6.

pretty little degree," but with " not too much really deep teaching."[1] Bro. Woodford wrote that " it is of late formation, and without offence may be termed a fancy grade."[2] A. E. Waite is more scathing, and terms it a " peculiar Mystery of Folly," refers to its " frivolity," and says that its teaching " might be spiritualized with equal efficiency in a schoolboy's exercise."[3]

Happily, however, in the Installation ceremonies of Commander Noah the Installing Officer produces a vessel of salt, explaining that " when the wild Arab of the desert has tasted salt with his guest, that guest is sacred to him.... Let us in like manner seal our vow of fidelity to Ark Masonry ". Then follows the hilarious rubric :—" All present take a pinch of salt...."

1. *The Higher Degrees Handbook*, p. 16.
2. *Kenning's Encyclopædia of Freemasonry*, p. 41.
3. *A New Encyclopædia of Freemasonry*, vol. II, pp. 380–381.

PART II

For thei conspiren many false errours aghenst the comyn fraternyte of Crist, that alle Cristene men token in here cristendom, and aghenst comyn charite and comyn profit of Cristene men . . . men of sutel craft, as fre masons and othere, semen openly cursed bi this sentence.

John Wyclif, The Grete Sentens of Curs.

VII

THE NEW COVENANT

Yet they still served up to me in those dishes glowing phantasies, than which better were it to love this very sun (which at least is true to our sight) than those illusions which deceive the mind through the eye. And yet, because I supposed them to be Thee, I fed upon them ; not with avidity, for Thou didst not taste to my mouth as Thou art, for Thou wast not these empty fictions ; neither was I nourished by them, but the rather exhausted. . . . With such empty husks was I then fed, and not fed.

St. Augustine, The Confessions.

"**M**ASONRY is a progressive science," the Craft ritual assures the initiate. Therefore, continues the argument of one who claims to have taken almost every degree in England and Scotland including the 30th, and is a regular communicant member of the Church of England, " we must look at the scheme of things *as a whole,* and not select passages from particular rituals or degrees which happen to suit our purpose."[1] The writer of this article, written in answer to one of my own, represents a widespread point of view put forward in shoals of letters with which I have been inundated, including many from the clergy. He goes on himself to pick out those very isolated aspects of the ritual discussed in earlier chapters which he claims are prophetic of Christianity. " What lies ahead ? " he asks. " What is here foreshadowed ? But at last we appreciate what the earlier ritual calls the relative dependency of the several parts when we proceed to the Eighteenth Degree or Rose Croix. Here, as the Church teaches, the Old Testament finds its completion in ' The New and Better Covenant,' and Hiram is indeed a forerunner of Christ."

This kind of argument is extremely popular with those Masons who have taken the Eighteenth Degree or who are Knights

1. *Theolog* (The Journal of the Faculty of Theology, King's College, London) Easter term, 1953. Article *Christian and Mason,* p. 10, anonymous. The author, however, is well known to me ; he wrote me that he remained anonymous because he feared " disciplinary action either by Grand Lodge, Great Priory, or the Supreme Council." It appears to be a Masonic offence to attempt to defend it from religious criticism.

Templar. Even those who have not gone beyond the Royal Arch will urge that as the Church uses the Old Testament in her lections and liturgy there is no reason why Masonry should not do the same, and thus at least provide a *preparatio Evangelii*.

Woolly thinking again ! Even if this symbolism and allegory could be accepted as patient of a far-fetched Christian prophetic interpretation (in the teeth of the historical evidence that Craft Masonry was deliberately de-Christianized in 1813), what would it prove ? The Church reveres and uses the Old Testament only in the context of the New. The Old Testament itself makes no claim to be a complete revelation, but ever looks forward to the redemption of the True Israel, and awaits the coming of the Messiah. Clearly a Church service which was entirely derived from the Old Testament, with nothing from the New, would not be a Christian service even if Messianic prophecies from the Book of Isaiah were included as lessons. Otherwise all Jews would *ipso facto* be Christians, which is absurd. No more absurd, however, than for the Craft Mason to claim that his ritual is Christian because he can here and there twist into it a Messianic prophecy, and that there are other degrees further on which claim to be fully Christian.

The Rose Croix Mason or the Knight Templar must first be a Craft Mason ; he cannot by-pass the first three degrees. He need not remain an active member of the Craft after his " perfection " but a very great number do. Here again is an anomaly. If Masonry is a progressive search for light, as is claimed, it is most curious that those who have gone on beyond the Craft to find the light of Christ in the higher degrees are unable to proclaim that light to their still-questing brethren in Craft Lodges where the name of Christ may not be mentioned or adored. How angry St. Paul would have been at this limitation ! He descended, so to speak, from the high degree of his Christian conversion to preach in the Craft synagogues of the Jews, but he preached Christ crucified, and Him only. He refused to bear witness anywhere where he could not bear witness to his divine Master.

Again, when the higher-degree Mason quotes that " Masonry is a progressive science " and implies that the progression leads inevitably and logically to the Rose Croix or Orders of the Temple, he ignores the fact that he is quoting out of context.

The " progressive science " of the Craft ritual leads to the Royal Arch and no farther, according to the ritual and Constitutions of Grand Lodge. The former declares that the Royal Arch is the " Supreme Degree, at once the foundation and keystone of the whole Masonic structure." The latter lays down authoritatively that " pure Antient Masonry consists of three degrees and no more... including the Supreme Order of the Holy Royal Arch." Not a hint is there of any further progress, for Craft and Chapter together claim to be a complete and entirely self-sufficient system from which all other degrees and orders were deliberately excluded in 1813. There is no recognition of any higher degrees, Christian or pagan. Officially they are all just fancy extras, extraneous systems later grafted on to the Craft foundation, optional extras for those interested. Few can claim any great antiquity.

There is a popular misconception about these degrees among non-Masons. Because the Ancient and Accepted Rite (incorrectly called the Scottish Rite in Britain, correctly so in America) has higher numerical titles to its degrees which stretch to thirty-three, it is often thought that this rite has also a higher authority. Nothing could be farther from the truth. The Supreme Council 33rd Degree would not dream of attempting the presumption of claiming any control over Grand Lodge, which is immeasurably the more influential and powerful body. An individual Mason who has the 33rd degree has no more precedence or authority in a Craft Lodge than any Master Mason.[1] He is not even allowed to wear the jewels and insignia of any higher order there, because they are not recognized as pure ancient Masonry at all. " Side degrees ", then, is really a more apt title for them, along with the Mark, the Allied and Cryptic degrees, the Secret Monitor, the Knights Templar, and the Royal Order of Scotland.

And this brings us to another snag in the facile argument that Christian degrees are the logical fulfilment of the Craft. They are in fact only one of many varying fulfilments. One can proceed through the Mark into the Cryptic degrees, which also cast further light on the Hiramic legend, but they are not Christian at all. Nor are the miscellaneous Allied degrees ; though some of them have a Templar content they are open to all religions.

1. That is, as a 33rd degree Mason. It so happens, however, that the Supreme Council do not normally confer this degree on any who have not already achieved Grand Lodge rank in the Craft.

The *Societas Rosicruciana in Anglia* claims to interpret and fulfil Craft Masonry in terms of Theosophy, and the amazing farrago of nonsense in its rituals derives more from Mme. Blavatsky's *Isis Unveiled* than from the New Testament. Its claim to be Christian in teaching is the sheerest impertinence or ignorance.[1] But Theosophists, too, can trace their symbolism and prophecies in the Craft degrees of Grand Lodge.

Even the thirty-three degrees of the Ancient and Accepted Rite do not present an orderly and logical sequence from the non-Christian to the Christian. The 18th or Rose Croix degree deals with the crucifixion and resurrection, but the Knights Kadosh or 30th degree (although of course composed only of those who have taken the eighteenth) reverts to innocuous philosophy of a very general kind and is mainly concerned with the ascent of a ladder whose rungs symbolize the seven sciences. The degrees over thirty become progressively more vague and pan-religiously platitudinous. In America there is a further order with a membership of over half a million called the Ancient Arabic Order of the Mystic Shrine, open only to Knights Templar and Masons of the 32nd degree.[2] Progression into this lands the aspirant into an idiotic absurdity of quasi-Moslem ritual and symbolism, though it is safe to pay it the compliment of assuming that its Nobles are incapable of taking the ritual seriously.

Hence the argument that Masonry is a progressive science which leads from the non-Christian to the Christian is not really convincing. One can progress through a bewildering labyrinth of degrees and orders of any or no religion before, or instead of, coming across the two or three Christian ones, and it is difficult to see by what right these two or three claim to be *the* fulfilment of the Craft. Christians may feel that they *ought* to be, and

1. The externals of this Rosicrucian order, like many other strange religious sects, such as the " Sanctuary " in Basil Street, Knightsbridge, before the war, the " Liberal Catholics", or the " Cathedral of the Good Shepherd " in Lower Sloane Street, London today, ape a good deal of Catholic ceremonial deprived of its Catholic content. The *Societas Rosicruciana in Anglia* has its altars, its thurifers, its torch-bearers, even its " celebrants." The Chaplain-General, according to the Ordinances as revised in 1918 must wear " Cassock, mantelletta and biretta of rose-red moiré silk. Indian cambric rochet edged with lace. Rose-red silk gloves. For full dress, in addition, red stockings or socks, gilt kid shoes and mozetta." The wearer of this ultramontane Masonic magnificence need not necessarily be a clergyman at all, still less a Cardinal !

2. See Appendix A.

possibly for them they are therefore, but Masonry as a whole does not confirm it, and Grand Lodge denies it by failing officially to recognize their very existence.

But finally, are these allegedly Christian degrees really Christian at all in any orthodox sense ? That is the next point to consider.

VIII

THE ANCIENT AND ACCEPTED RITE

O Sir, we quarrel in print ; by the book, as you have books for good manners, I will name you the degrees.
Shakespeare, As You Like It.

Trail'st thou the puissant pike ?
II King Henry V.

THE heyday of the multiplication of Masonic degrees and orders was the second half of the eighteenth century. Their most fruitful breeding ground was France. Here, then, is the time and the place to search for the origins of what is now known as the Ancient and Accepted Rite which was to superimpose an extra thirty degrees on top of the basic three of " pure ancient Masonry."

Some of these additional degrees represent a later development and elaboration of the original Masonic legend. Further incidents in the building of King Solomon's Temple are dramatized, and a good deal more is heard of the vengeance which overtook the assassins of Hiram the architect. Many of them, however, introduced entirely fresh matter quite alien to Masonic tradition. They are really different orders altogether, whose chief claim to the title of Freemasonry lies in their having made Lodge membership an essential prerequisite for entry into Chapter, Conclave, or Consistory.

It was a period of confusion and dissension. New rites and orders sprang up everywhere. Many of this bewildering chaos of degrees and orders were known as *grades écossais*, or Scottish degrees. The reason for this is not altogether clear. A popular explanation is that exiled Scottish Jacobites, in particular the Chevalier Ramsay, were largely responsible for their origin, but evidence for this is extremely scanty, and Ramsay, like Frederick the Great, has been credited with a larger Masonic role in popular imagination than he ever played in history. One myth in the Templar transmission theory is that exiled and persecuted knights fled to Scotland after the dissolution of the order encouraged by Robert the Bruce, and founded the Mother Lodge of Kilwinning ; this may account for certain degrees with a Templar content styling themselves Scottish. In any case, Scotland was supposed to be the cradle of Freemasonry (as indeed to a certain extent it was) and the most likely explanation therefore seems to be that the title was claimed as an alleged proof of antiquity and genuineness. If an irreverent simile may be pardoned, whisky is popularly claimed as " Scotch " the world over, wherever distilled—unless it is known to be Irish !

Many of these degrees and orders, " Scottish " and others, were short-lived and died a natural death. But the title of Scottish remained with some, to the irritation of the Grand Lodge of Scotland who would have nothing to do with them, and in America the Ancient and Accepted Rite is known as "Scottish Rite Masonry " to this day. The English Supreme Council dropped the title only in 1909.

In the course of the year 1758 a body arose styling itself *Conseils des Empereurs d'Orient et d'Occident* and its members as Sovereign Masonic Princes. It bestowed warrants for Lodges to work the higher degrees of " Perfect and Sublime Masonry " throughout Europe. This " Rite of Perfection," as it was called, consisted of twenty-five degrees, including the Royal Arch and the Rose Croix ; the twenty-fifth was the Sublime Prince of the Royal Secret. Not unnaturally its pretensions to superior Masonic status caused dissensions with the Grand Lodge (later known as the Grand Orient) of France, and there were schisms in both bodies which there is no point in tracing in detail here.

In 1761 the Council of Emperors granted an authority to a certain Stephen Morin to propagate the rite in the New World. It is generally believed that Morin was a Jew, but there is some evidence that he may have been of Huguenot extraction ; in any case no religious tests were demanded of initiates into the Rite of Perfection. Morin sailed immediately for the West Indies, and at Santa Domingo he started the dissemination of the rite, appointing Inspectors not only for the West Indies but also for the United States. Among others he conferred the twenty-five degrees on Moses M. Hayes, who appointed Isaac Da Costa as Deputy Inspector-General for South Carolina. In 1783 the

Grand Lodge of Perfection was established at Charleston,[1] which in 1801 became the Supreme Council, opened by John Mitchell, the Sovereign Grand Commander, and Frederick Dalcho, an Episcopalian clergyman. The other members of the first Supreme Council were Emanuel de la Motta, Abraham Alexander, Israel de Lieben, and Moses Clava Levy, who were Jews, and Thomas Bartholomew Bowen, Dr. Isaac Auld, and Dr. James Moultrie. At no time from the very beginning, then, was the Mother Supreme Council of Charleston a Christian body, even if her grand-daughter in England claims to be a Christian convert.

Up to this time nothing is known of any degrees in this rite higher than the twenty-fifth. But in 1802, sixteen years after the death of Frederick the Great of Prussia, eight further degrees were compiled from various European sources, and interpolated into this number. The legend went forth in a circular to all the Grand Lodges of the world that that Monarch had ratified a set of secret Grand Masonic Constitutions (alleged to have existed from time immemorial) and had established a Supreme Council of Sovereign Grand Inspectors General controlling thirty-three degrees. In these Constitutions " the higher power was conferred on a Supreme Council of nine brethren in each nation who possess all the Masonic prerogatives in their own districts, that His Majesty individually possessed, and are Sovereigns of Masonry."

This was patently a myth, if not a deliberate fraud. Nothing is known of it in the archives of the Berlin Lodge of the Three Globes, which might have been expected to know about it before it was proclaimed in Charleston, South Carolina. Frederick died in 1786, the year of these Constitutions, and had been in poor health for some time previously. His early interest in Masonry, such as it was, had in any case largely evaporated in later life. No serious Masonic historian today dreams of taking the story seriously, though unfortunately the *Official History of the Supreme Council* published in 1831 commits itself to the authenticity of the legend, and Albert Pike later defended it, disastrously for his reputation. The best that can be said of this fraudulent foundation for the rite is that it was a pious fraud born of hero-worship and a desire to attach a celebrity as an historical patron. Still,

1. The headquarters of the Southern Jurisdiction are now at Washington.

it was clearly a fraud clearly intended to deceive. The name of Frederick of Prussia continues to be used in the abbreviated ritual as the Word of the thirty-third degree, despite the embarrassment caused by its utterance in the 1914-18 war.

In 1813 a Supreme Council was constituted in New York, known as the Supreme Council for the Northern Jurisdiction. What in America is known as the Mason-Dixon line was roughly the frontier between these two bodies. The headquarters moved from New York to Boston in 1851.

Among Masons the most revered figure in the Ancient and Accepted Rite is undoubtedly Albert Pike, who more than any other man is responsible for the rapid spread and popularity of these higher degrees. Dr. Fort Newton, of the City Temple, London, said of him that he found Masonry a log-cabin and left it a temple. His most important work was his drastic revision of the rituals. Charles Joseph Jean Laffron-Ladebat had made some improvements in 1855, but Pike went much further. His rituals, with all their crude paganism and half-digested occultism (much of it lifted bodily without acknowledgement from the occultist Eliphas Levi) are still in use by the Southern Jurisdiction, of which he was Grand Commander from 1845. His other work, *Morals and Dogma*, a turgid, immensely lengthy, and monumentally boring commentary on the degrees, with many passages taken from other authors, is still accepted as the official monitor. Under his generalship the rite grew and prospered, and it is not without justification that he has been styled the master-genius of Masonry. That he was ever pope or absolute dictator of world-wide Masonry, however, is a figment of the anti-Masonic imagination, based on the forgeries of Gabriel Antoine Jogand-Pagès, better known as Leo Taxil, who formulated this legend in Paris only a few months after Pike's death in 1891, and backed it up with accusations of crude deliberate Luciferianism. Yet the fact remains that Pike's moral influence as Grand Commander of the Mother Supreme Jurisdiction was undoubtedly great wherever the rite was worked.

In England there is some evidence, but not a great deal, for the existence of a Supreme Council warranted directly from France as early as 1819. The evidence comes from France, and despite the known antipathy of the Grand Master the Duke of Sussex to the higher degrees, it seems that overtures were made to him regarding the formation of a Supreme Council, and that negotiations were entered into. If such a Supreme Council was actually formed, it seems to have existed only on paper, for there are no traces of its having functioned or issued any charters.

Yet there is evidence that Rose Croix Masonry was worked in England before the present Supreme Council was warranted. Encampments of Knights Templar used to work it. Those two museum cities of antique Masonry, Bristol and Bath, and also Newcastle and Portsmouth conferred the degree very early in the nineteenth century, the Antiquity Encampment at Bath apparently first worked it in 1793. But it was not until two years after the death of the Duke of Sussex that the Supreme Council of England and Wales, the Dominions and Dependencies of the British Crown was constituted, on October 26, 1845. The leading personalities were Dr. R. T. Crucefix, Dr. Henry Beaumont Leeson, and the Rev. George Oliver, the prolific writer referred to in an earlier chapter. Dr. Crucefix petitioned the Northern Jurisdiction of America for a warrant, which was issued on July 23, 1846. There was an inaugural festival, and the new Council was launched. By the end of the century there were one hundred and forty-four chapters. Today (1954) there are four hundred and seventy.

Owing to the loss of early minute-books there is not a great deal of information available about ritual revision. Existing minutes date from 1853, so it seems that the rituals must have taken shape before then. The most likely guess is that they are largely the work of Oliver, based on the ritual which would doubtless be sent from America with the warrant. The Council ordered the revised rituals of Laffron-Ladebat in 1857. Albert Pike sent copies of his revisions in 1872.

In England today the Ancient and Accepted Rite works only the eighteenth degree, and the thirtieth to thirty-third inclusive, the intermediate ones being conferred titularly, as explained in the rituals which follow. In London, however, there is an annual festival at which one of these intermediate degrees from the fourth to the seventeenth may be demonstrated in rehearsal as a museum piece for the interest of the Brethren, by the King Edward VII Chapter of Improvement. As they are not in regular use, however, I am informed, I know not with what accuracy, that the American rituals of the Northern Jurisdiction are used for these demonstrations. It is certainly true that Canon Covey-Crump's useful little book *The Intermediate Degrees of the A. & A. Rite* (1949) which summarizes the legends of these degrees, follows these American workings.

Any Master Mason of twelve months' standing may apply for " perfection " in the Rose Croix of Heredom,[1] the Royal Arch is not a necessary requirement. No one is eligible for the thirtieth degree until he is a Past Most Wise Sovereign in the eighteenth, and has been a member for at least three years. He must be recommended for the honour by his local Chapter.

The thirtieth degree is usually conferred in London, at the headquarters of the Supreme Council at 10 Duke Street, St. James's, S.W.1, and at least three Grand Inspectors General (thirty-third degree) must be present. Sometimes, however, special Chapters for this purpose are arranged in the provinces.

Promotion beyond the thirtieth degree is sparing, and depends on seniority and service. The thirty-first degree is limited to six hundred members, the thirty-second to two hundred and fifty. The 1954 Year Book lists seventy members of the thirty-third degree (one of whom has since died) and a further eight *honoris causa* from other jurisdictions. As there may be some interest in the identities of these so-called " top Masons " their names will be found in an appendix.

One also finds curiosity, and sometimes misgivings, over the foreign contacts and alleged alliances of the Supreme Council. It is therefore perhaps worth recording that there are ten other Masonic bodies with whom the Supreme Council of England and Wales is in full fraternal relations, and exchanges representatives. These are the Supreme Councils of Scotland, Ireland, Canada, the Northern and Southern Jurisdictions of the United States, the National Grand Lodge of Denmark, Norway, Sweden, Iceland, and the Supreme Council of the Netherlands.

1. Possible derivations of the word Heredom are :—
   a. From *Herodium*, a castle built by King Herod.
   b. From *Highrodian* (Highroadmen or wayfarers) an obscure Masonic degree worked at Gateshead in 1746.
   c. From *heredum*, genitive plural of *heres*, heir, implying that the degree was invented by the heirs of ancient Masons.
   d. From the *Harodim* or overseers (1 Kings, 16, and IX, 23).
   e. From the legend that Heredom was the name of a mountain in Scotland in which Masonic secrets were preserved.
   f. From the Greek *hieros domos*, holy house.
   The last is the most commonly accepted. The word also occurs in the first degree of the Royal Order of Scotland, Heredom of Kilwinning.

IX

THE RITUAL OF
THE ROSE CROIX OF HEREDOM

What knoweth then
The Brother of the Rosy Cross ?—But nothing
Save that he boasteth that all things created
Derive from three alone—salt, mercury,
And foetid sulphur.

Mundus Christopheri Filius (1619).

There is no question that the Eighteenth Degree, in its valid and orthodox form as the Word discovered and communicated, carries on the Rosicrucian claim to possess the Key of Masonry, to be its fons et origo and to deliver its final message. Its great success must be accounted for . . . in view of the talismanic magic which has always and everywhere encompassed the title of Rosy Cross.

A. E. Waite, The Brotherhood of the Rosy Cross.

IDEALLY there should be three rooms *en suite* for the conferment of this degree, the Black Room, the Chamber of Death, and the Red Room. There should be in addition an ante-room for the preparation of Candidates and for the conferment of the intermediate degrees ; sometimes, however, a separate room altogether can be devoted to this.

At the east end of the Black Room is an altar and a plinth of three steps. Above the altar is a transparency, lit from behind, on which are depicted three crosses, each upon three steps ; the central cross, higher than the other two, has on it the Mystic Rose surrounded by the Crown of Thorns. On the steps of the other two are depicted a skull and cross-bones. On the altar are a Bible, a pair of compasses, and an unsheathed sword. The altar has a frontal of black, fringed with silver. On it are worked five swords ; four in a St. Andrew's cross with the points towards the centre, and the fifth upright in the middle. The Most Wise Sovereign is seated on the north side of the altar, and the Prelate on the south. A pair of black curtains is hung in front of the altar, which completely conceal it when drawn.

In the centre of the space west of the curtains is spread a black floorcloth on which is painted a pelican surrounded by seven concentric white circles. The head of the pelican is towards the east.

In the south, west, and north are three black pillars surmounted by black pyramids with lights inside ; the sides of the pyramids facing inwards are pierced with eleven holes in a triangle surrounding translucent letters, H, C, and F respectively. A removable plate bearing the same letter is on each pillar.

The First General is seated in the north-west, the Second General in the south-west, and the Captain of the Guard at the entrance to the Red Room. The Outer Guard (corresponding to the Tyler in the Craft) is stationed in the ante-room.

All the furnishings are black, and there should be no lights at all other than those behind the transparency over the altar, and in the tops of the pillars shining through the holes and the translucent letters.

The Chamber of Death should have an entrance direct from the Black Room, and an exit direct into the Red Room. It is furnished entirely in black. On the floor are skulls and crossbones, and if possible a figure in a winding sheet laid out as a corpse. The room is lit only by lamps burning spirits of wine, and flambeaux fixed in skulls.

The Red Room provides a startling contrast. It is brilliantly illuminated, and furnished in bright red. In the east is a white altar, upon which are two super-altars each of four steps. On these are a profusion of red roses, and thirty-three lights arranged in three inverted triangles, with the white Cubic Stone in the centre. Also upon the altar, on the south side, are placed the Word (I.N.R.I.), a Bible, the alms-dish, and a taper. The altar has a white frontal, adorned with red and gold, bearing an equal-armed cross on which are five Hebrew characters in gold. The Most Wise Sovereign has his throne to the north of the altar, and in front of him is a pedestal on which are the Chapter Warrant, the seal, and copies of the regulations and by-laws.

In the west sit the First and Second Generals (with pedestals in front of them), the Marshal, and Raphael.

In the centre is the floor-cloth, strewn with roses, upon which is a ladder of seven steps. Upon each step is placed a movable letter, each covered by a rose. These letters, reading successively from west to east, are F.H.C.I.N.R.I. Between the ladder and the altar is a kneeling-stool.

The Officers of a Rose Croix Chapter are the Most Wise Sovereign, the Prelate, First and Second Generals, Director of

Ceremonies, Marshal, Raphael, Herald, Captain of the Guard, Organist, and Outer Guard. Others whose part is administrative and not ceremonial are the Treasurer, Recorder (Secretary), Almoner, Stewards, and assistants as required. A quorum of at least five Brethren, including the Most Wise Sovereign or Past Sovereign, is needed for the perfection of a Candidate.

All Brethren wear dark morning or evening dress, and (excepting members of the Thirty-Third Degree) white gloves. The regalia consists of apron and collar with jewel suspended from it, all reversible. The apron is of white satin, bordered with red. On it is embroidered in gold thread a pelican feeding its young, and a Latin cross, surrounded by a wreath. The reverse is of black watered silk, with a plain red Latin cross.

The collar is of red silk, embroidered in gold thread with the pelican and cross in the centre, a serpent having its tail in its mouth on the right, and the crown of thorns on the left. The reverse is of black silk, with three red Latin crosses.

The jewel is in the form of a pair of compasses enclosing a cross, and surmounted by a celestial crown. On one side of the jewel is the pelican feeding its young, on the other, a white eagle with extended wings. On both sides there is a rose on the joint of the compasses.

The black reverse of the regalia is displayed when the Chapter is assembled in the Black Room.

OPENING THE CHAPTER[1]

> (*The Most Wise Sovereign gives one knock, which is repeated by the First and Second Generals*).

M.W.S. Brethren, assist me to open the ...... Chapter of Princes Rose Croix of Heredom. (*All rise*).

M.W.S. Excellent and Perfect Marshal, see that the Castle Gates are duly guarded.

> (*The Captain of the Guard opens the door, and the Marshal satisfies himself that the Outer Guard is in his place, and reports*).

1. Rose Croix rituals are not sold to the public, though secondhand copies of earlier editions are reasonably available. A spurious version occurs in the *Text Book of Advanced Freemasonry* (Reeves and Turner) but authentic rituals are privately printed for the Supreme Council. An edition was printed in 1951, and later a list of errata and corrections appeared which were embodied in the latest 1952 edition. My own collection includes this, and almost every edition since 1876, and a manuscript ritual even earlier than this.

Mar.   Most Wise Sovereign, all is secure without.
M.W.S.   To order, Brethren, as Princes Rose Croix.

(All stand to order with the 3rd sign. The signs are described later in the ceremony when they are given to the Candidate).

M.W.S.   Excellent and Perfect First General, what is the hour ?
1st Gen. The ninth hour of the day.
M.W.S.   Then it is the hour when the Veil of the Temple was rent in twain and darkness overspread the earth, when the true Light departed from us, the Altar was thrown down, the Blazing Star was eclipsed, the Cubic Stone poured forth Blood and Water, the Word was lost, and despair and tribulation sat heavily upon us.

(Solemn pause)

M.W.S.   Since Masonry has experienced such dire calamities, it is our duty, Princes, to endeavour by renewed labours to retrieve our loss. May the benign influence of Faith, Hope, and Charity prosper our endeavours to recover the lost Word, for which purpose I declare this . . . . . . Chapter of Princes Rose Croix of Heredom duly open *(all drop sign)* in the Name of the Great Emmanuel.

(M.W.S. knocks 6.1., repeated by the First and Second Generals, the Captain of the Guard, and the Outer Guard. The Prelate opens the New Testament).

M.W.S.   Excellent and Perfect Prelate, the Chapter being open, what remains to be done ?
Prel.   To respect the decrees of Providence ; to render worship to God alone ; and with all humility and patience to endeavour to recover the Word.
M.W.S.   Yes, Princes, that shall be our aim. Do you, Excellent and Perfect Prelate, invoke a blessing on our labours.
Prel.   Almighty and Everlasting God, give unto us the increase of Faith, Hope, and Charity ; and, that we may obtain that which Thou dost promise, make us to love that which Thou dost command, through Jesus Christ, our Great Emmanuel. Amen.[1]
M.W.S.   *(Gives the first part of the second sign)* Save, we beseech Thee, O God in Heaven, Creator and Sovereign of all things, us Thine unworthy children.
Be seated, Brethren.

(The Minutes are read, and the business of the Chapter proceeds).

1. Except for the ending, this is the Collect for the fourteenth Sunday after Trinity in the Book of Common Prayer.

THE CEREMONY OF PERFECTION

1. RECEPTION

(When a Candidate presents himself for Perfection his qualifications are first examined, as follows):—

M.W.S. Excellent and Perfect Marshal, you will retire and ascertain if Brother ...... professes the Trinitarian Christian Faith, and, if he is willing to take an Obligation in the Name of the Holy and Undivided Trinity, you will ask him to sign the necessary Petition.

(The Marshal retires, and presents the Petition to the Candidate in the ante-room for his signature. The Petition is as follows) :—

I, the undersigned, most humbly supplicate the Most Wise Sovereign and Excellent and Perfect Princes now assembled, that you will be pleased to admit me to your Princely Order, presenting myself with humble desire to obtain perfection.

I do most solemnly promise true allegiance to the Supreme Council Thirty-Third Degree, duly, lawfully and constitutionally established on the 26th day of October, A.D. 1845, sitting at their Grand East in London for England and Wales, the Dominions and Dependencies of the British Crown.

I furthermore promise to hold no Masonic fellowship or communication with any Masons or Bodies of Masons which at any time have been or may hereafter be established anywhere by any authority whatsoever, except with such as are, or may be, duly acknowledged as being lawful and regular by the aforesaid Supreme Council.

In testimony whereof, I sign this my solemn promise and obligation.

(The Marshal returns and presents the completed Petition to the Most Wise Sovereign).

Mar. Most Wise Sovereign, Brother .... expresses himself willing to take an Obligation in the Name of the Holy and Undivided Trinity.

(The Sovereign satisfies himself that the Petition is in order. The Candidate is then balloted for, and if the ballot is favourable all go into the room where the Intermediate Degrees are to be conferred).

2. THE INTERMEDIATE DEGREES. (a) The lodge of Perfection

(The Candidate, who wears no Masonic clothing or regalia whatsoever, is admitted by the Marshal and placed before the Most Wise Sovereign).

M.W.S.   By virtue of the power vested in me by the Supreme Council Thirty-Third Degree, I declare this Lodge of Perfection open.

(Nine knocks. The Marshal opens the Bible).

M.W.S.   Brother ......, the position of a Prince Rose Croix to which you aspire requires that you have had conferred upon you seventeen Degrees of the Ancient and Accepted Rite of Freemasonry.

The Degrees of Craft Masonry, which you have already received, are accepted as equivalents of the first three Degrees of this Rite. In the ordinary course it would take many months, or even years, before you could acquire the whole, but it has pleased the Supreme Council Thirty-Third Degree to direct that the intervening fourteen Degrees may now be communicated to you by name. Are you willing to pledge yourself to preserve the secrets and mysteries of these Degrees ?

(The Candidate signifies his assent).

M.W.S.   Then you will kneel on both knees ; place your right hand upon the Volume of the Sacred Law ; and with your left hand hold this sword by the blade, hilt upward. State your names at length, and repeat after me :—

M.W.S.   I, ..., in the presence of God, Creator of the
& Can.   Universe, and calling upon these Brethren as witnesses, do upon this Sacred Book, most solemnly and sincerely promise that I will never illegally reveal any or either of the secrets or mysteries of or belonging to the several degrees of the Ancient and Accepted Rite from the First Degree to the Seventeenth Degree both inclusive, which heretofore have been known to me, or may at any future time, be communicated to me.

(The Marshal replaces the sword on the table).

M.W.S.   You will seal this once on the Volume of the Sacred Law.

(Candidate kisses the Bible).

M.W.S.   You will now rise.

I confer upon you the following Degrees by name :—

   4.   Secret Master,
   5.   Perfect Master.
   6.   Intimate Secretary,
   7.   Provost and Judge,
   8.   Intendant of the Buildings,
   9.   Elect of Nine,
 10.   Elect of Fifteen,
 11.   Sublime Elect,
 12.   Grand Master Architect,

M.W.S. 13. Royal Arch of Enoch,
        14. Scotch Knight of Perfection.

In the first eight of these Degrees (4th to 11th) the Legend of Hiram Abiff is continued in a series of allegories. Collectively they portray the confusion caused by the death of Hiram and the steps taken by Solomon to restore order and progress in the kingdom. The building of the Temple proceeds, and the successors of the three Grand Masters of Craft Masonry are shown in the 12th and 13th Degrees continuing the work with which they have been entrusted.
The 14th refers to the legend of the Secret Vault and its contents.
The whole group is known as that of the " Ineffable Degrees."
I now declare this Lodge of Perfection closed. (*Nine knocks*).

(b) The Council of the Princes of Jerusalem

M.W.S. By virtue of the power vested in me by the Supreme Council Thirty-Third Degree, I declare this Council of Princes of Jerusalem open. (*Knocks* 1, 2).
M.W.S. I confer upon you the Degrees of :—
        15. Knight of the Sword, or of the East,
        16. Prince of Jerusalem.
These two Degrees are variously known as the " Historical Degrees " and as " Orders of Chivalry." They give an account of the assistance received from Cyrus and Darius in the task of rebuilding the Temple after the Babylonian Captivity.
I declare this Council of Princes of Jerusalem closed. (*Knocks* 1, 2).

(c) The lodge of the Knights of the East and West

M.W.S. By virtue of the power vested in me by the Supreme Council Thirty-Third Degree, I declare this Lodge of Knights of the East and West open. (*Knocks* 2, 2, 2, 1).
I confer upon you the 17th Degree, Knight of the East and West.
The signs, tokens, and words are exchanged thus :—
Place your left hand, with the fingers straight, on my right hand, I cover it with my left hand, and you look over your right shoulder and say ABADDON, which refers to the Evil One.
I reply by touching your left shoulder with my left hand, and you touch my right shoulder with your right hand, thus forming a St. Andrew's Cross. Then

M.W.S. I look over my left shoulder and answer JAHABU-
LON, which means " The Lord is our help."
This Degree is the first of the " Philosophical Degrees," and forms a fitting preface to the principles of
Christianity represented in the 18th Degree. Studied
as allegories, these Intermediate Degrees continue the
teachings of Symbolic Masonry.
I close this Lodge of Knights of the East and West
with the knocks 2. 2. 2. 1.

*(The Marshal closes the Bible. The Sovereign and other
Princes pass to the Black Room, where members of the
18th degree reverse their aprons and collars).*

3. THE FIRST POINT

*(In the Black Room the Prelate opens the New Testa-
ment. The black curtains are drawn across, concealing
the altar, and all lights are extinguished except those
behind the transparencies and on the three pillars. The
Marshal conducts the Candidate to the door, and
knocks 2. 2. 2. 1.).*

2nd Gen. Most Wise Sovereign, an alarm.

M.W.S. Excellent and Perfect Second General, see who disturbs
this Chapter.

(The Second General opens the door).

2nd Gen. Wherefore this alarm ?

Mar. This worthy Knight of the East and West, having con-
fided to me a Petition which has been presented to the
Most Wise Sovereign, now begs to be admitted to receive
an answer.

2nd Gen. Wait while I report to the Most Wise Sovereign. *(Closes
the door)*. Most Wise Sovereign, a worthy Knight of
the East and West, having presented a Petition to you
by the hand of the Marshal, now requests to be admitted to receive your answer.

M.W.S. Summon our Excellent and Perfect Marshal to conduct
him hither.

*(The Second General admits them, and the Marshal
conducts the Candidate up to the drawn curtains).*

Mar. Most Wise Sovereign, I present to you Brother ......

M.W.S. Who and what are you ?

Mar. Nobly born and of the tribe of Judah.

M.W.S. What is your rank ?

Mar. Knight of the East and West.

M.W.S. Give me the Word.

Mar. ABADDON.

M.W.S. JAHABULON. What is your age ?

Mar. Thirty-three.

M.W.S.   Your petition has been favourably received by this Chapter ; but whilst we admire your zeal and courage, and your conduct inspires us with confidence and esteem, alas, you have come among us at the ninth hour of the day, when we are overwhelmed with grief and the deepest sorrow, and consternation spreads horror over our brows.

The earth quakes, the rocks are rent, the Veil of the Temple is rent in twain, darkness overspreads the earth, and the True Light has departed from us. Our Altars are thrown down, the Cubic Stone pours forth Blood and Water, the Blazing Star is eclipsed, our Shepherd is smitten, the Word is lost, and despair and tribulation sit heavily upon us.

(*Solemn pause*)

Nevertheless, it is well that you have arrived at this hour of peril ; since, as a courageous and valiant Knight, we trust that you will assist us in our endeavours to retrieve our loss and recover the Word ; in which case only shall we be able to confer upon you that distinction you so earnestly desire.

Mar.   We promise faithfully to aid you in your labours and to obey whatever commands you may be pleased to impose upon us.

M.W.S.   Then, worthy Knights, I direct you to travel thirty-three days ; eleven to the Pillar of Wisdom in the North ; eleven to the Pillar of Beauty in the South ; and eleven to the Pillar of Strength in the West ; returning to me in the East with whatever information you may obtain during your travels. I particularly commend to your meditation the beauties of the New and Better Covenant ; and that you may more completely appreciate its excellence, let us invoke guidance and direction from above.

(*All stand*).

Prel.   Almighty and Sovereign Architect of the Universe, who dost penetrate into the secret recesses of the hearts of men, purify ours with the Sacred Fire of Thy Divine Love. Banish from this Holy Sanctuary the impious and profane ; and grant that we, aided by the Power of Thy Spirit, may be enabled to distinguish the precious metal from the dross, and may not be deceived in the choice of him we are about to perfect. May our Order ever be adorned by service, good will, and peace. Now unto the King, Eternal, Immortal, Invisible, the only wise God, be the Kingdom, the Power, and the Glory for ever and ever. Amen.

(*The Brethren resume their seats*).

M.W.S. Depart in peace.
(The Marshal followed by the Candidate passes seven times round the Chapter. During the third circuit the Candidate is shown the Pillar of Wisdom in the north, and is given the letter F. During the fifth circuit he is shown and given the letter H from the Pillar of Beauty in the south. During the seventh circuit he is shown and given the letter C from the Pillar of Strength in the west. During the perambulations the Prelate reads Isaiah LIII. Solemn Music may be played during the reading).

Prel. " Who hath believed our report ? and to whom is the arm of the Lord revealed ? For he shall grow up before him as a tender plant, and as a root out of a dry ground : he hath no form nor comeliness ; and when we shall see him, there is no beauty that we should desire him.

" He is despised and rejected of men ; a Man of sorrows and acquainted with grief : and we hid as it were our faces from him ; he was despised, and we esteemed him not. Surely he hath borne our griefs and carried our sorrows : yet we did esteem him stricken, smitten of God and afflicted.

" But he was wounded for our transgressions, he was bruised for our iniquities : the chastisement of our peace was upon him, and with his stripes we are healed. All we, like sheep, have gone astray ; we have turned every one to his own way ; and the Lord hath laid on him the iniquity of us all.

" He was oppressed, and he was afflicted, yet he opened not his mouth ; he is brought as a lamb to the slaughter, and as a sheep before her shearers is dumb, so he openeth not his mouth. He was taken from prison and from judgment, and who shall declare his generation ?

" For he was cut off out of the land of the living : for the transgressions of my people was he stricken : and he made his grave with the wicked, and with the rich in his death, because he had done no violence, neither was any deceit in his mouth. Yet it pleased the Lord to bruise him, he hath put him to grief.

" When thou shalt make his soul an offering for sin, he shall see his seed, he shall prolong his days, and the pleasure of the Lord shall prosper in his hand : he shall see of the travail of his soul and shall be satisfied ; by his knowledge shall my righteous servant justify many, for he shall bear their iniquities.

" Therefore will I divide him a portion with the great, and he shall divide the spoil with the strong, because

Prel. he hath poured out his soul unto death ; and he was numbered with the transgressors, and he bare the sin of many, and made intercession for the transgressors."
(The Marshal, having timed the circuits with the reading, returns with the Candidate to the curtain. He passes through the curtain, leaving the Candidate outside, and gives the three letters F, H, C, to the Most Wise Sovereign).

M.W.S. I congratulate you on the success which has already rewarded your exertions. These letters are the initials of those Virtues by whose assistance you may be led to the discovery of the lost Word.
(The curtains are slowly drawn back, revealing the altar to the Candidate, and the Marshal returns to his side).

M.W.S. Before I can explain further, I must call upon you to take a solemn Obligation to keep inviolate the secrets and mysteries of our Order. Are you ready to take it ?
(The Candidate signifies his assent)

M.W.S. Then you will advance and kneel before the Holy Cross. *(Candidate kneels on both knees)*. Place your right hand upon the New Testament, whilst across your hand will be laid a sword and the compasses. *(The Prelate adjusts these. All rise)*. State your names at lenght, and repeat after me :—

M.W.S. & Can. I, ..., in the Name of the Holy and Undivided Trinity, before the Holy Cross, and in the presence of this Perfect Chapter, do hereby and hereon promise that I will never reveal the secrets or mysteries of this Order of the Rose Croix of Heredom to anyone in the world not lawfully entitled thereto, or whom I may believe not to have been duly qualified in a true and regularly constituted Chapter.
I furthermore pledge my sacred word of honour that I will, at all times, pay due allegiance to this Chapter and to the Supreme Council under whose authority it is held.
All this I solemnly pledge myself to observe : so help me God and keep me steadfast in this my obligation.
(The Prelate removes the sword and compasses).

M.W.S. You will seal that seven times on the New Testament. *(Candidate does so)*. Rise, newly obligated Brother. *(The Brethren sit. The Marshal takes the Candidate to the west of the floorcloth, where they face east).*

M.W.S. I now inform you that the seven circles round which you have travelled represent the seven periods of the world's existence, which will close with the Second Advent of our great Emmanuel, when time shall be swallowed up in eternity.

M.W.S.   I have already congratulated you on having found the
Initials of the three fundamental principles of our
Order—Faith, Hope, and Charity. Assisted by these
Virtues, we have no doubt that you will ultimately
succeed in attaining the end and object of all our
researches—that Word on which our eternal salvation
must depend.

M.W.S.   For Faith is the substance of things hoped for, the
or Prel.   evidence of things not seen. Hope maketh not ashamed
—Charity suffereth long and is kind ; Charity envieth
not ; Charity vaunteth not itself, is not puffed up,
doth not behave itself unseemly, seeketh not her own,
is not easily provoked, thinketh no evil, rejoiceth not in
iniquity, but rejoiceth in the Truth ; beareth all things,
believeth all things, hopeth all things, endureth all
things. Charity never faileth : but whether there be
prophecies, they shall fail ; whether there be tongues,
they shall cease ; whether there be knowledge, it shall
vanish away ; for we know in part, and we prophesy in
part, but when that which is perfect is come, then that
which is in part shall be done away.
Let us pray. (*All rise*).

Prel.   Almighty and Everlasting God, give unto us the increase
of Faith, Hope, and Charity ; and, that we may obtain
that which Thou dost promise, make us to love that
which Thou dost command, through Jesus Christ our
Lord. Amen.

M.W.S.   Having found the three fundamental principles of our
Order let us go forth in search of the lost Word.
*A Procession is formed. First the Most Wise Sovereign
and the Prelate, and members of the 33rd degree, if
any are present. Then members of the 32nd, 31st, and
30th degrees. Then those of the 18th. Finally the
Marshal and the Candidate. After passing the east once,
all bowing to the altar, the Sovereign, the Prelate, and
those of the 33rd degree leave the Black Room and pass
into the Red Room. After passing the east twice, those
of the 32nd, 31st, and 30th degrees similarly retire.
After passing the east thrice, members of the 18th
degree similarly retire, except for the Marshal. After
passing the east four times, the Marshal leads the
Candidate to the Captain of the Guard, who challenges
him).*

C. of G.   You cannot enter here unless you give me the Word.

Mar.   He cannot. He is travelling in search thereof, hoping
to obtain it by the practice of Faith, Hope, and Charity,
and by the help of the New and Better Covenant.

C. of G.   This attire is not compatible with that humility

C. of G. necessary for those who wish to recover the lost Word.
Clothe yourself in the garment of humility, and I will
then summon Raphael to your assistance.

*(A black crêpe veil is placed on the Candidate's head,
and the Marshal leads him into the Chamber of Death.
The Marshal then retires, and with the Captain of the
Guard passes into the Red Room, leaving the Candidate
alone. Solemn and funereal music may be played.[1]
After a pause, Raphael enters the Chamber of Death
with his sword at the carry).*

Raph. I am come to conduct you from the depths of darkness
and the Valley of the Shadow of Death to the Mansions
of Light.

You have undergone dangers, difficulties, and afflictions ; yet be of good cheer. Armed with the Virtues
you have already obtained, Faith will support you
when tempted to despair, Hope will cheer you on your
road, and Charity will sustain you in every trial, until
having travelled through the abyss of darkness, you
finally arrive at the Mansions of Light, whither our
Heavenly Sovereign has gone before. Approach and
follow me.

*(Raphael leads the Candidate through the skulls,
bones, corpses, etc., in the semi-darkness, and finally
into the Red Room).*

4. THE SECOND POINT

*(In the Red Room, brilliantly lit, the Brethren have
reversed their regalia again, coloured side out. The
music, if any, swells to a triumphant character as
Raphael leads the Candidate into the room, and to the
foot of the Mystic Ladder in the centre).*

Raph. Most Wise Sovereign, I bring with me this worthy
Knight who has travelled through dangers and
difficulties in search of the lost Word, and now
supplicates to be rewarded for his labours.

M.W.S. Excellent and Perfect Raphael, we doubt not that this
worthy Knight, assisted by your powerful aid, is
deserving of every distinction ; and I now call upon
him to ascend the ladder which leads from Darkness
to Glory and Perfection. But first, how came he
hither ?

Raph. Through the Valley of the Shadow of Death.

M.W.S. What supported him ?

1. The music recommended is Handel's Dead March from *Saul*, changing
to the joyful air of " Sound the Loud Timbrel o'er Egypt's Dark Sea "
when Raphael and the Candidate enter the Red Room.

Raph.	Faith, Hope, and Charity.
M.W.S.	What does he seek to obtain ?
Raph.	The Lost Word.
M.W.S.	Then, as he appears to have proceeded thus far aright and to be well prepared to ascend the mysterious ladder, he may advance, pausing at each step and replying to my questions with your assistance.

What is that virtue which leads from earth to Heaven ? (*The Candidate puts his left foot on the ladder. Raphael removes the rose over the letter with the point of his sword, and directs the Candidate to pick up the letter, and then to stand with both feet on the first step. This procedure is repeated for the subsequent steps. Raphael prompts the Candidate's replies*).

Can.	Faith.

(*Before the second step*) :—

M.W.S.	What Virtue supports you when oppressed by shame and sorrow ?
Can.	Hope.

(*Before the third step*) :—

M.W.S.	What is the perfection of every Christian Virtue ?
Can.	Charity.

(*Raphael takes the three letters F. H. and C. from the Candidate. Before the fourth step*) :—

M.W.S.	Whence come you ?
Can.	From Judaea.
Prel.	" Now when Jesus was born in Bethlehem of Judaea in the days of Herod the King, behold, there came Wise Men from the East to Jerusalem, saying :— 'Where is He that is born King of the Jews ? For we have seen His Star in the East, and are come to worship Him.' "

(*Before the fifth step*) :—

M.W.S.	By what village did you pass ?
Can.	Nazareth.
Prel.	" Philip findeth Nathaniel and saith unto him, ' We have found Him of whom Moses in the Law and the Prophets did write, Jesus of Nazareth, the Son of Joseph.' And Nathaniel said unto him, ' Can any good thing come out of Nazareth ? ' Philip saith unto him, ' Come and see.' "

(*Before the sixth step*) :—

M.W.S.	Who conducted you ?
Can.	Raphael.
Prel.	" He found Raphael that was an angel, and he said unto him, ' Canst thou go with me ? ' To whom the angel said, ' I will go with thee, and I know the way well.' "

(*Before the seventh step*) :—

M.W.S.	Of what tribe are you ?
Can.	Judah.
Prel.	" The sceptre shall not depart from Judah, nor a law-giver from between his feet until Shiloh come ; and unto him shall the gathering of the people be."
M.W.S.	Give me the Initials of the last four steps.
	(*Raphael takes the four letters I. N. R. I. from the Candidate, and gives them to the Sovereign*).
M.W.S.	Worthy Knight, by the aid of Faith, Hope, and Charity you have indeed succeeded in finding the lost Word.
	(*Raphael removes the black crêpe veil from the Candidate, and instructs him to step off the ladder*).
M.W.S.	By Faith you have found the Rose of Sharon, and you have been able to apprehend Him Who will neither leave nor forsake you.

By Hope you have obtained a Heaven-born blessing, which will console you under all difficulties and distresses and teach you under the afflictions of your earthly pilgrimage to look for a better and more enduring inheritance.

In Charity you behold the perfection of every Christian virtue.

Taking the Initials of the last four steps of your journey and putting them together, you have found the Name of Him Who is The Word, for St. John says, "In the beginning was the Word, and the Word was with God, and the Word was God. I am Alpha and Omega, the beginning and the ending, saith the Lord, which is, and which was, and which is to come, the Almighty."

Now, worthy Knight, having found the Word of the New Law, I request our Excellent and Perfect Prelate to affix it to its proper place.

(*All rise. The Prelate receives the Word from the Sovereign and places it on the Cubic Stone on the altar. All present, except Raphael and the Candidate, kneel on the right knee and point towards the Word with the right index finger. They then rise and give the first sign, with the word HOSANNA seven times. The Sovereign stands in front of the altar, facing west*).

M.W.S.	Let the Candidate approach.

Worthy Knight, I rejoice to confer upon you the reward you have so well earned, and I trust that, by the practice of those Virtues that have this day been commended to your notice, you will indeed be led to Him Who is the Way, the Truth, and the Life.

Kneel, therefore, and receive those honours to which you are now entitled.

(*The Candidate kneels on both knees. Raphael presents*

his sword to the Sovereign).

M.W.S. By virtue of the power and authority in me vested by the Supreme Council Thirty-Third Degree of England and Wales, the Dominions and Dependencies of the British Crown, I hereby make (*touches Candidate's right shoulder with the sword*) create, (*left shoulder*), and constitute (*head*) you, now and for ever, a Knight of the Pelican and Eagle.

(*The Sovereign returns the sword to Raphael*).

M.W.S. I seal you a Prince of the Order of the Rose Croix of Heredom with the Seal of Perfection.

(*The Sovereign raises the new Prince*).

M.W.S. Rise, Excellent and Perfect Prince Rose Croix, and receive the emblems of our Order. Princes, be seated.

(*The Director of Ceremonies takes away the kneeling-stool and presents the regalia*).

M.W.S. I invest you with the badge of the Order. (*Presents the apron, and then takes the Collar and Jewel in his hands*).

The Jewel worn in this Degree is a pair of Compasses with a rose on either side, and surmounted by a Celestial Crown.

The points of the Compasses are extended on the segment of a circle with a Cross between them. Beneath the Cross is the heraldic emblem known as a " Pelican in its piety " ; and on the reverse a White Eagle with wings extended as if rising in the air.

The Pelican is a symbol of Christ our Redeemer ; for, as it was reputed to feed its young with its own blood to save them from death, so our Saviour shed His Blood to save us from death eternal.

The Eagle reminds us that the Saviour is God Himself, as He said to the Israelites of old, " I bare you on eagles' wings and brought you unto myself."

The Rose is an emblem of secrecy and silence. In the Song of Solomon we find reference to the Saviour under the mystical title of the Rose of Sharon.

The Cross represents the Cross of Calvary, red with the Precious Blood.

The Red Collar is embroidered on the right side with the representation of a Serpent, the symbol of wisdom, having its tail in its mouth, thus forming a Circle, the emblem of eternity.

On the left side is embroidered a representation of the Crown of Thorns, worn by Him Who says unto us, " Be thou faithful unto death, and I will give thee a Crown of Life."

Thus the Rose and the Cross and the other symbols

M.W.S.   peculiar to this Degree should remind us, through the Eternal Wisdom, of Him who is The Word, and teach us to take up our Cross and follow Him here, that we may win the Crown hereafter.

I now invest you with the Collar and Jewel of the Order.

I present to you this Rose, an emblem of Him Who is the Rose of Sharon and the Lily of the Valley.

Be careful, by the exercise of Faith, Hope, and Charity, to continue to deserve these emblems, which are symbols of hidden truths known only to the Perfect Mason.

I will now communicate to you the signs and words of this Degree.

The first sign is called the sign of Adoration. It consists in interlacing the fingers, then lifting the hands to the forehead, palms outwards, and at the same time raising the eyes to Heaven and exclaiming HOSANNA, then dropping the hands on to the body.

The second sign is exchanged thus :—I raise my right hand to my forehead with the fingers closed except the index finger, saying HE ASCENDED. You reply by pointing downwards with the right hand, saying HE DESCENDED. The complete sign signifies that there is but One God in Heaven and Earth, Creator and Sovereign of all things.

The third is called the sign of the Good Shepherd or Pastor. It is given by crossing the arms on the breast, the left uppermost. It is answered in the same manner. We then approach each other with the third sign and mutually place our hands on the other's breast, thus forming two crosses. Then we exchange the letters I. N. R. I. alternately. These are the Initials of the superscription on the Cross, and stand for Jesus Nazarenus Rex Judaeorum.

The password EMMANUEL is given with the sign of the Good Shepherd, and is answered by PAX VOBISCUM given with the same sign. The sign is also given when addressing the Most Wise Sovereign and when entering or leaving a Chapter.

Excellent and Perfect Marshal, you will conduct the new Prince to the West and let him be duly proclaimed.

(*The Marshal and Raphael conduct the newly perfected Prince to the West and place him between and slightly in front of the Generals, and stand on either side of him facing East. All rise*).

Herald   (*Standing in the south west*) By command of the Most Wise Sovereign, I proclaim that our Brother ....

Herald   has this day been created a Knight of the Pelican and Eagle, and sealed and invested a Prince of the Order of the Rose Croix of Heredom. I summon him accordingly to take his seat in the Chapter.

(Fanfare. All resume their seats. The Director of Ceremonies leads the new Prince to the Sovereign who shows him the Warrant and presents him with a copy of the Rules and Regulations, and the by-laws of the Chapter. He is then conducted to his seat in the south east. The remaining business of the Chapter is then transacted. Alms are taken and presented at the altar. The Most Wise Sovereign rises thrice to enquire if anyone has aught to propose for the good of the Order in general, or of this Chapter in particular. Then all except members of the Thirty-Third Degree retire, and the room is prepared for the Third Point).

5. THE THIRD POINT.

(The ladder, floorcloth, and roses are removed, and a table with a red cloth is placed in the centre of the room. On the table are placed wafers, a chalice of wine, salt, and a second cup containing spirits. Gloves are removed, and the Princes enter the room in procession in inverse order of precedence, the Marshal and the new Prince first, others according to their degree, the Prelate and the Sovereign last. They circle the room, and when the Sovereign and the Prelate reach the East a complete circle is formed around the table. The members of the 33rd Degree take their places to the left of the Prelate. The Candidate is left outside the circle).

M.W.S.   Princes, we have now arrived at the perfection of Masonry ; let us then unite in forming the Living Circle as an emblem of Eternity.

(The Living Circle is formed with arms outstretched).

M.W.S.   Princes, let us receive him who has this day been admitted to our Order.

(The Marshal leads the Candidate into the Circle, on the right of the Sovereign. The Circle is again completed).

M.W.S.   Excellent and Perfect Prince, we receive you into the Living Circle of our hearts.

(After a brief pause the hands are dropped).

M.W.S.   Princes, we now invite you, according to Oriental custom, to break bread and eat salt with us ; at the same time pledging to each other our fidelity and friendship in the goblet of fraternal affection ; and let us invoke the blessing of Him Who is the Rose of Sharon and the Lily of the Valley, by Whose assistance

M.W.S. we hope to progress here on earth towards that perfection which can be consummated only when, rising from the tomb, we ascend to join our great Emmanuel and are united with Him for ever in a glorious and happy Eternity.

(The Director of Ceremonies presents the platter to the Sovereign, who takes a piece of wafer and presents it to the Prelate on his left, who breaks off a portion. Both dip their pieces into the salt and eat them. The Prelate repeats these actions with his next neighbour, and so on round the Circle. Then the Director of Ceremonies hands the chalice to the Sovereign, who turns to the Prelate and faces him. The Sovereign says EM-MANUEL, and the Prelate gives the sign of the Good Shepherd, saying PAX VOBISCUM. The Sovereign drinks and passes the chalice to the Prelate, who repeats the ceremony with the Brother on his left, and so on. The Prelate lights the spirit in the other cup with a taper kindled from the altar candles. When all have partaken) :—

M.W.S. All is consumed.

Prel. Gloria in excelsis Deo, et in terra Pax hominibus bonae voluntatis.

M.W.S. Princes, we rejoice to have united in this Feast of Fraternal affection. May we henceforth treasure up the sacred doctrines of the Order in the secret repository of our hearts.

Excellent and Perfect Prelate, I now request you to remove the Sacred Word, that it be not exposed to the eyes of the profane, but be consumed according to ancient custom as a perpetual memorial of our veneration of Him Who came to consummate the redemption of all those who faithfully and sincerely put their trust in Him, our risen Emmanuel.

(The Prelate removes the Word from the altar, passes to the west side of the table, faces east, and burns it in the cup of burning spirits. The fire is not extinguished but allowed to die down).

Prel. Consummatum est.

M.W.S. Princes, resume your seats.

CLOSING THE CHAPTER

(The Sovereign knocks once, repeated by the First and Second Generals).

M.W.S. Princes, assist me to close this .... Chapter. *(All rise).*

M.W.S. Excellent and Perfect Prelate, what is the hour ?

Prel. It is the first hour of the third day, being the first day of the week, the hour of a perfect Mason.

M.W.S. What is the hour of a perfect Mason ?

Prel. It is the hour when the Sacred Word is found and the Cubic Stone is changed into the Mystic Rose. The Blazing Star has reappeared in all its splendour ; our Altars are renewed ; the True Light restored to our eyes, the clouds of darkness dispersed ; and the New Commandment is given to love one another.

M.W.S. Let us then observe this New Commandment to love one another, the result and perfection of all preceding Masonry, which will enable us to erect an edifice in our hearts to the Glory of the Lamb ; to Whom belongeth Might, Majesty, Dominion and Power, Who liveth and reigneth world without end. Amen. (*All give the third sign, and after a pause, drop it. The Sovereign knocks 6. 1., repeated by the First and Second Generals, the Captain of the Guard, and the Outer Guard. The Prelate closes the Bible*).

M.W.S. The Chapter is now closed in the Name of the Great Emmanuel. Depart in Peace.

* * *

Whatever may be the meaning of this degree, it is first of all abundantly clear from the most superficial reading of it that it is presented as a solemn religious rite, with many of the external trappings of Christian worship. It sets up its altars, and offers acts of prayer and praise. It has mystic rites which lead the initiate " from darkness to glory and perfection". Secretly and behind locked doors the Princes of the Rose Croix of Heredom perform these ceremonies the aims of which a former Grand Chaplain declared differed from those of the Church " only in their pageantry." He furthermore wrote that " we join and pray, not as private men asking blessings for ourselves, but as a Religious Society."[1]

Even supposing this degree is perfectly orthodox in its Christianity, however, it remains a religious body outside the Church, unknown to the Church, resolutely refusing to disclose its teachings and its ritual to the Church, setting up its altars independently of the Church. There can, therefore, be no compari-

1. *The Origin and Progress of the Supreme Council 33° of the Ancient and Accepted (Scottish) Rite*, by the Rev. Arnold Whitaker, Oxford, 1933. The author was Grand Chaplain of the Rite from 1920–1948, than whom no one surely could be in a better position to make authoritative statements on its religious nature.

son whatsoever between such a rite and other devotional guilds and fraternities within, or at least harmoniously known to the Church. Therefore the corporate worship of the " Religious Society " of the Rose Croix is blatantly schismatic. The Churchman, and particularly the clergyman, who in the course of initiation swears fidelity to it, is guilty of a dual religious allegiance. By calling the Rose Croix a Masonic order rather than a Christian sect, its initiates blind themselves to this fact in what is really little more than a verbal quibble ; were these very same ceremonies, with appropriate changes of wording, widely advertised and performed publicly in chapels open to all, instead of secretly for the few, there can be no doubt that everyone would consider it a rather freakish Christian sect, not unlike that described in Ngaio Marsh's *Death in Ecstasy*. Many an Anglican cleric would denounce it as such if he found his parishioners sharing their allegiance between Church and Chapter. Even Bishops might then be found to take strong action if their clergy officiated in both. What a difference is made by a locked door !

Still supposing that the teachings of the Eighteenth Degree could be considered orthodox and Christian, a further problem arises in the fact that the English jurisdiction which makes this claim is still in full fraternal relations and intercommunion with the mother body, the Southern Jurisdiction of the Ancient and Accepted Scottish Rite in America, which not only makes no such claim, but specifically repudiates it. In its ritual of this degree it is stated that " All the Degrees of Scottish Masonry can be received by good men of every race and religious faith ; and any Degree that cannot be so received is not Masonry, which is universal, but some other thing, that is exclusive, and therefore intolerant. All our degrees have, in that, one object. Each inculcates toleration, and the union of men of all faiths ; and each erects a platform on which the Mohammedan, the Israelite, and the Christian may stand side by side and hand in hand, as true Brethren."[1]

Even in America, however, there is an exception to this toleration, for in the Office of Installation, the Master-Elect is asked, " Do you promise never to consent to the admission into a

1. *Liturgy of the Antient and Accepted Scottish Rite of Freemasonry for the Southern Jurisdiction of the United States of America* (1936) Part III, p. 173.

Chapter of Rose Croix of anyone who is or has been a Monk or a Jesuit, or is an Atheist ? "[1] The tenses are interesting ; there is always hope, it seems, for the Masonic conversion of an atheist, but none for the monk or Jesuit. The type of monk is not specified, and it would be interesting to know whether the ban includes the Buddhist monk and the Kelham Father (particularly the latter where the question is not wholly academic), as well as the Roman Catholic variety.

The structure of the American version of the Rose Croix is very similar to the English, but the interpretation differs. The pelican is not a symbol of Christ, but " represents the large and bountiful beneficence of Nature, from whose exhaustless bosom [sic] all created things draw their sustenance." And " the Eagle was, in Egypt, the living symbol of the God Mendes or Menthra, whom Sesostris-Rames made one with Amun-Ra, the God of Thebes and upper Egypt, and the representative of the Sun, itself a type of the infinite Supreme Reason of Intelligence." This same ritual points out that " the Cross, pointing to the four cardinal points, and whose arms, infinitely extended, would never meet, is an emblem of Space or Infinity...The Cross has been a sacred symbol from the earliest antiquity. It is found upon all the enduring monuments of the world— in Egypt, Assyria, India, and Persia. Buddha was said to have died upon one. The Druids cut an oak into its shape, and held it sacred, and built their temples in that form...The Cross also forms a part of the character representing each of the planets, Mars, Venus, Mercury, Saturn, and Jupiter." The fact that Our Lord was crucified is mentioned only in passing.

The rose, far from being identified with the Rose of Sharon, " was anciently sacred to Aurora and the Sun. It was a symbol of Dawn, of the resurrection of Light and the renewal of Life, and therefore of Immortality. The Cross also was a symbol of Life, and the two symbols, united, mean Immortality won by suffering and sorrow."[2] But the cross embroidered on the front of the American altar is the *crux ansata*, which is certainly not a Christian symbol, and the letters I.N.R.I. which flank it may be given the various interpretations of IGNE NATURA RENO-

1. *Chapter of Rose Croix Ceremonies*, revised, 1936. Published by the Supreme Council, Southern Jurisdiction.
2. *Liturgy*, pp. 176, 177.

VATUR INTEGRA,[1] or the alchemical IGNE NITRUM RORIS INVENITUR,[2] or the four elements in Hebrew, IAMAYIM, water ; NOR, fire ; RUAKH, air ; and IABASHAH, earth.[3]

The Northern Jurisdiction for this rite in America, though less emphatic in its Christian interpretation than the English rite, nevertheless angered Albert Pike by Christianizing it to some extent. Pike looked on the changes as " unnecessarily offensive to a Hebrew ", and he was not sure that it " would not exclude a Unitarian."[4] Clearly he would have disapproved even more strongly of the present English rite, and yet his successors maintain cordial relations with it, and of course enjoy the right of visitation in this country. There must, then, be a fundamental unity between them.

Hence the fact that the initiate to the Rose Croix in England must profess a belief in the Holy and Undivided Trinity seems to take a secondary place. It cannot rank as a landmark, as it is a regional peculiarity and not universal in the rite ; otherwise surely the Supreme Council in London would long ago have taken the same course with America as the United Grand Lodge of London took with the Grand Orient of France when the latter body ceased to make belief in the Great Architect as an essential of the Order. There is nothing in the English Rules and Regulations to prevent a Rabbi or a Dervish initiated in Alabama from joining an English Chapter and taking full part in its worship and religious observances, as long as they take the Oath of Allegiance to the Supreme Council, which is not taken in the name of the Trinity. In practice, however, this is unlikely to happen.

These are some of the arguments that can be brought against the secret ceremonies of the Rose Croix of Heredom even were these ceremonies compatible with Christian orthodoxy. Unfortunately they are not, which makes the argument ten times as strong.

Their ancestry, as we have seen, is not of great antiquity, nor was it orthodox. The Rosy Cross tradition, however, from which this degree derives its name and some of its symbolism and

1. " Entire nature is renovated by fire."
2. " By fire the nitre of the dew is extracted."
3. *The Inner Sanctuary*, by Albert Pike, p. 73 *et seq.*
4. *Proceedings* of the Northern Jurisdiction, 1877, p. 95.

teaching can be traced back possibly to the *Militia Crucifera Evangelica*, a German occult evangelical fraternity of the late sixteenth century. Little is known about it, for its chief literature, the *Naometria* of Simon Studion, is lost, and only partially known through the quotations of others. It appears to have been strongly Kabbalistic in inspiration. C. G. von Murr, who was certainly acquainted with the original, declared that it breathed the Rosicrucian spirit, and embodied real Rosicrucian doctrine.[1]

But although Rosicrucianism had its origins in the mystics and alchemists of the sixteenth century, it did not really enter history until the publication of the *Fama Fraternitatis Rosae Crucis* in 1614. This was an account of the legendary founder of the Order, Christian Rosenkreutz, his band of brethren seeking occult wisdom, his death, and the later discovery of the tomb. The story accounts, after its fashion, for the hypothetical transmission of secret knowledge from east to west. This was followed by the *Confessio Fraternitatis*, a manifesto of Rosicrucian principles, and the *Chemical Nuptials of Christian Rosenkreutz*, an elaborate allegory.

Although it certainly cannot be proved (and it has been hotly denied) that Freemasonry, either in the craft or higher degrees, grew directly out of Rosicrucianism, there is evidence of an overlap in Germany as well as England. A. E. Waite declares that " about the year 1777 the last transformation of German Rosicrucianism was drawing on the Masonic fraternity to recruit its own ranks...a Masonic qualification in Candidates was the first title for admission. We have further to remember that the Rosicrucian Mystery was one of Divine Rebirth, such indeed as we meet with—though under many veils—in the ceremonial of Masonry. It sought also that hidden knowledge which Masonry and several early aspects of the Secret Tradition in Christian times supposed to have been lost in Adam."[2] And in regard to the Eighteenth Degree in particular, " I am personally convinced that the whole arrangement of the Rose-Croix Grade, its clothing, its jewel, its entire *mise-en-scène*, the chambers in which it is worked are reminiscent of the older Order. The three points are in crude correspondence with the Hermetic Work in Alchemy—blackness, death, and finally

1. *True Origin of the Rosicrucian and Masonic Orders*, 1803.
2. A New Encylopædia of Freemasonry, vol. II, p. 375.

resurrection into the red or perfect state...It follows that the various Masonic writers who have denied any connection between the Eighteenth Degree and the Rosicrucian Order have either spoken with an extraordinary absence of even elementary knowledge or with considerable want of sincerity. The bond of kinship lies upon the surface of the subject, and those who have eyes can scarcely fail to see."[1]

However distant this alleged kinship, the main Rosicrucian symbol, a rose at the junction of a passion cross, is beyond all question a central emblem of this Masonic degree. If to the Rosicrucians it stood for the Cross of Calvary, red with the precious Blood, it also stood for the secret of the true light, or the true knowledge, which the Rosicrucian Brotherhood was to give to the world, for the rose symbolized secrecy, and the cross, light. As far as Rosicrucianism was Christian it was Lutheran and anti-Catholic in inspiration, but it owed much to the *Zohar*, the *Sepher Yetzirah*, and other books of the Kabbala.

The English rite of the Eighteenth Degree has been veneered with a good deal of conventional and orthodox Christian phraseology, but fundamentally it reverts to Gnosticism. Gnosticism is a difficult term to define precisely, as it covered many sects and mysteries based on *gnosis* or enlightenment. It was a theosophical philosophy, and in so far as it claimed to be Christian, it professed to reveal to an inner *élite* of initiates esoteric teachings concealed from the many. Dr. A. C. Headlam listed amongst its tendencies three points highly relevant to Freemasonry, " a syncretistic tendency combining in an artificial manner with some more or less misunderstood Christian doctrines, elements from classical, Oriental, and Jewish sources, or even from common magic; " " A tendency towards a Docetic Christology, i.e. one which looked upon the earthly life of Christ, or at any rate the sufferings, as unreal ; " and " a tendency to represent *gnosis* (knowledge) as something superior to mere faith, and the special possession of the more enlightened."[2]

If the Rose Croix Mason feels bewildered and incredulous at these accusations, another quotation before substantiating the charge of Gnosticism in detail may make the position clearer.

1. *The Brotherhood of the Rosy Cross*, p. 428.
2. *A Dictionary of the Bible*, edited by James Hastings, vol. II, p. 186.

" Gnosticism " says Fr. J. P. Arendzen[1] " threw itself with strange rapidity into Christian forms of thought, borrowed its nomenclature, acknowledged Jesus as Saviour of the world, simulated its sacraments, pretended to be an esoteric revelation of Christ and His Apostles...though in reality the spirit of Gnosticism is utterly alien to that of Christianity, it then seemed to the unwary merely a modification or refinement thereof."

The theosophical synthesis of pagan elements is more clearly apparent in the Royal Arch than the Rose Croix, though the American version of the latter is redolent of it, and it reappears implicitly in the English ritual of the thirty-first degree. The Rose Croix, however, is certainly Gnostic in its claims to hidden wisdom and esoteric enlightenment for the initiate only. The obligation pledges fidelity to the " secrets and mysteries of this Order," and the various emblems, principally the rose and the cross, are called " symbols of hidden Truths known only to the perfect Mason." The Word itself must " not be exposed to the eyes of the profane " (though it appears on almost every crucifix in every public place) but burned in a chalice. The Princes Rose Croix are bidden to " treasure up the sacred doctrines of the Order in the secret repository " of their hearts.

That a Docetic Christology underlies this degree is suggested by the fact that Christ's death and resurrection appear to be regarded, not as an objective act of redemption, but rather as a type of the experiences which the inititate must undergo in his quest for illumination. The emphasis seems to be on the initiate's impersonation of Christ in achieving his own salvation through enlightenment. He is aided, indeed, by faith, hope, and charity, but the fact that initials have been substituted in the Chapter for these words, with the Masonic craze for mystery, seems to imply that even these virtues should have a special and private significance for the Mason alone. The initiate gives his age as thirty-three, whatever it may be in reality. He travels for thirty-three days in seven concentric circles representing the seven periods of the world's existence. He passes through the blackness of death to his resurrection in the Red Room, and ascends the ladder to glory and perfection. He hears the Resurrection in the Closing ceremony described as " the hour of a perfect Mason ". This seems a little sinister, but far

1. *Catholic Encylopædia*, vol. VI, p. 594.

less so than the description of Our Lord's triumphant redemptive death on the Cross as a dire calamity for Masonry—a phrase which carries the unfortunate suggestion that the defeat of Satan is being mourned. But in any case, why a calamity for Masonry in particular, unless Masonry represents an inner circle of illuminati, more particularly concerned than the rest of mankind ? How absurd it would sound to call the Crucifixion a dire calamity for the Mothers' Union or the Church of England Men's Society !

The symbolic achievement of salvation by the Prince Rose Croix is attained without any acknowledgement or confession of sin, any cry of penitence or contrition, or any need for the divine forgiveness. It is laid down in the Rules and Regulations of the Order (No. 40) that " Good position and high moral character are indispensable requisites for admission as a Member of the Ancient and Accepted Rite," so perhaps the very idea of sin is insultingly superfluous, and a single reference to " us, Thine unworthy children " in the Opening is as far as an English gentleman of good position and high moral character can be expected to condescend without squirming. The defect is common to all Masonic degrees, however Christian, for respectability seems a more esteemed Masonic virtue than humility. But in this particular degree, based on the crucifixion and in a sense symbolically re-enacting it in each initiate, this defect has a special significance. Our Lord was crucified only incidentally by the wickedness or treachery of those immediately concerned. He died to pay the price of our sins, and the sins of the whole world, past, present, and future. He died that those sins might be forgiven to the penitent. But the Eighteenth-Degree Mason is given no clue of this, hence it is hardly surprising if the theology of atonement is warped and the Passion treated as a sort of dark night of the soul undergone by the Master-Hierophant, and followed by His Initiates, in the quest for illumination and glory.

The Feast of Fraternal Affection or Third Point is very similar, as Dr. H. S. Box has pointed out,[1] to the Valentinian Eucharist described in the Gnostic work *Pistis Sophia*. It has of course the nature of an *agape* or love-feast rather than a Mass or Communion. There is nothing approaching a consecration. Yet the

1. In a letter to the *Church Times*, April 13, 1951.

words *Consummatum Est* appear to establish a link with Calvary, and it is difficult to see how a Christian can be quite easy in his conscience when participating in such a rite. Neither Irenaeus nor Tertullian nor any of the Fathers engaged in the struggle against Gnosticism would have tolerated loyal sons of the Church participating in such secret and macabre mysteries. Is that of no significance to the Church of England today ?

A Masonic Bishop in the Craft degrees is reported to have said,—I know not to whom, or on whose authority—" Play about with King Solomon and his Temple by all means, if you must. But let's leave our dear Lord out of it."

X

THE RITUAL OF THE GRAND ELECTED KNIGHT KADOSH

Though stale, not ripe ; though thin, yet never clear ;
So sweetly mawkish, and so smoothly dull.
Alexander Pope, The Dunciad.

It is impossible to genuflect on the top of a ladder.
Adrian Fortescue, Ceremonies of the Roman Rite Described.

WHEN worked " in ample form " as the phrase is, three rooms and an ante-room are required for the conferring of this degree. The three rooms represent the Cavern, the Temple of Wisdom or Council of the Aeropagus, and the Senate. The first two, however, may be one room divided by black curtains.

The first room is hung wholly with black. The second is also black, with a table at the far end covered in blue, behind which sit the principal officers. There is a brazier with charcoal, on which grains of incense are cast. The room is lit with three candles.

The Senate Chamber is hung with red and black, with red crosses. In the east is the throne, bearing on its canopy the crowned double-headed eagle holding a sword in its claws, with the motto *Deus Meumque Jus*. On either side of the throne are two standards. In this room is the mystic ladder, with six steps up and six steps down, and a platform on top. The room is illuminated with nine candles.

The Intermediate Degrees are conferred in the ante-room.

CLOTHING.

Sash. Four-inch black watered silk ribbon, worn from the left shoulder to the right hip. Upon it in the centre over the breast, the Ancient Order of Heredom Kadosh, that is, an eagle soaring towards the light, holding the Anchor of Hope in his talons, and on the extremity the red flag of England and Wales, bearing three golden lions crossed by the banner of the Supreme Council, and below a red Teutonic cross. The point is fringed with silver bullion.

Breast Jewel. A Pattée cross in red enamel, the number 30 in gold upon the blue enamel in the centre.

Eagle. A black double spread-eagle, surmounted by a crown, and holding a sword in its claws is worn from the neck on a black ribbon, one and a half inches wide, with a narrow silver edging.

Sword. Gilt grip and mountings, black scabbard.

Sword-belt. Black leather.

MARGINAL INITIALS.

G.C.	(Most Puissant Sovereign) Grand Commander.
G.D.C.	(Very Illustrious) Grand Director of Ceremonies.
Jan.	Janitor.

CEREMONY OF OPENING A GRAND CHAPTER[1]

G.C.	Very Illustrious Grand Director of Ceremonies, are we securely guarded ?
G.D.C.	We are well defended, within and without.
G.C.	(*Gives one knock*). Illustrious Knights, assist me to open this Grand Chapter. (*All Rise*).
G.C.	Very Illustrious Grand Director of Ceremonies, review your columns and assure yourself that all present are Grand Elected Knights Kadosh.
G.D.C.	I vouch for them as for myself.
G.C.	Illustrious Brother, are you elected ?
G.D.C.	I am.
G.C.	How came you to be elected ?
G.D.C.	Fortune decided in my favour.
G.C.	What proof can you give me of your reception ?
G.D.C.	A cavern was witness to it.
G.C.	What did you do in the cavern ?
G.D.C.	I executed my commission.
G.C.	Have you penetrated any farther ?
G.D.C.	I have.
G.C.	How shall I know it ?
G.D.C.	My title is Knight Kadosh. Once I bore a fuller name.
G.C.	I understand you. Is the just vengeance of our Order perfected ? [2]

1. As far as I am aware, this authentic English ritual of the 30th degree has not hitherto been published at all, but exists only in manuscript. A sketchy and extremely spurious version, however, appears in *The Text Book of Advanced Freemasonry*, Reeves and Turner.

2. This appears to be the only oblique reference remaining in the English workings to revenge for the death of Jacques de Molay. In the brief Lecture (see p. 154) where this phrase is explained, the enemies are Despotism, Ignorance, and Intolerance. The use of the term " just vengeance of our Order " (rather than, say, " just warfare ") would appear to indicate more than mere hostility or spiritual combat, and that there was a victory of these enemies to be specifically avenged.

G.D.C. It is not. One of our enemies still continues powerful ; another is struggling for existence ; and the third is grovelling in darkness.

G.C. What is the hour ?

G.D.C. That of profound silence.

G.C. Since it is the hour of silence let us continue our labours till time shall consummate our exertions. Very Illustrious Grand Director of Ceremonies, give me a sign to convince me of your knowledge, and to show that you are prepared against surprise. (*G.D.C. gives sign*).[1]

G.C. Let us unanimously resolve to maintain the sacred principles of our Order at the expense of our lives.

Omnes (*All make sign*). We resolve.

G.C. Illustrious Knights, the Chapter is open. (*One knock*). Be seated, Brethren.

CEREMONY OF RECEPTION

1. THE PRELIMINARY DEGREES

As the intermediate degrees between the Rose Croix and the Knight Kadosh are not worked in this country, they are conferred titulary in an anteroom by the Grand Director of Ceremonies, in the following form :—

G.D.C. You seek to be admitted to the degree of Grand Elected Knight Kadosh, being the thirtieth degree of the Ancient and Accepted Rite, but it is first necessary that you should possess the preliminary degrees from the nineteenth to the twenty-ninth inclusive. I, therefore, by virtue of the authority vested in me by the Supreme Council of the 33rd Degree, confer upon you the degrees of :—

19 Grand Pontiff,
20 Venerable Grand Master,
21 Patriarch Noachite,
22 Prince of Libanus,
23 Chief of the Tabernacle,
24 Prince of the Tabernacle,
25 Knight of the Brazen Serpent,
26 Prince of Mercy,
27 Commander of the Temple,
28 Knight of the Sun,
29 Knight of St. Andrew.

G.D.C. The sign of a Knight of the Sun and St. Andrew is given by extending the hand, thumb and forefinger making a circle, points not touching, and looking

1. See p. 154.

G.D.C.   through the circle.

The pass word is STIBIUM ALKABAR, I compass the Sun.

(After conferring the preliminary degrees the G.D.C. returns to the Grand Chapter and reports to the Most Puissant Sovereign Grand Commander, as follows) :—

G.D.C.   Most Puissant Sovereign Grand Commander, there is in attendance a candidate who has been duly elected and now seeks admission to the degree of Grand Elected Knight Kadosh. Is it your pleasure that he should be admitted to the Temple of Wisdom ?

G.C.   Very Illustrious Grand Director of Ceremonies, let him be introduced in due form, and I will ask Most Illustrious Brother . . . . (name) to repair to the Temple of Wisdom for this purpose.

(At least three Sovereign Grand Inspector Generals should take part in the ceremony in the Temple of Wisdom. The G.D.C. conducts the Candidate to the Cavern).

2. THE CEREMONIES IN THE CAVERN.

(Outside the door the Janitor is found asleep upon the ground. The G.D.C. gives one knock).

J.   Who art thou ?

G.D.C.   A Knight of the Sun and St. Andrew.

J.   What wouldst thou ?

G.D.C.   Permission to enter the Temple of Wisdom.

J.   Why troublest thou my repose ?

G.D.C.   I would not do so willingly, but you obstruct the path that leads to the consummation of my wishes.

(Janitor disappears. G.D.C. knocks twice, then thrice, then four times).

G.C.   Who art thou ?

G.D.C.   In the cavern adjoining the Aeropagus there is a Candidate for the rank of Grand Elected Knight Kadosh, who has proved himself to be a Knight of the Sun and St. Andrew.

G.C.   We place the fullest reliance on your knowledge and discretion, and if the Candidate proves himself otherwise qualified we are prepared to admit him to the exalted rank to which he aspires, but you must warn him of the danger he incurs should his courage and virtue fail him.

G.D.C.   *(To Candidate)* I am here to guide you, but I warn you that if you do not feel courage to face the greatest danger, you had better retrace your steps.

G.C.   Do unto others as thou wouldest they should do unto thee.

2nd Judge	Do not unto others that which thou wouldest not they should do unto thee.
3rd J.	Love thy neighbour as thyself.
4th J.	Succour the unfortunate.
5th J.	Adore the Supreme Being and Worship Him.
6th J.	Be true and free from falsehood.
7th J.	Be patient, and bear with the failings of thy Brethren.
8th J.	Be faithful to thy engagements, and remember that discretion is a virtue.
9th J.	Be patient under adversity.
G.C.	Such are the duties of a philosopher.
G.D.C.	(*To Candidate*) Now, my Brother, that you are acquainted with our chief duties, do you think that you are able to put them into practice ?
Can.	I do.
	(*G.D.C. knocks* 2.3.4.)
G.C.	Who comes here ?
G.D.C.	A Knight of the Sun and St. Andrew who seeks to be admitted to the Temple of Wisdom.
G.C.	Tell him that he alone can learn our mysteries who reverences and adores Him who is the Eternal All-Wise Creator, and devotes himself to the acquisition of true wisdom. If he feels that he possesses the virtues characteristic of a Philosopher permit him to enter the Temple of Wisdom.

(*The black curtains are drawn back, and the Candidate is admitted to the Temple of Wisdom*).

3. THE TEMPLE OF WISDOM

G.C.	Supplicate with me the God of Wisdom, Sanctity and Truth.
G.D.C.	To order, Brethren.
Grand Chaplain	Grant us, O God, to be enkindled with Thy Spirit ; strengthened with Thy Power ; enlightened with Thy Brightness ; filled with Thy Grace ; and led forward by Thine Aid even to our lives' end in Thy Service and Thy Love, through Jesus Christ our Lord,
Omnes	Amen.
G.C.	Pursue your course.
G.D.C.	Be seated, Brethren.

(*The G.D.C. leads the Candidate round, placing grains of incense on the brazier as he passes. The Candidate follows suit*).

G.C.	My Brother, the course of truth in which we are engaged requires from every one entrusted with our secrets the utmost fidelity and discretion. We shall therefore call upon you to make a solemn promise to

G.C.   hold inviolate whatever information relative to the Order may be entrusted to you. With your right hand on your heart, repeat after me :—
(*One knock. All rise*).

OBLIGATION

I promise and bind myself by all that is most sacred never to reveal any of the secrets of a Grand Elected Knight Kadosh, which have hitherto been entrusted to me, may now, or hereafter be communicated to me. I promise not to assist in conferring this degree on any Brother who has not, to the best of my belief, the necessary virtues and qualifications ; nor then except in the presence of three Sovereign Grand Inspectors General. I promise to maintain at the peril of my life the sacred principles of the Order and to preserve them by all means in my power against error. Lastly, I promise to execute all that is prescribed by the Supreme Council Thirty-Third Degree, and to conform to the Laws and Statutes of the Order. So help me God.

G.C.   Child of Wisdom, retire and meditate on the mysteries you have already learnt, and collect your energies for further trials.
(*The Candidate retires with the Grand Director of Ceremonies. The Members of the Supreme Council Thirty-Third Degree, and the other Brethren present in the Temple of Wisdom return to the Grand Chapter*).

4. THE GRAND CHAPTER.

(*The ascent to the Ladder is guarded by two stalwart Knights in black cloaks, with masks, and armed with battle-axes*).

G.D.C.   Most Illustrious Members of the Supreme Council, I bring with me this Philosopher, Knight of the Sun and St. Andrew, who having been received into the Temple of Wisdom renews his prayer to be admitted to the Grand Chapter.

G.C.   Permit him to enter the Outer Sanctuary.

G.D.C.   (*To Candidate*) I am not here to prevent you from accomplishing your destiny, but to warn you that after having taken the first step, if you recoil you are lost. Choose to advance or retire.
(*Candidate indicates his desire to advance by taking one step forward*).

G.D.C.   Most Illustrious Members of the Supreme Chapter, I venture to supplicate you to admit into your Chapter

G.D.C.   this Child of Wisdom ; who by the practice of virtue, and the observance of his duty, merits your approbation.

G.C.   You well know, my Brother, that we admit none to these important mysteries but those whose integrity, unspotted reputation, and tried probity, distinguish them among their fellows. If, my Very Illustrious Brother, you are sufficiently acquainted with the Candidate to declare that he possesses these qualifications we will willingly consent to his undergoing our further trials of his firmness and courage.

G.D.C.   (*After turning and surveying the Candidate*) I answer for him as for myself.

G.C.   Let the Candidate be admitted.
(*Candidate stands in the West*).

G.C.   My Brother, you aspire to be admitted to this Sanctuary, not knowing the force of the engagements into which you are about to enter ; but, as we would not bind you in matters of which you are ignorant, we will call upon our colleagues to explain them to you.
(*Other members of the Supreme Council present then pronounce the following sentences in order*).

1st.   Discretion, an essential attribute, for on it depends the safety of our Order.

2nd.   Execution of our Laws and Statutes ; these require nothing repugnant to the virtuous man.

3rd.   The sacrifice of all, even life itself, for the good of the Order.

4th.   The worship of the Great Architect of the Universe.

5th.   The acquisition of knowledge for the good of mankind.

6th.   A vindication of all truth.

7th.   And last ; to practise all virtue and be in truth a philosopher.

G.C.   Are you willing to attempt all these ?

Can.   I am.

G.C.   My Brother, have you well considered the trials and difficulties which await you ?

Can.   I have.

G.C.   Do you still wish to proceed ?

Can.   I do.

G.C.   Then we will cause you to pass over the Mysterious Ladder, and will explain the meaning of its steps, which are all veiled in allegory, representing the road that must be travelled in order to arrive at the *Ne Plus Ultra*, or Perfection of Wisdom.

G.C.   The right side of the Ladder is called OHEB ELOAH, and is the first of the fundamental principles of the Order which impresses upon us the duty of love to

G.C. God.
The left hand side is called OHEB KEROBO, and is the emblem of the second basis of our Order, for it enjoins us to love our neighbour as ourselves.
(*Candidate ascends the first step of the ladder, and halts*).

G.C. The first step is called TSEDAKAH ; it signifies that our physical and mental powers must always be employed in succouring the unfortunate.
(*Candidate takes the second step*).

G.C. The second step is called SHOR LABAN ; it signifies that we should do to others as we would they should do to us ; and that we should not do to others what we would not they should do to us.
(*Candidate takes the third step*).

G.C. The third step is called MATHOK ; it signifies that we must support adversity with resignation.
(*Candidate takes the fourth step*).

G.C. The fourth step is called EMOUNAH ; it signifies that we must be true and avoid falsehood.
(*Candidate takes the fifth step*).

G.C. The fifth step is called HAMIL SAGHAI ; it signifies the necessity of labouring in order to make ourselves perfect.
(*Candidate takes the sixth step*).

G.C. The sixth step is called SABHAL ; it signifies that we ought to bear with the failings of the Brethren.
(*Candidate takes seventh step*).

G.C. The seventh step is called GEMUL BINAH TEBU-NAH;[1] it signifies that we must be faithful to our engagements, and recollect that discretion is one of the first virtues of a philosopher.
(*The Grand Director of Ceremonies and the Assistant Director of Ceremonies cross their wands before the Candidate. One knock*).

G.C. NE PLUS ULTRA.
(*The Organist plays a chord or cadence*).

G.C. My Brother, as the seven steps you have just ascended form the basis of our moral labours, so our material labours are indicated by the seven steps you will now descend. Each of the former pointed out to us that to arrive at the wished for end it is indispensable to practise each of the virtues which they symbolically represent ; so these latter require us to acquaint ourselves with the sciences, and thus enable us to fulfil our appointed duties.
(*The Candidate descends the seven steps, passing each*

1. There are certain slight variations in these words on the steps of the ladder. I have chosen what I believe to be the most usual forms.

step while the Grand Commander says) :—

G.C.   The first step represents Grammar ; the second, Rhetoric ; the third, Arithmetic, Geometry and Mathematics ; the fourth, Physiology, the knowledge of organic life ; the fifth, Chemistry ; the sixth, Harmony as illustrated by poetry and music ; and the seventh represents Astronomy.

(The Candidate is placed before the Pedestal, facing East. The cloaks and visors of the Guardians of the Ladder are now removed, and the axes replaced).

G.C.   My Brother, as a Sovereign Grand Inspector General, and Prince of the Royal Secret, I can assure you that before we can confer upon you the purpose and object of our Confederation and those secrets by which we secure efficiency of action and prompt obedience to the Sovereign Power of our Order, that it is indispensable we should have ample assurance that we may confide in and rely upon you.

Be not, however, too hastily urged forward by imprudent zeal. It may be that we are only permitted to prepare the way for others, and must wait patiently and in silence for the hour and the opportunity. Let us not increase our ranks by admitting even our most intimate friends unless assured of their discretion.

My Brother, we appreciate the satisfactory nature of the credentials with which you approach us today, but before we can say more we are compelled to require of you another and more binding promise. Be certain before you determine to proceed that you will not hesitate to comply with every part of this promise, which, if you advance, you must pronounce with me, and it will bind you to us forever.

(The Grand Director of Ceremonies directs the Candidate to take one pace forward with the left foot. The Grand Commander gives one knock. All rise).

G.C.   Firstly. Do you promise by all that you hold most dear that you will hereafter consider yourself the soldier of truth, justice, law, order, and suffering humanity ; that you will practise mercy, and live and die in submission to the Will of God ?

(The Candidate is instructed to extend the forefinger of his right hand, and is prompted in making the answers to these promises).

Can.   I promise. TSEDAKAH.

G.C.   Secondly. Do you promise that you will be modest in all your actions, and that you will never receive into this Degree anyone you believe unworthy to be your friend ?

Can.   I promise. SHOR LABAN.

G.C.   Thirdly. Do you promise at all times to be gentle and affectionate towards your Brethren ; to aid them in their necessities ; visit and assist them in sickness, and love, and cherish those who are near and dear to them ?

Can.   I promise. MATHOK.

G.C.   Fourthly. Do you promise in your conversation to be governed by truth, and in your actions by sincerity and frankness ?

Can.   I promise. EMOUNAH.

G.C.   Fifthly. Do you promise that you will labour zealously for the good of the Order, and that you will at all times follow what shall be prescribed to you by the Illustrious Grand Inspector General under whom you may happen to serve ?

Can.   I promise. HAMIL SAGHAI.

G.C.   Sixthly. Do you promise to practise the virtues and cultivate the sciences commended to you by the steps of the Mysterious Ladder ?

Can.   I promise. SABHAL.

G.C.   Seventhly and Lastly. Do you promise that you will aid in punishing and bringing to disgrace all traitors to Masonry, and that you will bear true faith and allegiance to the Supreme Council of the Thirty-Third Degree ?

Can.   I promise. GEMUL BINAH TEBUNAH.

G.C.   The Candidate will kneel.

        (*The G.D.C. presents the sword to the Grand Commander*).

G.C.   (*Giving the accolade*) By the seven promises you have now made, I hereby nominate, constitute and create you a Grand Elected Knight Kadosh, Knight of the Black and White Eagle, and I invest you with all the dignities and prerogatives thereto appertaining.
Rise, Grand Elected Knight Kadosh. Be brave, discreet, and virtuous.
        (*G.D.C. receives back the sword, and directs the Brethren, other than the Candidate, to be seated*).

LECTURE

G.C.   Illustrious Brethren : To explain the purpose of our Order I must recall to your notice the dark period of the world's history which followed on the dissolution of the Roman Empire in the West. Thereafter for centuries the principles of justice which underlie our civilization were forgotten ; our ancestors lived in a state of continual unsettlement in the pursuit of their

G.C. everyday occupations. Despotism was unchallenged in civil governments, and even when the time came later for the organization of society under the Feudal System the majority of men were regarded as mere chattels. The small but growing power of the Christian Church with which our knightly predecessors were so honourably identified was threatened by superstitions and ignorance, and clouded by intolerance.

It was only when the renewal of the old learning and all that we associate with it forged anew the weapons of true philosophy that these enemies of Christianity and civilization could be again placed in subjection. The Knights Kadosh preserve these weapons as their most cherished possession, and for this reason you have been reminded of them today. Despotism, Ignorance, and Intolerance still live. Our vigilance is continually called for. Our vengeance is by no means fully perfected. It is by the pursuit of Truth, and Truth only, that full liberty of soul, mind, and body can be won, and the purpose of our Order accomplished. There is a call for work by all of us. No man can master all the knowledge that is indicated to us in passing the Mysterious Ladder, but our Order contains many members of eminent wisdom and experience, and we welcome you as a re-inforcement of their number today, being well assured that the high rank you now enjoy will be regarded by you, not as the summit of your ambition, but rather as the starting point of further efforts for the spread of those principles and practices you have proved to have so much at heart.

(*The Grand Commander, who has been standing near the front of the dais while giving the accolade and the Lecture, now invests the Candidate, and communicates the secrets*).

The Sign is given thus :—place the right hand upon the heart with the fingers extended, let it fall on the right thigh, bending the knee.

The Token is as follows :—toe to toe, knee to knee, present the right hand with fingers clenched and thumb erect. (*Demonstrates*) Enclose his thumb with your hand, showing eight fingers, and the thumb erect. Unclose or slip the thumb. (*The same is done by the other who demonstrates, changing over*). Unclosing, each recoils a pace with the arm upraised, as if to strike.

The one says, BEKOLGOL, To be united.

The other, PARASH KOL, All is explained.

Very Illustrious Grand Director of Ceremonies, you

G.C.   have my commands to place our Illustrious Brother in the West, and to proclaim that he has been duly advanced to the Degree of Grand Elected Knight Kadosh.
(The G.D.C. after conducting the Candidate to the West, calls the Grand Chapter to order, the Supreme Council remaining seated).

G.D.C.   Illustrious Brethren, to order.
(Fanfare on the organ).

G.D.C.   By command of the Supreme Council for England, Wales, the Dominions and Dependencies of the British Crown, I proclaim that Illustrious Brother .... has this day been advanced to the Degree of Grand Elected Knight Kadosh, Knight of the Black and White Eagle, and I accordingly summon him to take his seat in the Grand Chapter.
(Fanfare on organ).

G.D.C.   Illustrious Brethren, be seated.

CEREMONY OF CLOSING A GRAND CHAPTER

G.C.   *(Gives one knock)* Illustrious Knights, assist me to close this Grand Chapter.
(All rise. The G.D.C. comes to the dais, takes the Sword of State, and stands facing the Grand Commander half way between the dais and the Ladder).

G.C.   Most Illustrious Brother ......, will you circulate the Word, and report the same to me in the East ?
(The G.D.C. conducts the appointed Brother to the head of the Ladder, and stands behind him while the word is circulated round. It is then reported back to the Grand Commander).

G.C.   Illustrious Brethren, I have received the Word, and it is correct.
Let us unanimously resolve to maintain the sacred principles of our Order at the peril of our lives.

Omnes   *(Making the sign as at the Opening)* We resolve.

G.C.   Illustrious Knights, this Grand Chapter is now closed. Depart in peace.
(Note :—the Word circulated is ADONAI, Lord).

*   *   *

Clearly there is nothing very sinister or Satanic in the prosy platitudinous moralizings of the ritual of the Knights Kadosh as worked in England today. After the mawkish, if exciting, sentimentality of the Rose Croix it comes as somewhat of an anticlimax, and the genuine student of philosophy can but smile at it. Nevertheless the ritual has been included here in its entirety to disprove the allegation that " Masonry is a progressive science " leading ever onwards and upwards to the full revelation of Christianity. One prayer, it is true, has a Christian ending, but the broad generalities of this degree, the appeal to God as a supreme being and great architect take us back again to the pan-religious atmosphere of the Craft. It breathes the spirit of old-fashioned liberalism, of salvation through ethical enlightenment and education.

Nor is there any return to Christianity in the degrees beyond. The thirty-first degree, that of Grand Inspector Inquisitor Commander, indulges in even broader generalities, and is mainly concerned with illustrating the twin virtues of *Justitia* and *Equitas* from imaginary extracts from such world thinkers as Zoroaster, Confucius, and Alfred the Great. There is little of any interest or meaning in the thirty-second degree, and none in the thirty-third, which is almost entirely an administrative grade.

Thus the English version of the Knights Kadosh ritual has been watered down and made comparatively innocuous. It is interesting, however, to compare it with the original from which it was derived. In the United States the thirtieth degree is more Templar in tone, and bitterly anti-Catholic. As we have seen in considering the Rose Croix, there is full intercommunion and amicable fraternal relations between the English Supreme Council and the mother body, the Southern Jurisdiction at Washington. Some of the same problems and anomalies arising from this intercommunion, therefore, are to be found in this degree as in the Eighteenth.

The initials of Jacobus Bergundus Molay continue to appear on the American jewel of the Kadosh, and it is explained that the appearance of these same initials J.B.M. in the Craft, (standing for Jachin, Boaz, and Mahabone), indicate that the true teaching of the third or Master Masons' degree is that Hiram is a disguised figure of Jacques de Molay, and that his death represents the martyrdom of the last General of the Knights Templar put to death for heresy. In this context the celebrated and irritating words of Albert Pike still appear :—" The Blue Degrees are but the outer court or portico of the Temple. Part of the symbols are displayed there to the Initiate, but he is intentionally misled by false interpretations. It is not intended that he shall understand them ; but it is intended that he shall imagine he understands them. Their true explication is reserved for the Adepts, the Princes of Masonry...it is well enough for the mass of those called Masons, to imagine that all is contained in the Blue Degrees ; and who so attempts to undeceive them will labour in vain, and without any true reward violate his obligation as an Adept. Truly Masonry is the veritable Sphynx, buried to the head in the sands heaped round it by the ages."[1]

The English ritual certainly indicates that the Reformation was a blessing in that it dispelled by true learning the superstitious tyranny of the middle ages, but this is pale platitude compared with the forthright anti-Romanism of the parent Masonic body. " Now from the tomb in which after his murders he rotted, Clement the Fifth howls against the successors of his victims, in the Allocution of Pio Nono against the Freemasons. The ghosts of the dead Templars haunt the Vatican, and disturb the slumbers of the paralysed Papacy, which, dreading the dead, shrieks out its excommunications and impotent anathemas against the living."[2]

And again :—" The Pope no longer sets his foot on the necks of kings, nor by a bull from the Vatican places realms under interdict, and dethrones emperors..Realm after realm, Rome has lost the brightest jewels of her tiara, since the preaching of Luther and Melancthon shook the foundations of her power as with an earthquake. Even Catholic countries no longer tolerate the indignities of the Inquisition, nor permit the once terrible Order of Jesus to exist and plot within their limits ; and in Portugal, Spain, and Brazil, Freemasonry publicly avows its existence and purposes ; its Dignitaries hold high civil office, and its halls are dedicated with public ceremonies. The Grand Orient of Italy sits at Rome. Truly, the world moves ! "[3] " The night draws towards its close. Fantacism is pale with terror, and Intolerance protests that she has been misunderstood, and that it is a mistake to suppose that she ever persecuted."[4]

1. *Liturgy of the Ancient and Accepted Scottish Rite of Freemasonry for the Southern Jurisdiction of the United States.* Part IV, Charleston, 1944, pp. 260–261. The same passage is also found in Albert Pike, *Morals and Dogma*, p. 819.

2. *Liturgy*, p. 225. Also *Morals and Dogma*, p. 814.

3. *Liturgy*, p. 268.   4. ibid., p. 274.

"If it (Masonry) cannot prevent the crimes that disgrace humanity, it will denounce those who commit them, and make their names infamous all over the world."[1]

That these sentiments are no mere ritual archaisms may be seen by the most cursory perusal of almost any number of *The New Age*, the monthly official organ of the Southern Jurisdiction. The tone is bitterly anti-Catholic, and particularly outspoken in opposing all parochial schools in America, whether Roman or Lutheran. However non-political Masonry may be in this country, the Ancient and Accepted Scottish Rite in America stand four-square for purely secular education, and the ritual of this degree hints at the reason. " Admitting into the ranks of her initiates, on terms of perfect equality, men of all creeds and countries who are worthy of such fellowship, she labours to emancipate men from their own ignorance, prejudices and errors, which enslave them, in order that they may emancipate themselves from the bondage of despotism and the thraldom of spiritual tyranny."

1. ibid., p. 242. In fairness it must be stated that Rome is not the sole culprit ; along with the Albigenses and the victims of the Massacre of St. Bartholomew, Huss, Ridley and Cranmer, are listed Socrates, Jesus of Nazareth, and the victims of Nero, Claverhouse, and Judge Jeffreys.

XI

MASONIC ORDERS OF CHIVALRY

He then ...
Doth but usurp the sacred name of Knight,
Profaning this most honourable order,
And should, if I be worthy to be judge,
Be quite degraded, like a hedge-born swain
That doth presume to boast of gentle blood.

Shakespeare, I King Henry VI.

I do not call to mind that I have yet read of a Grocer errant : I will be the said Knight.... Hence, my blue apron !
Beaumont and Fletcher, The Knight of the Burning Pestle.

IT is not surprising that the Knights Templar have captured the imagination of the world. The fighting orders were the backbone of the Crusades, the militant arm of Holy Church in her warfare against the Saracen, wholly dedicated to the service of Christ and His vicegerent on earth, the Holy Father of Rome. The history of the order from its foundation by Hugo de Payens in 1128 to its suppression in 1312 has inspired the lover of chivalry, the poet, the ballad-writer and the novelist of every generation.

And yet undoubtedly in the later years of the order there was a darker side to the picture. Showered with benefactions and endowments the Knights Templar ceased to be the " poor fellow-soldiers of Jesus Christ " and became exceedingly rich and powerful. Strange rumours became current of occult practices, heresies, obscenities and forbidden rites. It is difficult to assess the truth of these accusations for the evidence is conflicting ; some of the confessions were wrested under torture and are therefore far from reliable. There seems no doubt, however, that there were some grounds for some of the charges against them. It is unlikely that they actually worshipped a head or idol called Baphomet, or that unnatural practices were more prevalent among them than in other military or monastic communities. It seems beyond question that there was some curious ceremony of rejecting the cross, but its significance has never

159

been fully ascertained. Perhaps it was a test of implicit obedience. It is generally believed that elements of Catharism crept into the order through the initiation of Albigensians, and to the Cathari the cross was to be despised as the means of our Lord's death, not reverenced as the token of His victory.

It is possible that long residence in the Near East on terms of intimacy with adherents of other religions had further infected them with heresies. The very fact that the Templars were to some extent a secret order was enough to arouse suspicion and distrust. Philip le Bel of France may perhaps be compared with Henry VIII of England who exaggerated or even trumped up charges against the morals of the monastic orders in order to possess himself of their wealth ; Pope Clement V was clearly not entirely without justification in proceeding against the Templars for heresy.

Justly or unjustly, Jacques de Molay perished in the flames, with many of his Knights. The Order disappeared, leaving scarce a wrack behind except a tradition, and some magnificent Templar Churches including the well-known one in London.

It is not surprising that the passion for secret orders and grades in the eighteenth century should have turned men's minds to the Templars for inspiration and imitation. The Templars built churches, therefore they must have been skilled stonemasons. They had their own symbols and secret traditions, therefore they must have been not only masons, but Freemasons, at least in embryo. Not all the Knights Templar were put to death, in England some were pensioned and sent to other monasteries. Others, probably the Serving Brothers, were secularized and disbanded—is it not reasonable to suppose that some at least, with their experience of building, found employment in the masons' gilds, bringing with them and spreading their secret arts and hidden mysteries ? So ran the argument, and Masonic Templar grades became fashionable. The celebrated Discourse of the Chevalier Ramsay in Paris in 1737 maintained that Masonry derived from the Crusading orders, and this doubtless contributed to the popularity of Masonic Templar grades.

More specific traditions arose of an actual lineal descent of Masonry from the Knights Templar. The first is based on the supposition that the Knights Templar in Scotland, introduced by King David I, were never really suppressed at all, but thanks

to their services in the army of Robert the Bruce and their share
in the victory of Bannockburn they escaped the penalties
suffered in other countries, evolved, so to speak, into Freemasons, and were admitted into the Rosy Cross grade of the
Royal Order of Scotland by Robert the Bruce himself at
Kilwinning.

The second tradition states that the Templar General for
Auvergne at the time of the suppression, Pierre d'Aumont, fled
with seven companions disguised as stonemasons to the Isle of
Mull. So that the order might be continued d'Aumont was
elected Grand Master. In 1361 the body moved to Aberdeen
and from thence Freemasonry spread all over Europe. This was
the tradition of such Templar bodies as the Chapter of Clermont
in France, from which Baron von Hund founded the Strict
Observance in Germany in 1754, a Masonic reform on Templar
lines contending for the doctrine that every true Freemason is a
Knight Templar. Unfortunately von Hund, a man of personal
integrity and boundless Masonic zeal, suffered from credulity ;
when an adventurer styling himself Mr. Johnson (probably a
Jew whose real name was Leucht) imposed himself on the Rite
by claiming himself to be the secret emissary of " unknown
superiors " in Aberdeen, von Hund for some time accepted his
claims at their face value before he became suspicious and expelled him. Ragon, a not very reliable historian hostile to the
Strict Observance, declares that von Hund was a party to the
fraud, and accepted Johnson to bolster up the claims of his
rite, but of this there is little evidence.

The Strict Observance, however, flourished, and extended to
province after province in Europe before it was rent into a
schism and finally declined and faded out of existence. Its influence may be noted in the Masonic rituals of Scandinavia,
however, to this day.

The third transmission theory is French, and includes an
actual line of succession. This is the Charter of Larmenius,
which states that Jacques de Molay during his last imprisonment
in 1313 secretly conferred the Grand Mastership of the Knights
Templar on Johannes Marcus Larmenius, who drew up the
Charta Transmissionis and appointed Theobaldus Alexandrinus
as his successor, after which each Grand Master in turn received
the document and added his name in unbroken succession down

to and including Bernard Raymond Fabré-Palaprat in 1804. This document was discovered and presented to the Great Priory of England, where it now hangs in the Council Room at Mark Masons' Hall in Kingsway, London.[1] Apart from the fantastic improbability of the story, the document is clearly a forgery which is taken no more seriously than the family tree hanging in Windsor Castle which purports to prove the lineal descent of Queen Elizabeth II from King David.

The Charter of Larmenius, however, formed the spurious title-deeds of the *Ordre du Temple* in Paris, a body connected with the name of Fabré-Palaprat, whose name appears last on the Charter. The *Ordre du Temple*, however, can be called only quasi-Masonic. It admitted both sexes, made much of their own spurious version of St. John's Gospel, and required no Masonic qualification, although it imitated certain Masonic ceremonies and grades, and was probably inspired or at least suggested by the Strict Observance. Hence even if Fabré-Palaprat and his successors could substantiate their fraudulent claim to be the legitimate successors of Jacques de Molay, the Charter of Larmenius would still be quite irrelevant to the Masonic Knights Templar.

The one genuine organization which could claim continuity with the Knights Templar of old is the Order of Christ in Portugal, and this has nothing whatsoever to do with Freemasonry. It was a revival, almost a continuation of Templarism constituted by Pope John XXII in 1319. The Knights Templar in Spain and Portugal were less tainted with heresy than elsewhere, and hence their suppression was accomplished with less bitterness and prejudice. The King of Portugal later became the Grand Master of the Order of Christ, which was a strictly Catholic and non-secret order of chivalry, comparable with the English Garter. In 1879 it was secularized, but its cross remained a highly prized distinction amongst the Portuguese nobility. It survived certainly until the recent overthrow of the Monarchy.[2]

1. A transcript of this document appears in *Ars Quatuor Coronatorum* vol. XXIV, also in J. S. M. Ward's *Freemasonry and the Ancient Gods.*

2. As " The Supreme Equestrian Order of the Army of Our Lord Jesus Christ " this same order survives as a Papal Knighthood. General Franco was admitted to it in February, 1954.

It is not surprising, perhaps, that Masonic Templarism, eager to prove continuity, cast hungry eyes at the Order of Christ. It seems that Fabré-Palaprat attempted to strengthen his claims by fabricating a connection with it ; Clavel reports that a certain Francisco Alvaro da Sylva Freyre de Porto, a Knight of the Order of Christ, was admitted into the Order of the Temple and became Grand Master's secretary, and that Fabré-Palaprat applied for recognition of his Order and of his own position as successor to Jacques de Molay from John VI of Portugal in 1804. Needless to say, this application was simply ignored. A Portuguese adventurer called Nunez turned up in Paris in 1807 claiming the authority to confer the Order of Christ. He established a Masonic rite of nine grades alleged to be adapted from the genuine Portuguese Order, but it attracted little interest and quickly died out.

Yet another transmission theory comes from Sweden. It is similar to that of the Strict Observance (which indeed was not without influence in Sweden) and claims that Count Beaujeu, a nephew of Jaques de Molay and also a Knight of the Portuguese Order of Christ, inherited the Grand Mastership. He brought the ashes of Molay with him to Sweden where they were buried at Stockholm, and secretly continued the rite. The source of this legend is unknown.

The French occultist Eliphas Levi records yet another theory, probably drawn from the ritual of some lesser French grade. He affirms that Jacques de Molay just before his death organized and constituted occult Masonry as a continuation of Templarism, and established four Metropolitan Lodges, at Naples for the east, Edinburgh for the west, Stockholm for the north, and Paris for the south.

In Scotland there is a persistent but groundless legend connecting the Knights Templar with Jacobitism, and it is even said that Prince Charles Edward was Grand Master in 1745.

Not one of these traditions, however, is cited or drawn upon by the Military and Religious Order of the Temple and Holy Sepulchre, to give the Knights Templar of England and Wales their full title today. There is no pretended succession, no derivation from unknown superiors, no appeal to the Isles of Scotland, to Aberdeen, Edinburgh, or Kilwinning. In Ireland, to be sure, there was at one time a legend in the Templar province of Munster that their statutes were transcribed from a document found in 1540 under the high altar of the Temple Church in London[1] but in England, although there are ritual references implying identity with the original Order, in particular the reference to Simon of Syracuse, the Knights Templar have never accounted for themselves by the help of a traditional history.

The first known reference to Anglo-Saxon Masonic Knight Templary comes from pre-revolutionary America. In the minutes of St. Andrew's Royal Arch Lodge, Boston, holding under the Grand Lodge of Scotland, for August 28, 1769 it is recorded that Bro. William Davis received the four steps of Excellent, Super-Excellent, Royal Arch, and Knight Templar. In 1774 advertisements appeared in certain Dublin newspapers which indicated that the Irish Knights Templar dined together with other Masonic bodies on St. John's Day in the summer of 1774. In England the Knights Templar appear to derive from the Baldwyn Encampment at Bristol, where it may have been worked as early as 1772.[2] The great figure associated with the growth of the Order in England is Thomas Dunckerley (1724–1795), who consolidated and organized the small number of enthusiasts who were already Templars. He was the first Grand Master of the Order, from 1791 until his death, and some early correspondence published by Henry Sadler[3] is illuminating. A group of Templars wrote to him from York in 1791 who " waited with the most fervent anxiety till the time sh'd arrive that we were able to look up to a Grand Master under whose patronage the Knights Templar sh'd again flourish, & the happy moment has now come, in which we most cordially congratulate our Most Excellent and Exalted Bro. Comp'n Knight, & Grand Master, Sir Thos. Dunckerley as our Head and Chief." To which Dunckerley replied, " Being Grand Superintendent of the Royal Arch Masons at Bristol, I was requested by the Knights Templar of that city (who have had an Encampment from time immemorial) to accept the Office of Grand Master, which I had no sooner comply'd with than Petitions were sent to me for the

1. An account is given of this by J. W. Chetwode Crawley in *Ars Quatuor Coronatorum*, vol. XXXVI.
2. See the *History of Freemasonry in Bristol*, by A. C. Powell and J Littleton, for an assessment of these claims.
3. In *Thomas Dunckerley, His Life, Labours, and Letters*.

same purpose from London 1, Bath 2, the first Regiment of Dragoon Guards 3, Colchester 4, York 5, Dorchester 6, and Bideford 7. I suppose there are many more Encampments in England which with God's permission I may have the happiness to revive and assist. It has already been attended with a blessing, for I have been but *two* months Grand Master & already have 8 Encampments under my care."

Before 1791 the Knights Templar, then, had no separate organization of their own, but the grade was often conferred in Royal Arch Chapters particularly among the Ancients. We have seen in an earlier chapter that the Union of 1813, and particularly the hostility of the Duke of Sussex to higher and Christian degrees led to the confinement of pure and ancient Masonry to the three degrees of the Craft plus the Royal Arch, and that the exception in the Articles of Union permitting Royal Arch Chapters to confer orders of chivalry became a dead letter.[1]

The Order of Knights Hospitaller of St. John of Jerusalem, Palestine, Rhodes and Malta, commonly known as the Knights of Malta, has been curiously and anomalously wedded to the Knights Templar as a higher degree, for in history the original orders were bitter rivals and even enemies. In any case its revival as a Masonic order seems unfortunate, for the original still survives as an order of chivalry under the legitimate custody of the Church which gave birth to it, and is conferred to this day as a Papal honour.

A much-disputed transcript of 1790 provides the earliest reference to the Masonic revival, which claims that it was conferred in the Ancient Lodge of Stirling as early as 1745; 1780, however, is a less unlikely date. Vague legends that the ritual was imported from Malta are of course totally without foundation. The Jerusalem Conclave at Manchester appears to contain a reference to Knights of Malta in 1786, but this again is open to question. The Order lapsed into obscurity, and it was not until the second half of the nineteenth century that it became popular. It contains little of interest, and the ritual is no more than a barren memorial. The Mediterranean Pass or Knight of St. Paul, its preliminary degree, seems unknown to antiquity (though A. E. Waite, without quoting references, calls it the

1. The Duke of Sussex, however, consented to act as Grand Master of the Knights Templar from 1812–1843.

oldest part), and it seems to have been introduced merely because the episode recorded from the Book of Acts also concerned the island of Malta.

There was extensive revision of the rituals of the Temple and of Malta in 1873 under a commission set up by the Great Priory. If Carlile's version of the earlier ritual in the *Manual of Freemasonry* of 1825 is at all to be relied on (and in spite of its spurious origin it has been cited in evidence by Masonic scholars) the overhaul was fairly drastic. My own earliest version of the new ritual was printed in 1876, and apart from some minor editing, and a new form of opening the Preceptory, it is substantially that in use today.

Great Priory is now administered from Mark Masons' Hall in London. The 1953–54 *Liber Ordinis Templi* lists three hundred and thirty-nine Preceptories in England, Wales, and the Dominions and Dependencies of the British Crown, and close on ten thousand members. There are fraternal relations and exchange of representatives with the Great Priories of Scotland, Ireland, and Canada, the Grand Encampment for the United States, the Grand Priory of Helvetia (Switzerland) and the National Grand Lodge of Sweden. The present Most Eminent and Supreme Grand Master is the Rt. Hon. Lord Harris, M.C.

XII

THE RITUAL OF THE KNIGHTS TEMPLAR AND KNIGHTS OF MALTA[1]

" It's my own invention," said the White Knight.
Lewis Carroll, Alice Through the Looking-Glass.

THE apartment in which the ceremonies are held represents a Chapel of the Order of Knights Templar. In the east is an Altar, on which are a cross and two candlesticks, flower vases, an alms dish, and a book of the Gospels.

In the centre of the apartment is the Sepulchre. On it is a crucifix (veiled for the first part of the Installation ceremonies) placed in a triangle ; at the points of the triangle are three large candlesticks, and on the three sides three smaller ones, making twelve in all. Arranged on the Sepulchre are also emblems of the lamb, the cock, and the dove ; skull and cross-bones, a book of the Gospels, a cup of wine, a cube, a pen, and a set of armour for the investiture of the Candidate. To the west of the Sepulchre is a kneeling-stool.

In the west end of the apartment is a table furnished with bread and water.

The Eminent Preceptor sits in the east, on the north side of the Altar, the Chaplain on the south side of it. The First and Second Constables are stationed in the south-west and north-west respectively, with the Marshal and the Deputy Marshal between them. The Captain of the Guard is stationed in the west, by the door.

The regalia consists of mantle, tunic, cap, and sword and dagger. The mantle is of white, with a hood, and with a Maltese cross on the left shoulder. Preceptors' and Past Preceptors' mantles are lined with red silk, with cords and tassels of the same

1. Rituals are " privately printed for the Great Priory of England and Wales, etc." from Mark Masons' Hall. My most recent copy is the sixth reprint of the 1936 edition, which I am informed is the latest. A spurious and inaccurate version occurs in the *Text Book of Advanced Freemasonry*.

colour. The tunic is of the same material as the mantle, and must cover the knees. A plain red Latin cross in front extends to the full length of the tunic. The cap is of crimson velvet, with a cross in front. Prelates, Chaplains, and Almoners, if in holy orders, may wear cassock and cotta instead of the tunic, and a biretta instead of the cap ; Great and Provincial Prelates wear copes instead of mantles.[1] The sword is straight, with a straight cross-hilt and with a black scabbard. The sword-belt is of brown leather. Knights may also wear a ring, enamelled with a cross. In addition, the insignia of the Order consists of a black watered silk ribbon four inches wide to be worn over the right shoulder, adorned for officers with gold fringe ; Provincial officers have a white stripe in the centre, and Great officers three white stripes. Prelates, Chaplains, and Almoners if in orders wear this ribbon as a stole. The Knights also wear a silver seven-pointed faceted star with a passion cross in red enamel on a white ground surrounded by a black enamel garter, on which is the motto in silver *In Hoc Signo Vinces*. Also a cross pattée an inch and a half wide in red enamel with gilt edges, suspended from the left breast by a scarlet ribbon edged with white. Officers' insignia becomes progressively more elaborate.

OPENING THE PRECEPTORY

(*An " Arch of Steel " is formed by a company of Knights, with the following procedure*).

Marshal Arch of Steel in the West.

(*The Knights forming the Arch rise and draw swords, taking their time from the Marshal*).

Mar. Flankers take Post.

(*The two flanking Knights of each column take their posts, two facing each other at a distance of three paces at the western corners of the Sepulchre, and two by the door, marking the ends of the north and south columns of the Arch*).

Mar. North and south columns, on your flankers— March.

(*The remaining Knights of the north and south columns march forward and fill the spaces between the flankers, making two lines stretching from the door to the*

---

1. The present Great Prelate, the Rev. Joseph Moffett, is a Presbyterian Minister of, I believe, northern Irish descent. I am informed, however, that this successor of John Knox wears his cope and swings incense in the ceremonies of Great Chapter with distinction.

Sepulchre. The order is given to dress, if necessary. When the procession of Officers approaches) :—

Mar.   Engage.

(The Knights raise aloft their swords, each making an arch with the Knight standing opposite. When the Eminent Prior and the Officers have passed through, the Arch of Steel is dismissed, as follows) :—

Mar.   Carry Swords.

(The Knights hold their swords at the " carry ", that is, forearm horizontal, hand in front of the elbow, elbow close to the side, the blade vertical, with the cross-bar resting in the hollow between the thumb and the first knuckle-joint).

Mar.   North and south columns—To your stations— March.

(The columns turn to face their seats and march back to their places).

E.P.   Brother Knights. To Order.

(The Knights draw their swords, spring to attention, and bring their swords to the " carry ").

E.P.   Assist me to open this Preceptory. Are the approaches properly guarded ?

(The Marshal proceeds to the door and sees the Captain of the Guard at his post. He opens the door and sees the Guard at his post outside. He closes the door and reports).

Mar.   Eminent Preceptor, the approaches are properly guarded.

E.P.   See that none are present but Brethren of the Temple.

(The Marshal looks round the Preceptory and satisfies himself that this is so. He gives the sign of a Crusader and reports).

Mar.   Eminent Preceptor, none are present but true Brethren of the Temple.

E.P.   Brother Registrar, call the Roll.

(Each Knight on hearing his name says " here " and gives the sign of a Crusader).

E.P.   Brother Knights, let us pray to God to send His Holy Grace amongst us.

Chaplain *(Standing in front of the Altar facing east)* Let us— pray.

(At " let us " the Knights bring their swords to the recover, that is, with the blade vertical, back of the hand to the front, elbow close to the body, cross-bar on hilt of sword in line with the mouth and about one inch from it. At the word " pray " the sword is dropped to the front to the full extent of the right arm, with the point of the sword about six inches from the ground.

At the same time the left hand covered with the mantle is raised to the forehead. This is the position adopted for prayers throughout the ceremonies).

Chaplain Merciful Redeemer of perishing mankind, Who has promised that Thou wouldst be in the midst of those assembled in Thy Holy Name ; look down upon us, Thy humble servants, with an eye of tender compassion, and so direct us that our labours may be begun, continued and ended in love to Thee, affection to our companions, protection to the distressed, and obedience to our Order. Amen.

O Lord our Heavenly Father, high and mighty, King of Kings, Lord of lords, the only Ruler of princes, Who dost from Thy throne behold all the dwellers upon earth. Most heartily we beseech Thee, with Thy favour to behold our Most Gracious Sovereign Lady Queen Elizabeth, and so replenish her with the grace of Thy Holy Spirit that she may always incline to Thy will and walk in Thy way. Endue her plenteously with heavenly gifts, grant her in health and wealth long to live, strengthen her that she may vanquish and overcome all her enemies, and finally after this life she may attain everlasting joy and felicity ; through Christ our Lord. Amen.

Our Father, which art in heaven, hallowed be Thy name. Thy kingdom come. Thy will be done, in earth, as it is in heaven. Give us this day our daily bread. and forgive us our trespasses, as we forgive them that trespass against us. And lead us not into temptation, but deliver us from evil. For Thine is the kingdom, the power, and the glory, for ever and ever. A—men.

(At " A— " the Knights drop the left hand. At " —men" they "carry swords ").

E.P. Exhorting you, my Brethren, to bear always in mind the solemn and sacred ties by which we are bound to the Order, and to one another, I now, in the name of the Holy, Blessed and Glorious Trinity, and in the name of Christ our Prophet, Christ our Priest, Christ our King, declare this Preceptory to be open.

(During these last words, spoken slowly, the Knights salute three times with the sign of a Crusader. The Eminent Preceptor takes his seat).

Mar. Brother Knights, I call upon you to salute our Eminent Preceptor with three.

(The Knights bring their swords from the " carry " to the " recover " and by three distinct outward movements

elevate them to the right front, exclaiming "A Beauceant!"[1] at each movement. The sword is raised higher for each of the three salutes, the third being at the full extent of the right arm).

Mar. Brother Knights. Be seated.

(The Knights return their swords into the scabbards, and sit down. In all sword drill, they take their time from the Marshal, or the Knight who is nearest to the east on the south side. The Chaplain opens the Bible on the Altar. The Marshal opens that on the Sepulchre at St. John, Chapter I).

CEREMONY OF INSTALLATION

(The Candidate is prepared, dressed as a Pilgrim with a brown mantle, a cord round his waist, a scrip over his left shoulder, a wallet over his right shoulder, and a pilgrim's hat. He has a staff in his right hand. The Guard conducts him to the entrance of the Preceptory, and gives four knocks).

Capt. of Guard Brother Second Constable, there is an alarm.

2nd Con. Ascertain the cause thereof.

(The Captain of the Guard opens the door and sees the Candidate. He closes the door, and reports with the sign of a Crusader).

C. of G. Eminent Preceptor, a stranger is endeavouring to enter our Preceptory.

E.P. Be cautious, and see who the intruder is.

(The Captain of the Guard again opens the door).

C. of G. Who comes here ?

Guard Companion . . . ., a pilgrim on his travels, weary and fatigued, having heard of this Preceptory of Knights Templar, is anxious to take refuge therein, and, if possible, to be admitted to the privileges of the Order.

C. of G. What recommendation does he bring ?

Guard The sign and first Word of a Royal Arch Mason.

C. of G. *(To Candidate)* Show me that sign and communicate the Word.

(The Candidate gives the Reverential or Hailing Sign of the Royal Arch, bowing the head slightly, left hand raised to the forehead as if shielding the eyes, and the right raised to the left breast. He gives the Word, JEHOVAH).

C. of G. Wait, while I report to our Eminent Preceptor.

---

1. " *Au Beauceant !* " was a battle-cry of the original Knights Templar.

(The Captain of the Guard closes the door, faces the Eminent Preceptor, and salutes him with the sign of a Crusader).

C. of G. Eminent Preceptor, Companion ...., a pilgrim on his travels, weary and fatigued, having heard of this Preceptory of Knights Templar, is anxious to take refuge therein, and if possible to be admitted to the privileges of the Order.

E.P. What recommendation does he bring ?

C. of G. The sign and first Word of a Royal Arch Mason.

E.P. Let him be admitted with caution.

E.P. Brother Knights, to order.
(or M.)

(Knights stand to attention with swords at the " carry." The Pilgrim is admitted by the Captain of the Guard and received by the Marshal. He is conducted to the Second Constable, who presents his sword to the Pilgrim's breast).

2nd C. Who are you who dares to penetrate thus far into our Preceptory ?

Mar. *(Parrying the thrust with his sword)* Companion ...., a pilgrim on his travels, weary and fatigued, having heard of this Preceptory of Knights Templar, is anxious to take refuge therein, and if possible to be admitted to the privileges of the Order.

2nd C. What recommendation does he bring ?

Mar. The sign and first Word of a Royal Arch Mason.

2nd C. *(To Candidate)* Show me that sign and communicate the Word.
(Candidate does so).

2nd C. *(With sword at the " carry ")* Pass in the name of JEHOVAH.
(The Marshal then leads him to the First Constable, who challenges him, and is answered, in the same way. The Marshal then places the Candidate in the west, between the Constables).

Mar. Salute the Eminent Preceptor with the same sign and Word. *(Candidate does so).*

E.P. Welcome in the name of JEHOVAH ; rest yourself and partake of bread, the staff of life, and water, the only refreshment we can at present offer you.
(The Candidate is seated in the Marshal's chair and refreshed with bread and water from the table in the west. After he has partaken he is instructed by the Marshal to rise).

E.P. Pilgrim, you have sought refuge in our Preceptory, and desire to be admitted to the privileges of our Order, let me therefore demand of you, on whom in the hour of danger do you rely ?

Can. (*Prompted in his replies*) On God.

E.P. And in whom do you put your trust for eternal salvation ?

Can. In our blessed Saviour Jesus Christ.

E.P. Can you give me any proof of your sincerity ?

Can. I am willing to undertake any task, however perilous, which may entitle me to admission under your banner as a Soldier of the Cross.

E.P. Then as a proof of your faith, I enjoin a seven years' pilgrimage. This you will figuratively perform by proceeding seven times round the Preceptory.

E.P. or Brother Knights. To order. Guard the Sepulchre.
Mar.

(*The Knights stand to order. On receiving the order to guard the Sepulchre, the Marshal gives these commands :—" Brother Knights—March." The Knights who formed the Arch of Steel at the Opening Ceremony take the necessary number of paces forward, turn toward the east, and march up the sides of the Sepulchre. " Halt." The columns halt, and the leading Knight and the westernmost Knight of each column take one side pace toward the centre. " Outwards, Turn." The two Knights at the east end of the Sepulchre stand fast the remainder face outwards. The Marshal conducts the Candidate round the Preceptory, preceding him with a drawn sword. They make three rounds*).

2nd Con. Halt.

(*The Marshal and Candidate halt, facing east*).

2nd Con. (*Saluting with the Sign of a Crusader*) Eminent Preceptor, the Pilgrim has performed three years of his pilgrimage, and having evinced great zeal and fidelity, I beg to request that you will remit the remainder of the term.

E.P. Brother Second Constable, I readily accede to your request, and remit the remainder of the term.

E.P. (or Brother Knights, resume your stations.
Mar.)

(*The Knights at the east and west ends of the two columns take one pace outwards. The Marshal commands " Toward the west—turn." The Knights at the west of each column stand fast, the remainder turn towards the west. " March." Both columns march towards the west and resume their places*).

Chaplain (*Standing in front of the Altar facing east*) Let us pray.

(*The Eminent Preceptor rises. The Knights take their positions for prayer as before. The Candidate makes the sign of Fidelity, his right hand on his heart).*

Chaplain O great Emmanuel, our heavenly Captain, look down, we beseech Thee, on this Preceptory and impart Thy Holy Grace to the Candidate now before Thee, that he may acquit himself as a good and faithful Soldier of the Cross, and henceforward with a firm resolution shun all occasions of offending Thee, and so become worthy of Thy acceptance and salvation. Amen.

E.P. Let the Pilgrim now approach the Holy Sepulchre and, kneeling on both knees and placing both hands on the Holy Gospels, enter into a solemn obligation.

(The Marshal removes the Candidate's pilgrim hat and staff. The Candidate kneels, places his hands on the Gospels, and the First and Second Constables cross their drawn swords on his hands. Other Knights stand with their swords at the " Carry ").

E.P. Pilgrim, you will state your Christian Names and Surname, and say after me :—

I, ..., in the name of the Holy, Blessed and Glorious Trinity, and in the presence of the Knights here assembled, do hereby and hereon most solemnly promise and swear never to reveal the secrets of a Knight Templar to anyone beneath that rank, unless it be to a Candidate for the same, in a lawful Preceptory of Knights Templar, and then only whilst acting as a regularly installed Preceptor. I furthermore solemnly promise, that I will faithfully defend and maintain the holy Christian faith against all unprovoked attacks of its enemies ; that I will not shed the blood of a Knight Templar in wrath, unless it be in the just wars of sovereign princes or states ; but on the contrary, will defend him, even at the risk of my life, where or whensoever his life or his honour may be in danger. That I will, to the utmost of my power, protect the near and dear relatives and connections of Knights Templar, and if possible prevent all harm, danger, or violence to which they may be exposed. Lastly, I do most sincerely promise to be obedient to the supreme authorities of the Country in which I do, or may, reside ; strictly to observe and maintain the Ancient Laws and Regulations of the Order, and the Statutes of the Great Priory of England and Wales ; and to answer and obey, so far as lies in my power, all summonses sent to me, the same being duly marked. To all these points I swear fidelity, without evasion, equivocation, or mental reservation of any kind, under no less a penalty than loss of life, by having my head struck off and placed on the point of a pinnacle or

E.P. spire, my skull sawn asunder, and my brains exposed to the scorching rays of the sun, as a warning to all infidels and traitors. So help me Christ, and keep me steadfast in this my solemn obligation.
You will seal that solemn obligation seven times with your lips on the Holy Gospels.
(*The Candidate does so. The Constables raise their swords and engage them over his head*).

E.P. Arise, Novice of our Order.
(*The Candidate stands up. Constables carry swords and resume their stations*).

E.P. Brother Knights, be seated. (*Candidate remains standing*). Let the Novice be divested of his pilgrim's habit and assume the garb of a Soldier of the Cross.
(*The Marshal takes off the pilgrim's habit from the Candidate, and invests him with the tunic. The Standard Bearers take their posts to the north and south of the Sepulchre, and the Deputy Marshal behind the Candidate*).

E.P. The Novice will now attend to a portion of Holy Scripture.

Chaplain " Finally, my Brethren, be strong in the Lord, and in the power of His might. Put on the whole armour of God, that ye may be able to stand against the wiles of the devil. For we wrestle not against flesh and blood, but against principalities, against powers, against the rulers of darkness of this world, against spiritual wickedness in high places. Wherefore take unto you the whole armour of God, that ye may be able to withstand in the evil day, and having done all, to stand. Stand, therefore, having your loins girt about with truth (*Marshal invests Candidate with the belt*) and having on the breastplate of righteousness (*invests with breastplate*) and your feet shod with the preparation of the gospel of peace ; (*puts on spurs*) above all, taking the shield of faith (*gives Candidate the shield*) wherewith ye shall be able to quench all the fiery darts of the wicked. And take the helmet of salvation (*Candidate puts on helmet*) and the sword of the Spirit, which is the word of God."[1] (*He is girded with the sword*). *He retains the belt, shield, and sword ; the helmet is removed and replaced by the red velvet cap of the Order*).

E.P. Brother Knights, to order. (*Done*). Being now armed as a soldier of the Cross, I must request you to make those professions which were made by our sainted predecessors ; you will repeat after me, suiting the action to the words.

1. Ephesians VI, 10–17.

(The Preceptor rises, and draws his sword carrying it to the right front above his head to the full extent of his arm).

E.P. I draw my sword in defence of the Holy Christian Faith. *(Candidate, in each case, copies his actions and repeats his words).*

E.P. I draw my sword in defence of all Knights Templar.

I draw my sword in defence of the near and dear relatives and connections of Knights Templar.

You are now about to proceed on a seven years' warfare, and as you may be stopped and subjected to an examination as a Soldier enrolled under the banner of the Cross, I will entrust you with the sign and Word of a Crusader, whereby you will gain confidence and support.

The sign is given thus. *(The sign of a Crusader is a sign of the Cross made normally with the sword ; first, downwards, then across about level with the eyes. The Candidate copies it).* This sign should always be given when addressing the Eminent Preceptor or on entering or leaving the Preceptory. It may be given with the hand on certain occasions when the sword is not drawn.

The Word is GOLGOTHA. *(Candidate repeats it).*

E.P. Thus prepared, you may prosecute your crusade, which you will figuratively perform by proceeding seven times round the Preceptory, and be prepared to defend yourself with your sword.

(The Candidate, accompanied by the Marshal, proceeds round the Preceptory and is stopped on the first round and challenged by a Past Preceptor in the south-east.

Past P. Who comes here ?

Can. *(Prompted by Marshal)* A Soldier of the Cross.

Past P. Give me the sign and Word of a Crusader.

(Candidate gives sign).

Can. GOLGOTHA.

Past P. Pass, GOLGOTHA.

(On the second round, the Candidate is challenged by the First Constable in the south-west, with the same reply. On the third round he is similarly challenged by the Second Constable in the north-west, and gives the same reply).

1st Con. (To Marshal). Halt.

(Marshal and the Candidate halt, and face east).

1st Con. *(Saluting with the sign of a Crusader)* Eminent Preceptor, the Novice has zealously prosecuted the campaign up to the present time ; is it your will to remit the remainder of the term ?

E.P.   Most willingly I remit the remaining four years of his probation as a Crusader.
(The Marshal conducts the Candidate to the foot of the Sepulchre).

E.P.   With the point of your sword you will assist the Marshal to unveil the Cross, and you will then notice the scroll thereon. *(Done).* That scroll bears the initials of the Latin inscription placed over our Saviour at his Crucifixion.
Brother Knights, Be seated.

E.P. or Chaplain Worthy Brother, now a Novice of our Order, the ceremonies in which you are engaged are calculated to impress your mind deeply, and I trust will have a lasting effect upon your future character. You were first, as a trial of your faith and humility, enjoined to perform a seven years' pilgrimage ; it represented the pilgrimage of life, through which we are all passing ; we are all weary pilgrims, advancing toward that haven where we shall cease from our labours and be at rest for ever. You were then, as a trial of your courage and constancy, directed to perform seven years of warfare. This represented to you the constant warfare with the lying vanities and deceits of the world, in which it is necessary for us always to be engaged. You are now about to perform a year of penance as a further trial of your humility and of that faith which will conduct you safely over the dark gulf of death, and land your enfranchised spirit in the peaceful abodes of the blessed.
Let the emblems of life and death which lie before you remind you of the uncertainty of our earthly existence, and teach you to be prepared for the closing hour of your mortal life ; and rest assured that a firm faith in the truths revealed to us will afford you consolation in the gloomy hours of dissolution, and insure your ineffable and eternal happiness in the world to come.

E.P.   Brother Knights, To Order. Reverse Swords.
(The Knights turn their swords over to the left until horizontal, grasping the blade with the left hand half way between the cross-bar on the hilt and the point. They then continue to turn with the left hand until the sword is vertical in line with the centre of the body. The right hand is dropped, heads are bent forward, eyes fixed on the hilt of the sword. All lights, except the candles on the Altar and the Sepulchre, may be extinguished).

E.P.   You are now about to undergo one year of penance and mortification ; you will therefore take that skull in your left hand *(the Marshal gives the skull to the*

E.P.   *Candidate, the skull with face to the Candidate*) and one of those small lighted tapers in your right (*Marshal gives Candidate a lighted taper*) and banishing all worldly thoughts, and mentally invoking the blessing of heaven on your undertaking, you will figuratively perform a year of penance by walking slowly round the Preceptory, keeping your eyes fixed on those emblems of life and mortality.

(The Candidate proceeds slowly by himself once round the Preceptory carrying the skull and the lighted taper. A solemn dirge may be played during the perambulation. He returns to his position facing the Eminent Preceptor)

E.P.   You will now repeat after me these Imprecations :—
May the spirit which once inhabited this skull rise up and testify against me, if ever I wilfully violate my obligation of a Knight Templar.
Seal it with your lips seven times on the skull.

(The Candidate does so. The Marshal then replaces it on the Sepulchre).

E.P.   May my light also be extinguished among men, as was that of Judas Iscariot for betraying his Lord and Master, and as I now extinguish this light.

(The Candidate blows out the taper, which is replaced, unlighted, by the Marshal).

E.P.   Brother Knights, Carry swords. (*Done*).

E.P.   You are about to retire to meditate upon the ceremony through which you have just passed, and to prepare yourself for the honour of Knighthood. And to enable you to gain re-admission, I will entrust you with the casual sign and Grand Password of our Order : the Chaplain will read a portion of Holy Writ.

Chaplain " I gave my back to the smiters, and my cheeks to them that plucked off the hair ; I hid not my face from shame and spitting."[1]

E.P.   The sign is given thus. (*By pretending to pluck hair from the cheek with the thumb and forefinger of either hand. Candidate copies*).

E.P.   The Chaplain will read a further portion of Holy Writ.

Chaplain " Moreover the Lord said unto me, take thee a great roll, and write in it with a man's pen concerning Maher-shalal-hash-baz."[2]

E.P.   The Grand Password is MAHER-SHALAL-HASH-BAZ, and is contained in the portion of Scripture which has just been read to you by the Chaplain. It is in the Hebrew language and it signifies, In making speed to the spoil he hasteneth the prey.

1. Isaiah I, 6.   2. Isaiah VIII, 1.

E.P. You may now retire.
  (*The Candidate gives the sign of a Crusader with his hand and retires*).
E.P. Brother Knights, be seated.

PART TWO

(*The Guard from without knocks* 5. 2.)
C. of G. Brother Second Constable, there is a report.
2nd C. (*Rising and giving the sign of a Crusader with his hand*) Eminent Preceptor, there is a report.
E.P. Inquire who seeks admission.
2nd C. (*To Captain of the Guard*) See who seeks admission.
  (*The Captain of the Guard opens the door, sees the Candidate, closes door, and reports with sign*).
C. of G. Eminent Preceptor, our new Companion-in-Arms.
E.P. Admit him.
  (*The Candidate is admitted, and gives the casual sign and the Grand Password to the Captain of the Guard. He is conducted by the Marshal to the west of the Sepulchre*).
Mar. Salute the Eminent Preceptor with the sign of a Crusader with your hand.
E.P. Our new Companion-in-Arms will now attend to a portion of Holy Scripture.
Chaplain " Dearly beloved, I beseech you as strangers and pilgrims, abstain from fleshly lusts, which war against the soul ; having your conversation honest among the Gentiles, that whereas they speak against you as evildoers, they may by your good works, which they shall behold, glorify God in the day of visitation. Submit yourselves to every ordinance of man for the Lord's sake ; whether it be to the king, as supreme ; or unto governors, as unto them that are sent by him for the punishment of evil-doers and for the praise of them that do well. For so is the will of God ; that with well-doing ye may put to silence the ignorance of foolish men : as free, and not using your liberty for a cloak of maliciousness, but as the servants of God. Honour all men. Love the brotherhood. Fear God. Honour the king."[1]
E.P. Brother Marshal, let the cup of memory be presented to our new Companion-in-Arms.
  (*The Marshal presents the cup to the Candidate*).
E.P. Brother Knights, to order.
  Worthy Brother, at your first admission you were refreshed with bread and water ; we now invite you to

1. I Peter II, 11–17.

E.P.   refresh yourself with the cup of memory. You will repeat after me :—

To the memory of Moses, Aholiab and Bezaleel, the Three Grand Masters who presided over the Holy Lodge.

To the memory of Solomon King of Israel, Hiram King of Tyre and Hiram Abiff, the three Grand Masters who presided over the Sacred Lodge.

To the memory of Zerubbabel the prince of the people, Haggai the prophet, and Joshua the son of Josedech the High Priest, who presided over the Grand or Royal Lodge.

To the memory of St. John the Baptist, the Forerunner of Christ.

To the memory of St. John the Evangelist, the Beloved Apostle of Our Lord, who finished by his learning what St. John the Baptist had commenced by his zeal.

To the pious memory of all those valiant Knights who sealed their faith with their blood, under the banner of the Cross.

To all Knights Templar, wheresoever dispersed over the face of earth or water.

(The Candidate drinks after each of these toasts, and the Marshal replaces the cup on the Sepulchre).

E.P.   Brother Knights, Be seated.

You will now attend to another portion of Holy Scripture.

Chaplain " He that hath an ear, let him hear what the Spirit saith to the Churches : To him that overcometh will I give to eat of the hidden manna, and will give him a white stone, and in the stone a new name written, which no man knoweth saving him that receiveth it."[1]

E.P.   Worthy Brother, it was customary at the period of the institution of our Order for each Novice to be required to sign his name with his blood on the north-east corner of the Mystical Stone before he could obtain the Sacred Word which it enshrines ; are you prepared to sign your name on the Stone which is now presented to you ?

(Marshal hands pen and stone to the Candidate. With his left hand he takes the Candidate's left wrist, and with his right he directs the point of the dagger thereto).

Mar.   Are you prepared to conform to the ancient ceremony of the Order ?

Can.   I am.

Mar.   Whence will you have the blood drawn ?

1. Rev. II, 17.

Can.	My arm.
Mar.	Eminent Preceptor, the Novice is ready.
E.P.	Worthy Brother, accepting your ready acquiescence as a sufficient proof of your devotion to our Order, we dispense with the observance of the custom (*the Marshal releases Candidate's wrist*), further than to require you to moisten the pen with your lips, and write your initials with it upon the Stone.

(*Candidate does so. The stone is replaced on the Sepulchre and a small one is presented to him in turn*).

E.P.	You will carefully preserve that memorial, for should you wish to gain admission into a Preceptory of Knights Templar, you will, on presenting that Stone and explaining the circumstances under which you received it, be recognized and received as a Knight of our Order.

Approach my Brother, and receive the highest honour I can at present bestow upon you.

Brother Knights, To Order.

(*The Marshal assembles an escort in the north-west carrying the regalia on cushions. On his command " Escort—March " they proceed to the east. The Eminent Preceptor stands in front of the Altar, facing west, and the Candidate kneels before him for the accolade*).

E.P.	In the name of the Holy, Blessed and Glorious Trinity, and by the authority vested in me as a Preceptor of the Order, I make thee a Knight of the Temple and Holy Sepulchre.

(*The Preceptor lays the sword first on the Candidate's left shoulder, then on his right, and then on his head during the following words*) :—

E.P.	Be loyal, brave, and true!

(*The Preceptor returns sword to the Marshal. He takes the new Knight by the hand*).

E.P.	Arise, Brother Knight.

(*The Constables present the regalia to the Preceptor, who decorates and invests the new Knight*).

E.P.	Wear this Ribbon, the ensign of our Order ; this Cross, and this Star, an emblem of the reward which the great Captain of our Salvation has promised to those who conquer in His Name ; he being the Bright Morning Star, whose rising brought peace and salvation to mankind, and light to those who sat in darkness and in the shadow of death. Bear this ever in mind, and continue His faithful soldier until death. We clothe you with this mantle of pure white, ennobled with the Red Cross of the Order ; symbol of the

E.P.   Christian's Faith and Hope.

Lastly I present you with this sword. Never draw it without cause nor sheathe it without honour.

Return your sword, Brother Knight.

(The Preceptor, who has been holding it by the blade, directs it into the scabbard).

E.P.   I will now entrust you with the Grand Sign, the Grand Grip, and the Grand Word of the Order.

(The Grand Sign is made by imitating, " in all reverence " our Lord on the Cross. The Knight stands with his head bowed to one side, his arms outstretched, palms forward, and his feet crossed. The Grand Grip is given by grasping each other's arms across, above the elbows, representing a double triangle or the cross-bones. The Grand Word is EMMANUEL.

(The new Knight is conducted to the west accompanied by his escort, and seated in the Marshal's chair. The Constables resume their stations, the Marshal with the Standard Bearers on either side of him stands behind the new Knight, all facing east. The Standard bearers slightly dip their standards).

E.P.   Heralds, you will now proclaim.

(The Marshal draws his sword, the Heralds take their posts, and the Standards are raised).

1st Herald   *(In the south-west, facing east)* Brethren of the Temple. Be it known that our Brother and Companion, ..., is this day installed a Knight of our Illustrious Order, and I call upon you to salute him, taking the time from the Marshal.

Mar.   Brother Knights, with three.

(The Knights give the Salute of the Order thrice, as described in the Opening Ceremony).

2nd Herald   *(In the north-west, facing east)* Long life, honour, and prosperity to our Most Eminent and Supreme Grand Master, the Great Officers and all other Knights of our Order, and I call upon you to salute our newly-installed Knight ...., taking your time from the Marshal.

(The Knights salute thrice as before. The Heralds and Standard-Bearers resume their places).

E.P.   Brother Knights. Be seated.

(The Marshal directs the new Knight to rise, and conducts him to the Sepulchre, where the Preceptor stands at the north-east corner of it).

E.P.   I will now explain to you the symbols of the Order. The Three Great Lights placed at the angles of the equilateral triangle represent the three favourite Apostles of our Saviour ; namely, Peter, James, and John, of whom

E.P. the last-named was the most beloved ; for, leaning on our Saviour's bosom, he received those instructions which he communicated so faithfully to the other Disciples. The Nine Smaller Lights, distributed equally between those already noticed, are emblematic of the nine other Apostles, one of whom, represented by the taper extinguished by you, betrayed his Lord and Master. You will now relight and replace the taper. (*The new Knight does so*).

Chaplain (*With right hand raised, if in holy orders. Or it may be pronounced by the Preceptor*). So may our Saviour lift up the light of His reconciled countenance upon you, and keep you from falling.

E.P. The skull and cross-bones, the emblems of mortality, are placed at the foot of the Cross ; these collectively remind us of the place called in Hebrew Golgotha, unto which Simon of Cyrene was constrained to bear the Cross on which our Saviour was crucified. The skull also reminds us of the fate of one Simon of Syracuse, who was admitted into our illustrious Order, but violated his obligation by betraying his trust to the Infidels. They, although they profited by the treason, despised the traitor and caused his head to be struck off and sent to the Grand Master of the Knights Templar, who ordered it to be placed on the point of a pinnacle or spire, the skull to be laid open, and the brains exposed to the scorching rays of the sun, as a warning to all others. It is in allusion to this circumstance that the penal sign of a Knight Templar had its origin.

(*The Preceptor demonstrates this sign, and the new Knight copies it. It is given by closing the fingers of the right hand, the thumb upright, the tip of the thumb pressing under the chin, representing the head stuck on a spire*).

E.P. The Lamb, the Dove and the Cock are sacred symbols of the Order. The first is emblematic of the Paschal Lamb, slain from the foundation of the world. The Dove is symbolical of the Almighty Comforter, which descended like a Dove on Christ at His baptism, whereby His divine mission was indicated to St. John the Baptist. The Cock is the monitor of the Order, for as his crowing heralds the morn, so let it at that still hour call to our remembrance our duties as Knights Templar, and remind us thus early to ask for assistance to perform them throughout the coming day. May we ever welcome that sound as a friendly caution and not have reason to fear it as the periodical reminder of a

E.P.   broken vow.

(The Preceptor resumes his seat. The Marshal conducts the new Knight to the east, where the Preceptor shows him the Warrant and gives him a copy of the Statutes, and the by-laws of the Preceptory).

E.P.   In a former part of the ceremony your attention was called to the inscription on the Cross. Whenever that mark (that is, I.N.R.I.) is on your summons it will be your duty, in accordance with your obligation, to attend. If this is not possible, you must inform the Eminent Preceptor of the reason.

(The new Knight is then conducted to a seat in the north-west of the Preceptory).

CLOSING THE PRECEPTORY

(The alms are collected).

E.P.   Brother Knights, have you aught to propose for the advancement of the Glory of the Cross, or for the honour of our Order ?

(Any propositions are now made).

E.P.   Brother Knights, we may now close this Preceptory, for, praise be to God, all is well, and God grant that it may so continue, and goodness be every day increased. Brother Knights. To order. Listen to our Precepts.

Chaplain Love, honour, and fear God ; walk after His commandments. Maintain and defend the Christian Faith, and the honour, dignity and interests of our Order. Be loyal to your Sovereign, dutiful to the Grand Master, and obedient to those who rule over you. Prefer honour to wealth. Be just and true in word and deed. Give no willing cause of offence to any ; but, while opposing wrong and injustice, deport yourselves courteously and gently. Assist the distressed, the widow and the fatherless. Eschew all debasing employment, recreation, and company ; abhor pride and selfishness and so raise the standard of chivalrous honour, striving for the welfare of your Brethren.

(Psalm CXXII may now be read).

I was glad when they said unto me, Let us go into the house of the Lord.

Our feet shall stand within thy gates, O Jerusalem.

Jerusalem is builded as a city that is compact together.

Whither the tribes go up, the tribes of the Lord unto the testimony of Israel, to give thanks unto the name of the Lord.

For there are set thrones of judgment, the thrones of the house of David.

Chaplain Pray for the peace of Jerusalem ; they shall prosper that love thee.

Peace be within thy walls, and prosperity within thy places.

For my brethren and companions' sakes, I will now say, Peace be within thee.

Because of the house of the Lord our God, I will seek thy good.

(*Standing at the Altar and facing east*) Let us pray. O merciful Lord, grant Thy Holy protection and salutary blessing to this Preceptory. Enlighten its rulers with the rays of Thy Brightness that they may see the just ways of our Heavenly Captain, and may by their example teach the Knights committed to their charge so to follow them through this wilderness of temptation, that, being armed with the Shield of Faith and the Breastplate of Righteousness, they may overcome the enemies of Thy Holy Name, and finally arrive at the Heavenly Jerusalem, through Jesus Christ our Saviour. Amen.

(*The Knights carry swords*).

E.P. In the name of the Holy, Blessed and Glorious Trinity, and in the name of Christ our Prophet, Christ our Priest, Christ our King, I close this Preceptory. (*During these words the Knights salute thrice with the sign of a Crusader, as at the Opening*).

Chaplain (*Closes the Bible, and faces west in front of the altar*) May the blessing of our Heavenly Captain descend upon us, and remain with us now and evermore.

(*Or if the Chaplain is in holy orders*).

Chaplain Pax et Benedictio Dei Omnipotentis, Patris, Filii, et Spiritus Sancti, in vos descendat, et vobiscum maneat in saecula saeculorum. Amen.

(*The Marshal closes the Bible on the Sepulchre. An Arch of Steel is formed in the west, and the Officers leave in procession*).

* * *

THE ORDER OF KNIGHTS HOSPITALLER OF ST. JOHN OF JERUSALEM, PALESTINE, RHODES, AND MALTA,

Also

KNIGHT OF ST. PAUL, OR MEDITERRANEAN PASS

This is a " higher degree " of the Templar Order, and no one can be admitted unless he is a Knight Templar.

Two rooms are needed for these ceremonies. A large room

represents the Chapter House or Council Chamber of the Priory. A smaller room serves as the Guard Room. There should also be an ante-room for the preparation of candidates.

At the eastern end of the Chapter House is a five-sided table, with a red cover on which is worked the upper limb of a white cross. A Bible is placed at the western point of the table. Five Officers sit at the sides of this table, the Eminent Prior, the Captain-General, the Lieutenant-General, the First Lieutenant, and the Second Lieutenant.

At the west of the Chapter House is an octagonal table with a red cover on which is worked a white eight-pointed Maltese cross having a centre circle divided into four parts. On these four quarters are depicted an ancient galley ; a ladder of five rounds bearing the letters B, L, D, R, and A, and a speaking trumpet ; a hand and a viper ; and a skull with a spear and sword. The following eight Officers sit at the eight points of the table : the Mareschal, the Hospitaller, the Admiral, the Conservator, the Baillie, the Turcopolier, the Chancellor, and the Treasurer. These Officers are said to represent the Heads or Priors of the respective " langues " or provinces of which the Order consisted, that is, Provence, France, Arragon, Germany, Auvergne, Italy, England, and Castile.

Inside the door ranged along the north wall are five banners, guarded by five knights. From west to east, these banners represent : Palestine, 1099 (white) ; Cyprus, 1291 (red) ; Rhodes, 1310 (black) ; Candia, 1523 (purple) ; and Malta 1530 (gold). These five banners correspond to the Birth, Life, Death, Resurrection, and Ascension respectively of Our Lord, hence the five initials on the octagonal table. The explanation of all this is given in the lecture at the end of the ceremonies. There are two further banners of the Order, the Standard of St. John, to the north side of the Prior in the east, and the Standard of Malta to the south side.

The Captain of the Outposts is seated in the west, near the door, the Guard outside the door. Great Officers and Past Priors sit in the east, the former on the north side, and the latter on the south side of the pentagonal table. The Chaplain has his place in the south-west corner.

Sword drill, the " carry," the call to order, and so on, are the same as in the previous degree.

The Guard Room has a table covered with a black cloth, on which are a New Testament open at Acts XXVII, and a drawn sword. It is in this room that the Mediterranean Pass is given.

The Mantle of the Order of Malta is of black stuff, with the hood lined in white, with white cords and tassels. The white eight-pointed (Maltese) Cross of the Order is worn on the left shoulder. A red tunic may be worn, with a similar cross on the breast. The cap is of black velvet, with the eight-pointed cross in white enamel on the front. The sword and belt are the same as in the Order of the Temple. Knights of Malta also wear the eight-pointed Maltese cross in white enamel and gilt suspended from the left breast by a black ribbon.

Knights of Malta, however, may appear in the Priory in their habit as Knights Templar, except that the Knight Templar ribbon is not worn.

There is of course no distinctive dress or regalia for the Mediterranean Pass or Knights of St. Paul, which is a mere preliminary degree conferred by the Priory before installation as a Knight of Malta.

OPENING THE PRIORY

Mar.	Brother Knights. To order.
	(*The Officers enter in procession and take their places*).
Mar.	Brother Knights. Be seated.
E. Prior	Worthy Captain-General, what is the first and most essential care of a Knight of Malta ?
Capt.-Gen.	To see that our Brethren-in-Arms are properly protected from all opposers of the Gospel of the Saviour of fallen man.
E.P.	Worthy Lieutenant-General, do your duty and see that the Priory is properly guarded.
	(*The Lieutenant-General goes to the door and knocks 1, 12. The Guard replies from outside. The Lieutenant-General returns and reports*).
Lt.-Gen.	Eminent Prior, all is guarded without.
E.P.	Worthy Captain-General, what is our next duty ?
C.-G.	To see that every Warrior present proves himself a true brother of our Order.
E.P.	See that they be so.
Mar.	Brother Knights. To order.
	(*The Captain-General and the Lieutenant-General draw their swords and prove the Knights with the Rowing sign, and the words KING OF KINGS, answered by*

LORD OF LORDS. *They return to their places and report*).

C.-G.   (*With Penal Sign*) Eminent Prior, the Companion Warriors present have proved themselves true Brethren of our Order.

E.P.   Let us implore a blessing upon our present meeting.

Chaplain Let us pray.

O Thou Great Emmanuel and God of Infinite Goodness, look down upon this Priory with an eye of tender compassion, and incline our hearts to Thy Holy Will in all our actions, through Jesus Christ our Lord. Amen.

E.P.   In the name of the Holy Trinity, I declare this a duly opened and constituted Priory of Knights of Malta.

(33 *knocks are given, five by each of the five Officers at the pentagonal table, given with the pommel of the sword, and one knock each from the eight Officers at the octagonal table*).

Mar.   Brother Knights, be seated.

(*The five Officers at the pentagonal table lay their swords in the lines marked on the table, points to the centre. The eight Officers at the octagonal table also lay their swords in order on the table. The Deputy Mareschal opens the Bible at the Gospels*).

THE MEDITERRANEAN PASS

(*When the Candidate is ready the Guard knocks* 5, 2. *The Captain of the Outposts goes to the door, receives from the Candidate the sign and Word of a Crusader, and requests him to wait while he makes a report*).

C. of O.   Eminent Prior, Bro. ...., a Knight of the Religious and Military Order of the Temple stands without, humbly soliciting to be admitted to the secrets and privileges of the Mediterranean Pass, and if found worthy he hopes to be elected a Member of the Ancient Order of St. John of Jerusalem, Palestine, Rhodes, and Malta.

E.P.   Worthy Captain of the Outposts, far be it from us to interpose any obstacle to the fulfilment of his desire. Can you vouch that he is in possession of the sign and Word of a Crusader ?

C. of O.   I can, Eminent Prior.

E.P.   Is it your pleasure, Brother Knights, that Bro. ...., be elected a Member of our Order ?

(*The Brethren signify their assent by show of hands*).

E.P.   I declare Bro. ...., duly elected a Member of our Order ; and you, our Worthy Chaplain, and you,

E.P.   our Worthy Mareschal, will accompany me to the Guard Room ; and do you, our Worthy Captain-General, be pleased to assume my seat during my temporary absence and take charge of this Priory.

Dep.-Mar.   Brother Knights, rise while the Eminent Prior retires.

(The Prior, Chaplain, and Mareschal leave the Chapter House and enter the Guard Room. The Prior and Mareschal take their swords, the Chaplain the New Testament, which he places on the table open at Acts XXVII, and takes his place on the south side of the table. The Prior places his sword on the front of the table.

The Candidate, wearing the garb of a Knight Templar, is conducted into the room by the Mareschal, and faces the Prior, whom he salutes with the sign of a Crusader).

E.P.   Bro. ...., before I place you in possession of the secrets of the Mediterranean Pass, are you willing to pledge yourself to keep inviolate the secrets and mysteries of the degree of a Knight of St. Paul ?

Can.   I am.

E.P.   Then you will assume the sign of Fidelity.

Do you solemnly promise on your Knightly honour that you will never improperly reveal the secrets which we are about to impart to you ?

Can.   I solemnly promise. *(Drops sign).*

E.P.   You will now attend while the Chaplain reads a portion of Holy Scripture.

(The Chaplain reads Acts XXVII and XXVIII, 1-6. But the portions in brackets are frequently and permissively omitted).

Chaplain " And when it was determined that we should sail into Italy they delivered Paul and certain other prisoners unto one named Julius, a centurion of August's band. And entering into a ship of Adramyttium, we launched, meaning to sail by the coasts of Asia ; one Aristarchus, a Macedonian of Thessalonica, being with us.

(" And the next day we touched at Sidon. And Julius courteously entreated Paul, and gave him liberty to go unto his friends to refresh himself. And when we had launched from thence, we sailed under Cyprus, because the winds were contrary. And when we had sailed over the Sea of Cilicia and Pamphylia, we came to Myra, a city of Lycia. And there the centurion found a ship of Alexandria sailing into Italy, and he put us therein. And when we had sailed slowly many days, and scarce were come over against

Chaplain Cnidus, the wind not suffering us, we sailed under Crete, over against Salmone ; and, hardly passing it, came into a place which is called the Fair Havens ; nigh whereunto was the city of Lasea).

" Now when much time was spent, and when sailing was now dangerous, because the fast was now already past, Paul admonished them, and said unto them, Sirs, I perceive that this voyage will be with hurt and much damage, not only of the lading and ship, but also of our lives. Nevertheless the centurion believed the master and the owner of the ship, more than those things which were spoken by Paul. And because the haven was not commodious to winter in, the more part advised to depart thence also, if by any means they might attain to Phenice, and there to winter ; which is an haven of Crete, and lieth toward the south-west and north-west. And when the south wind blew softly, supposing that they had obtained their purpose, loosing thence, they sailed close by Crete. But not long after there arose against it a tempestuous wind, called Euroclydon. And when the ship was caught, and could not bear up into the wind, we let her drive.

(" And running under a certain island which is called Clauda, we had much work to come by the boat : which when they had taken up, they used helps, undergirding the ship ; and fearing lest they should fall into quicksands, strake sail, and so we were driven. And we being exceeding tossed with a tempest, the next day they lightened the ship ; and the third day we cast out with our own hands the tackling of the ship).

" And when neither sun nor stars in many days appeared, and no small tempest lay on us, all hope that we should be saved was then taken away. But after long abstinence Paul stood forth in the midst of them, and said, Sirs, ye should have hearkened unto me, and not have loosed from Crete, and to have gained this harm and loss. And now I exhort you to be of good cheer : for there shall be no loss of any man's life among you, but of the ship. For there stood by me this night the angel of God, whose I am, and whom I serve, saying, Fear not, Paul ; thou must be brought before Caesar ; and lo, God hath given thee all them that sail with thee. Wherefore, sirs, be of good cheer, for I believe God that it shall be even as it was told me. Howbeit, we must be cast upon a certain Island.

(" But when the fourteenth night was come, as we were

Chaplain driven up and down in Adria, about midnight the
shipmen deemed that they drew near to some country ;
and sounded, and found it twenty fathoms : and when
they had gone a little further, they sounded again,
and found it fifteen fathoms. Then fearing lest we
should have fallen upon rocks, they cast four anchors
out of the stern, and wished for the day. And as the
shipmen were about to flee out of the ship, when
they had let down the boat into the sea, under colour as
though they would have cast anchors out of the
foreship, Paul said to the centurion and to the soldiers,
Except these abide in the ship, ye cannot be saved.
Then the soldiers cut off the ropes of the boat, and let
her fall off. And while the day was coming on, Paul
besought them all to take meat, saying, This day is
the fourteenth day that ye have tarried and continued
fasting, having taken nothing. Wherefore I pray you to
take some meat : for this is for your health : for there
shall not an hair fall from the head of any of you. And
when he had thus spoken, he took bread, and gave
thanks to God in the presence of them all : and when
he had broken it he began to eat. Then were they all
of good cheer, and they also took some meat. And
we were in all in the ship two hundred threescore and
sixteen souls. And when they had eaten enough, they
lightened the ship, and cast out the wheat into the sea.
And when it was day, they knew not the land ; but
they discovered a certain creek with a shore, into
which they were minded, if it were possible, to thrust
in the ship. And when they had taken up the anchors,
they committed themselves unto the sea, and loosed
the rudder bands. and hoisted up the mainsail to the
wind, and made toward shore).

" And falling into a place where the two seas met, they
ran the ship aground ; and the forepart stuck fast, and
remained unmoveable, but the hinder part was broken
with the violence of the waves.

(" And the soldiers' counsel was to kill the prisoners,
lest any of them should swim out and escape. But the
centurion, willing to save Paul, kept them from their
purpose ; and commanded that they which could
swim should cast themselves first into the sea, and get
to land : and the rest, some on boards, and some on
broken pieces of the ship. And so it came to pass, that
they all escaped safe to land).

" And when they were escaped, then they knew that
the island was called Melita. And the barbarous
people shewed us no little kindness : for they kindled

Chaplain a fire, and received us every one, because of the recent rain, and because of the cold. And when Paul had gathered a bundle of sticks, and laid them on the fire, there came a viper out of the heat, and fastened on his hand. And when the barbarians saw the venomous beast hang on his hand, they said among themselves, No doubt this man is a murderer, whom, though he hath escaped the sea, yet vengeance suffereth not to live. And he shook off the beast into the fire, and felt no harm. Howbeit they looked when he should have swollen, or fallen down dead suddenly : but after they had looked a great while, and saw no harm come to him, they changed their minds, and said that he was a god."

E.P.   I will now entrust you with the sign, token and Words of this Degree.

The sign is shaking the hand, as if shaking off a viper, as St. Paul did.

The grip or token is given by taking hold of the little fingers and throwing up the hands, and then, with the forefinger and thumb, alternately laying hold of the skin on the back of each other's hand.

The Mediterranean Pass is MELITA ; the pass words are FEAR NOT PAUL.

(*The Prior takes up the sword, and the Chaplain the New Testament, and return to the Chapter House. The Mareschal remains with the Candidate*).

CEREMONY OF INSTALLATION

(*As the Prior and Chaplain enter the Chapter House, the Deputy Mareschal rises*).

Dep.-Mar. Brother Knights, Rise. (*When Prior and Chaplain have taken their seats*), Brother Knights, be seated.

(*The five Knights who act as Guards to the Banners take their posts with drawn swords opposite their respective banners, forming an avenue up which the Mareschal and the Candidate approach the east. When they come to the door of the Chapter House the Mareschal knocks 5, 2*).

Cap. of Out. Who comes ?

Mar.   A worthy Knight and Soldier of the Cross seeks admittance.

C. of O. To what Order does he belong ?

Mar.   The Knights Templar.

C. of O. Has he the necessary qualifications ?

Mar.   He has.

C. of O. Halt while I report to the Eminent Prior and Knights in Council.

(The Captain of Outposts closes the door and reports).

C. of O.   Eminent Prior, a worthy Knight and Soldier of the Cross seeks admittance.

E.P.   Admit him.

(The Captain of Outposts opens the door).

C. of O.   I have received orders to admit you. Give me the pass words.

Can.   FEAR NOT PAUL.

(The Mareschal and Candidate enter and advance towards the banners. As they approach the first, the Knight guarding it points his sword at the Candidate's breast and challenges him).

1st Guard.   Give me the Mediterranean Pass.

Can.   MELITA.

(The First Guard carries sword, and gives the name of his banner, PALESTINE. The Candidate approaches the second banner, and the Knight guarding it challenges him).

2nd G.   Give me the word of the first banner.

Can.   PALESTINE.

(The Second Guard carries sword, and gives him the name of the second banner, CYPRUS. The Candidate approaches the third banner).

3rd G.   Give me the word of the second banner.

Can.   CYPRUS.

(The Third Guard carries sword, and gives the name of his banner, RHODES. The Candidate approaches the fourth banner).

4th G.   Give me the word of the third banner.

Can.   RHODES.

(The Fourth Guard carries sword, and gives the name of his banner, CANDIA. Candidate approaches the fifth banner, and is challenged again as before).

5th G.   Give me the word of the fourth banner.

Can.   CANDIA.

(The Fifth Guard carries sword, and gives the name of his banner, MALTA. The Candidate is then placed between the pentagonal and octagonal tables, facing the Prior).

E.P.   Brother Knight, is it your wish to join our Order and fight against all opposers of the Gospel of our Lord and Saviour under our Holy Banner ?

Can.   It is.

E.P.   Have you any further proof ?

(The Candidate bows to the Prior, and points to the cross on his breast).

Can.   I have this.

E.P.   Give me the word of the fifth banner.

Can.	MALTA.
E.P.	Are you prepared to conform yourself to our rules and regulations and to walk in strict accordance therewith?
Can.	I am.
E.P.	Will you swear ?
Can.	I will.
E.P.	Then you will kneel, and enter into the obligation of a Knight of Malta.

(The Mareschal conducts the Candidate to the faldstool at the west of the pentagonal table, and tells him to draw his sword and place it across the open Bible, to put his right hand on the Bible and sword, and to kneel on his right knee. The Candidate repeats the obligation after the Chaplain, who stands in front of him facing west).

Chaplain and Can. I, ..., do hereby and hereon promise and vow, on the honour of a Knight Templar, never improperly to divulge the secrets about to be entrusted to me ; and in all respects to conform to the rules and regulations of this Ancient Order, as contained in the Statutes of the Great Priory of England and Wales, under no less a penalty than that of having my skull cleft[1] from crown to chin. So help me God.

E.P. You will seal this obligation three times on the Holy Gospels.

(Candidate does so. The Prior leaves his place, and stands in the east, facing west. The Mareschal raises the Candidate, tells him to return his sword, and conducts him to the east in front of the Prior, instructing him to kneel on both knees. The Prior then places a sword on the right shoulder of the Candidate, and invests him).

E.P. By virtue of the power and authority vested in me by the Great Priory of England and Wales, and in the name of St. John the Baptist, the Patron Saint of the Order, I make thee a Knight Hospitaller of St. John of Jerusalem, Palestine, Rhodes, and Malta.

(The Prior transfers the sword to his left hand and raises the new Knight).

E.P. Arise, Brother Knight, Be Valiant, Bold, and True. Brother Knight, draw your sword.

I will entrust you with the grip, Words, and sign of the Order.

The grip is given thus. With the sword in the right hand, interlace the fingers of the left hand as if rowing. *(Demonstrates).*

The Words are KING OF KINGS, which are answered by LORD OF LORDS.

1. Or sometimes, *cloven.*

E.P.   Brother Knight, return your sword.
The Grand Word is JESUS EMMANUEL.
The penal sign is given thus: draw the thumb down
the centre of the face. (*Candidate copies*).
The sign of Adoration is given by pointing upwards
with the index finger. (*Candidate copies*),
I now invest you with the jewel of this Order. (*Does
so*).

Mar.   Brother Knights, Be seated.
(*The Candidate is placed by the Mareschal on the
south side of the Chapter House, facing north. In
the following address, when the Prior refers to each
banner the Guard of it extends it on the point of his
sword, returning to the "carry" and lowering the banner
when the explanation is finished*).

E.P.   Worthy Brother Knight, it is now my duty to direct
your attention to a brief résumé of the history of the
Order, and its bearing on our present ceremonies.
This Order was originally founded in Jerusalem, during
the first Crusade, about the year of our Lord 1099,
by the association of many pious Knights with the
Fratres of St. John's Hospital, an establishment
previously founded in 1048 for the relief of Pilgrims
proceeding to worship at the Holy Sepulchre.
The name Palestine, and the date on the Banner of
Birth, commemorate the country of our Lord's
Nativity, and have reference to this earliest period of
our Order, and also to the place where the Order was
founded. After a troubled existence in the Holy Land,
and in consequence of being deprived, by the wars
raging in Europe, of their looked-for assistance, the
Order was compelled to evacuate Palestine and, in the
year 1291, established itself in the Island of Cyprus.
The name and date on the Banner of Life are in
memory of this refuge of the Knights of St. John.
In 1310, the Island of Rhodes became the property of
the Forces of the Order, which had a few years before
(in 1307) been strengthened in numbers and enriched
by the properties of the Templars, who were at that
time suppressed by the cruelty and avarice of Pope
Clement V and Philip le Bel, King of France. The
remains of the fortifications erected in Rhodes by the
Knights still bear testimony to their architectural
talent and their engineering ability. The Banner of
Death has reference to this period of our history.
In 1522, the Island of Rhodes was besieged by the
Turks, under the Emperor Solyman II, and after a
memorable defence fell into the hands of the infidels ;

E.P.   the garrison, however, was permitted to depart with all the honours of war. From 1523 the Order found refuge in the Island of Candia and elsewhere ; and in 1530 the Emperor Charles V ceded the Island of Malta to the Order, on condition of using all their abilities to repress the ravages of the Moorish rovers, who at that period infested the southern part of the Mediterranean. These periods of our history are designated by the Banner of Resurrection and the Banner of Ascension. (*The Guards to the Banners resume their seats*).

E.P.   The legend of the approach of the Knights to this their final resting-place has given rise to the distinguishing words of the Order. The story runs, that on coming to take possession of the island they approached the shore rowing their galleys, two men to an oar, the oars in their left hands and their swords in their right hands, singing a psalm in the words " King of Kings and Lord of Lords." The natives of the island seeing their approach in a warlike guise, hailed them through a speaking-trumpet, saying in the Arabic tongue: ...., ..., ..., which means " Do you come in peace ? " To this the Knights replied ...., ..., ..., " We do come in peace," to which the natives rejoined, ..., ..., ...,[1] " Then come in peace." It is worthy of remark that these are to this day the common forms of salutation between an Arab and a stranger.

The Mediterranean Pass, which you have received in the introductory degree of Knight of St. Paul, was instituted at an early period of our Order, so that the Pilgrims might distinguish one another from the Moorish rovers who tried to bar their passage to the Holy Land.

Five Officers of the Priory, namely, the Eminent Prior and his bodyguard, are seated in the east of the Council Chamber at a table on which is represented the upper limb of a Cross. Their swords are all pointing to one spot, that where the Heart of Our Lord was supposed to have rested, figurative in a degree of the holy character of the Order. The number five has also an allusion to the Five Wounds, and is again repeated in the number of rounds of the ladder, depicted on one of the divisions of the circle forming part of the Jewel represented on the

---

1. I have continued to leave these words blank, because there is really no uniformity or standard version. Priors give them as best they can. The three words are, of course, made up in various ways from the syllables of SALAAM ALEIKUM.

E.P.   second table. These five formed the personal staff in attendance on the Grand Master of the Order.

The eight other Officers are placed at an octagonal table in the west. This table has on it the eight-pointed star or cross which is well known as the Emblem of the Order.

(The Hospitaller points with his sword to each object as it is mentioned by the Eminent Prior, replacing his sword on the table when the explanation is over).

E.P.   On the centre are four divisions, with representations of a ship, or ancient galley ; a ladder of five rounds, with the letters B. L. D. R. A. on the rounds, and a speaking trumpet ; a cloven skull, a double-handed sword, and a spear ; and a hand and viper. The ancient galley is a representation of the vessels formerly used in carrying corn from Egypt to Rome ; the ladder has letters in the rounds corresponding with those on the five banners ; the skull is typical of the penalty of death to traitors to the Order ; the double-handed sword was in use by the Knights in the earlier period of the Order ; the spear reminds us of the weapon which pierced the side of our Lord ; and the hand and viper refer to the history of St. Paul in connection with the Island of Malta.

The eight Officers sitting there represent the heads of the eight Langues or Tongues into which the Order was divided. These were Provence, Auvergne, France, Italy, Aragon, England, Germany and Castile. These eight Priors also held the several offices in the Order of Mareschal, Hospitaller, Admiral, Conservator, Baillie, Turcopolier, Chancellor, and Treasurer.

The thirty-three knocks given at the Opening and Closing of the Priory refer to the thirty-three years of the life of Our Lord on earth.

The practical lessons to be drawn by us from the study and contemplation of the Birth, Life, Death, Resurrection, and Ascension of Our Blessed Lord and Saviour will be more particularly brought to your notice during the Ceremony of Closing the Priory, to which your attention will presently be directed.

My Brother, be seated.

CLOSING THE PRIORY

E.P.   Worthy Captain-General, what is the last duty of our Brethren-in-Arms ?

Capt.-Gen.   To close the Priory in peace and good will with all our Companions-in-Arms, and in Christian charity

	with all mankind.
E.P.	How can we best effect this noble and Godlike purpose ?
Capt.-	By proving to friends and foes the Birth, Life, Death,
Gen.	Resurrection, and Ascension of Christ, the Saviour of Mankind.
E.P.	Pray, Worthy Captain-General, what do we learn from His Birth ?
Capt.-	That the great Captain of our salvation was born to
Gen.	redeem fallen mankind.
E.P.	Worthy Lieutenant-General, what do we learn from His Life ?
Lieut.-	All requisite for us to follow, He being the Way, the
Gen.	Truth, and the Life.
E.P.	Worthy First Lieutenant, what do we learn from His Death ?
1st	That our debt of nature is fully paid, and the rigour
Lieut.	of the law satisfied.
E.P.	Worthy Second Lieutenant, what do we learn from His Resurrection ?
2nd	He, being the Day Star of Mercy, has risen to conduct
Lieut.	our feet into the paths of truth and peace.
E.P.	Thus, my Companions-in-Arms, by the Birth, Life, Death, and Resurrection of Our Blessed Lord and Saviour, we are taught to live and die as Christians ; and it is now my province to close this Priory, previously declaring that by His glorious Ascension He is gone before to open the Door of Everlasting Life ; for He hath said : In my Father's house are many mansions, but I go to prepare the way, and open the gates of Paradise, that where I am My servants may be also.
Mar.	Brother Knights, to order.

(The Chaplain advances to the centre of the Chapter House, between the two tables, and receives from the Deputy Mareschal the Bible. He presents the Old Testament to the five Senior Officers, who advance towards him, kneel on their right knee, and place the points of their swords on the Old Testament. They then salute the Old Testament, rise, and resume their seats, replacing their swords on the table.

The Chaplain then turns to the west, and presents the New Testament to the eight other Officers who advance, kneel on their left knee, placing the points of their swords on the New Testament. They salute the New Testament, rise, and resume their seats, placing their swords on the table. The Chaplain returns to his place in the east).

Chaplain Let us pray.

(*The Officers at the tables rise and elevate the left hand covered with the mantle to their foreheads, but do not take up their swords during prayer*).

Chaplain Most merciful God, grant, we beseech Thee, that we may ever show forth in ourselves the lessons taught by the Birth, Life, Death, Resurrection, and Ascension of Thy Son Jesus Christ our Saviour, so that, at the last, we may be found acceptable in Thy sight and worthy to be numbered with Thine elect. Amen.

E.P. In the name of the Holy Trinity I declare this Priory of the Knights of Malta duly closed, to remain so until it is my will and pleasure, or the will and pleasure of some other duly authorized person, to open the same again.

(*The Officers take their swords from the tables, and the* 33 *knocks are given in full, as in the Opening*).

Mar. Brother Knights. Return swords.

Brother Knights, you will remain standing while the Eminent Prior, attended by the Officers of the Pentagonal and Octagonal Tables and accompanied by the Chaplain and the Great Officers, leaves the Chapter House.

(*The Eminent Prior and Officers leave in procession. The Knights disperse*).

* * *

There is a significant difference between the nature of the Masonic Knights Templar and the Rose Croix of Heredom. The former professes to defend the Christian faith against all its enemies, but does not greatly concern itself with the content of that faith. It believes in the Holy Trinity, and stresses the triple function of Christ as Prophet, Priest and King, and there, generally speaking, it leaves the matter. Its ritual is an imaginary, naïve, and rather Boy-Scoutish reconstruction of ancient orders of knighthood with plenty of clashings of swords, military drill, secret passwords, and the most magnificent and pretentious costume of any English Masonic order, but unlike the Rose Croix its legend does not concern our Lord himself. It is not engaged in the quest of hidden wisdom or with the re-discovery in Christian guise of a lost word, but with the defence of what has been already revealed. Apart from the fact that it has a Masonic qualification for membership, and the Candidate must come with the word and sign of a Royal Arch Mason, it really has practically nothing to do with Masonry at all. It is less theologically objectionable than the Antient and Accepted Rite—but on the other hand it is so completely different from and outside the normal Masonic tradition that it is surely impossible to claim that it is in any sense a Christian Masonic fulfilment of the non-Christian craft, even though the first three libations toast the memories of the three Lodges under the old covenant. It is assumed that the Royal Arch Mason seeks at once to be enrolled as a Soldier of the Cross, and there is, so to speak, a break and a fresh start as a Christian, rather than any development or continuity of teaching.

The oath, however, has all the objectionable characteristics of the Masonic oaths in the Craft, with the added one that instead of being sworn in the name of the Great Architect, it is sworn specifically in the name of the Holy, Blessed, and Glorious Trinity, and ends, " So help me Christ." With his hands on the Holy Gospels the Candidate swears fidelity " without evasion, equivocation, or mental reservation of any kind " under a penalty of having his head struck off, his skull sawn asunder, and his brains exposed to the scorching rays of the sun. Here again is the consent to a murder pact sworn on the Gospels, indefensible by any rules of Christian moral theology concerning a just and reverent oath. Here again is the old dilemma that the symbolical interpretation placed upon it in practice by those administering it is expressly ruled out by the declaration that it is sworn without evasion, equivocation or mental reservation— words which surely mean that the oath ought to be taken literally and mean what it says. There is no preliminary assurance, as in the Craft, that the oath contains nothing contrary to moral or religious duties, and again we are faced with the fact that the Candidate is swearing allegiance and secrecy in a religious organization that teaches he knows not what—which again is clean contrary to Christian moral theology. If taken literally, therefore, it is rash swearing. If taken symbolically, it is vain swearing or profanity.

The solemn imprecations, too, are objectionable. To walk round the darkened Chapter carrying a skull and a lighted taper may seem childish and macabre ; to pray that the spirit which once inhabited that skull may rise up and testify against one if found unfaithful is sheer witchcraft. To kiss the skull seven times is merely nauseating. Plastic skulls are in common use today, but many an older Chapter still possesses the genuine article. Fortunately the habit of drinking the libations from the skull is no longer followed in this country, though it continues in America.

" May my light also be extinguished among men, as was that of Judas Iscariot," says the novice, as he blows out the taper. That is a truly dreadful thing to say. Judas Iscariot committed suicide, and was doomed to everlasting hell because, although he may have suffered remorse, he died impenitent after betraying our Lord. Can the violation of a secret society oath, the disclosure of a password unmistakably initialled in printed rituals anyway, the ignoring of a Chapter summons without grave cause, can these seriously be compared with the sin of Judas ? Is no repentance possible, no forgiveness offered ? This horrible imprecation is trifling with our eternal salvation, which no Christian has the right to do.

Only traces can be found of Gnosticism and the tradition of a secret wisdom confined to the initiate. The explanation of the Great Light on the Sepulchre representing St. John the Evangelist hints at the Johanite heresy that that disciple was, while leaning on Our Lord's bosom, entrusted with secret teachings which were not for the Church at large. J. S. M. Ward considers the possibility that the Skull is Baphomet, the head that the Templars of old were reputed to worship. Then he asks, "Whose skull was this ? Some say it was Simon the Traitor. Who was this traitor ? Does it refer to that other Simon, who bore the cross of our Lord, and, if so, is there any reference to the Gnostic heresy that it was Simon the Jew, and not Christ, who actually died on the cross ? " And, again, referring apparently to the kissing of the skull, he writes, " In the Egyptian mystery legend of Osiris we are told that, on discovering the dead body of the murdered Osiris, Isis threw herself on the corpse and had intercourse with it, and from this came the birth of Horus, the avenger of Osiris. To prevent a repetition of this, Set tore the body of Osiris into many pieces and scattered them throughout Egypt. This Templar ceremony would be the mystic marriage, old symbol of the attainment of a divine union. Here we get death and the tomb, and after the tomb, a birth or rebirth. The body, female, dies ; but the spirit, male, rejuvenates it, and a new life begins ; above all a skull and cross-bones, the age-old emblems in all the mysteries of the world, emblems of death, and, since death does but lead to a new birth, the emblems also of life. Perhaps, then, we have here in our modern ritual the last relics of the old ceremony, now shorn of most of its interest. Is the name Simon a corruption of this Lord of Sidon ? "[1]

All of which is a little far-fetched, but J. S. M. Ward has the sufficient hesitancy of his opinions to be generous with question-marks. More people are likely to be disturbed by the sheer bad taste of this Order than by its implicit Gnosticism. There is too much playing about with sacred things and words. Jesus Emmanuel, at whose name every knee should bow, of things in Heaven and in earth, is used as a Masonic word. The imitation of Our Lord on the cross of Calvary becomes a Masonic sign. "*Rex Crucifixus*," accompanied by a thrusting of the finger into the palm of the hand, in imitation of St. Thomas proving the reality of the sacred wounds, will identify one as an installed Masonic Prior.[2] Is nothing sacred in this game of pretending to be Knights ?

It is surely paradoxical that an Order professing to be devoted solely and whole-heartedly to the defence of the Christian faith, if it is to be taken seriously and not as a childish romp, should not only be outside the Church which is the true guardian of that faith, but unrecognized by the Church, keeping its secrets from the Church, and, as an Order, having nothing to do with the Church. It was when the Knights Templar of old allowed too great a spirit of independence, and the infiltration of secret and heretical teachings into their Order, that they fell away from the Church, and suffered suppression.

When the Christian lad is confirmed, when he is initiated, so to speak, into the true mystery of the Mystical Body of Christ, he promises, without any frills or threats of decapitation, that he will be Christ's faithful soldier and servant until his life's end. Is this Sacrament of Holy Church in need of being supplemented by these bizarre schismatic secret rites ? What, exactly, do they add to it, and why ?

1. *Freemasonry and the Ancient Gods,* p. 306 *et seq.*
2. This word and grip appear in the inner workings of the installation of the Eminent Prior.

APPENDIX A

THE MYSTIC SHRINE

Their dress was Moslem, but you might have guessed
That these were merely masquerading Tartars,
And that beneath each Turkish-fashioned vest
Lurk'd Christianity ; which sometimes barters
Her inward grace for outward show, and makes
It difficult to shun some strange mistakes.

Lord Byron, Don Juan.

The Ancient Arabic Order Nobles of the Mystic Shrine is a purely American degree which indeed would not be tolerated by British Freemasons. Members must be either Knights Templar, or Masons of the 32nd degree of the Ancient and Accepted Scottish Rite.[1]

The legend that this order with its ritual was imported to America from Mecca, Cairo, or any other Moslem centre, or that it has any history at all before about 1870 is regarded by Shriners themselves as purely mythical. A certain Dr. Walter M. Fleming of New York, the first Grand Potentate, together with a Mr. Florence, and the celebrated liturgist of the Northern Jurisdiction Ancient and Accepted Rite Charles T. McClenachan seem to have been mainly responsible for the adolescent and occasionally Rabelaisian nadir of drivelling tomfoolery and burlesque blasphemies which serves as its ritual.

It may be freely admitted at the outset that no Shriner dreams of taking it at all seriously ; they do not accept the religion of Islam, and it is purely in a spirit of frolic that the Mohammedan Allah is invoked. The shrine is a sort of Masonic playground, the most serious side of which is the truly magnificent work which they finance for crippled children. Their hospitals and infantile paralysis research work are beyond all criticism.

1. See *History of the Imperial Council, Nobles of the Mystic Shrine*, Cincinnati, 1919 ; *Early History of the Ancient Arabic Order of the Nobles of the Mystic Shrine in North America* (1918) by James McGee ; and *Mecca, the Parent Temple* (1894) by Dr. Walter M. Fleming and William S. Paterson.

The ritual[1] is mainly concerned with tests of bravery and endurance on the same mental plane as the undergraduate hazings indulged in by the Greek-letter fraternities in American colleges and universities. The whole absurd business might be dismissed at once as a harmless frolic were not the joke in such extremely poor taste, to say the least of it.

The Solemn Obligation, in view of what follows, is utter blasphemy. It is sworn upon the Bible and the Koran jointly, and contains the following phrases :—"I do hereby, upon this Bible, and on the mysterious legend of the Koran, and its dedication to the Mahommedan faith, promise and swear and vow...I do here register a sacred vow...I here register this irrevocable vow, subscribing myself bound thereto as well as binding myself by the obligation of the prerequisite to this membership, that of a Knight Templar or that of a thirty-second degree A. and A. Scottish Rite Mason, in wilful violation whereof may I incur the fearful penalty of having my eyeballs pierced to the centre with a three-edged blade, my feet flayed and I be forced to walk the hot sands upon the sterile shores of the Red Sea until the flaming sun shall strike me with livid plague, and may Allah, the god of Arab, Moslem and Mohammedan, the god of our fathers, support me to the entire fulfilment of the same. Amen, Amen, Amen."

After which the Illustrious Potentate calls upon him to seal the oath by kissing the Bible " *in token of his sincerity !* "

The secrets protected by this sacred and irrevocable Bible-Koran oath consist, among other puerilities, of what is known as the Bung-Hole Test, in which two blindfolded initiates crawl into opposite ends of a metal tube, and of course stick in the middle. In the course of the further ceremonies are a mock hanging, a mock beheading, and a mock drinking of the blood of

---

1. A pirated edition of the Shrine ritual is issued by Ezra A. Cook, Publisher, Chicago. I laid this aside as spurious and utterly incredible until I compared it later with the official ritual issued by an Ohio Temple, lent me by an American Shriner who vouched for its authenticity and showed me his own Shrine certificates. The two rituals agreed almost *verbatim*, and entirely so in the portions which I quote. A third version from the Allen Publishing Co. of New York came to hand later and again was identical with the other two. The secrecy is supposed to be such that only officers are allowed to possess rituals. The punishment for lending a ritual to a Noble not an officer is, for the first offence, a fine ; for the second, expulsion.

the victim, all carried out with as much macabre realism as grease-paint and subdued lighting will allow. Interspersed among these more gruesome matters, however, may be culled the following mystic gems of impeccable refinement.

The blindfolded candidate is stretched on the floor. " While in this position a small dog or one who can imitate a dog is caused to give a sharp yelp, just after a few drops of warm water have been squirted on the candidate's face, with the remark, " Take that dog out, he has just p......d in the face of Mr......."

Afterwards " He is then conducted to the Illustrious Potentate, whom he is commanded to approach with humble and great reverence, stooping very low on his knees, his head near the ground, his buttocks elevated, where he receives the ' Grand Salaam,' that is a blow on his buttocks with two pieces of board between which are placed some torpedoes that explode with a loud report when they come together. This is called the Grand Salaam or stroke of introduction."

After the minor discomfort of being stripped to his drawers and made to sit on a sponge full of ice water he comes to his most embarassing test. Still stripped and blindfolded, he is led around the room several times and then halted.

" Conductor (to Candidate): This is the place where our brethren stop to sprinkle the Devil's Pass with urine. You will contribute a few drops of urine to commemorate the time and place where all who pass here renounce the wiles and evils of the world to worship at the Shrine of Islam. Only a few drops will do.

" Candidate begins to obey instructions when the blinder is jerked from his eyes and he beholds before him a group disguised as women..."

It is not altogether clear from the ritual whether the Bible remains present and open during these mystic rites ; probably by this time the candidate has forgotten that it has played any part in the ceremonies, or that he has so recently saluted it with a kiss. The lecture included in the closing ceremonies, however, gives a certain element of moral uplift and a strange spiritual interpretation to the last rite quoted :—

Illustrious Potentate From where to what place have you travelled ?

Chief Rabban	To the East over the hot burning sands of the desert.
Ill. P.	Where were you stopped at ?
C.R.	At the Devil's Pass.
Ill. P.	What were you required to do ?
C.R.	*I was required to pray.*
Ill. P.	Why were you required to do this ?
C.R.	As a token of my renouncing the wiles and evils of the world, and be granted permission to worship at the Shrine.

More than half a million American masons demonstrate their retarded adolescence by being Nobles of the Mystic Shrine. Even Bishops of the Protestant Episcopal Church, I am told, have not found it derogatory to exchange their mitres for the jaunty red fez of the Order, to join in these preposterously unbecoming capers. Crippled children indeed may rise up and call them blessed, but surely there are more becoming ways of banding men together in the sacred cause of benevolence. O Charity, what inanities are committed in thy name !

APPENDIX B

ANGLICAN CLERGY IN HIGHER DEGREES

It must be emphasized that this is very far from being a complete list of all Anglican Masonic clergy ; it gives only those in the degrees for which there is a Christian qualification for membership, that is, the Ancient and Accepted Rite, and the Knights Templar. A complete list of all the clergy in the Craft would be many times larger.

It does not include the clergy of the Scottish Episcopal Church, the Episcopal Church in the United States, or of the Church in Canada, except where they are under English or Irish Masonic jurisdiction.

Figures and initials in brackets after the name indicate the degree as follows :—

(18) *Knight of the Pelican and Eagle, Sovereign Prince Rose Croix of Heredom*

(28) *Chevalier du Soleil, or Knight of the Sun (worked only under Irish jurisdiction)*

(30) *Grand Elected Knight Kadosh, Knight of the Black and White Eagle*

(31) *Grand Inspector Inquisitor Commander*

(32) *Sublime Prince of the Royal Secret*

(33) *Grand Inspector General*

(K.T.) *United Religious and Military Orders of the Temple and Hospital (Knight Templar)*

BISHOPS

BARNE, the Right Rev. George Dunsford, former Lord Bishop of Lahore (33, K.T.)

CRICK, the Right Rev. Douglas Henry, Lord Bishop of Chester (K.T.)

DE MEL, the Right Rev. Hiyanirind Lakdasa Jacob, Lord Bishop of Kurunagala (Ceylon) (K.T.)

HALWARD, the Right Rev. Nelson Victor, Assistant Bishop of British Columbia (K.T.)

HAVARD, the Right Rev. William Thomas, Lord Bishop of St. David's (18)

HERBERT, the Right Rev. Percy Mark, Lord Bishop of Norwich (K.T.)

HILLIARD, the Right Rev. William George, Bishop Coadjutor of Sydney (30)

HUBBACK, the Right Rev. George Clay, former Metropolitan of India (32, K.T.)

HUGHES, the Right Rev. Albert Edward, former Lord Bishop of Kilmore, Elphin and Ardagh (30)

KERR, the Right Rev. William Shaw, Lord Bishop of Down and Dromore (32)

KNIGHT, the Most Rev. Alan John, Lord Bishop of Guiana, Archbishop and Metropolitan of the West Indies (31, K.T.)

KNYVETT, the Right Rev. Carey Frederick, Lord Bishop Suffragan of Selby (30)

McCANN, the Most Rev. James, Lord Bishop of Meath (18, K.T.)

PARHAM, the Right Rev. Arthur Groom, former Lord Bishop Suffragan of Reading (18, K.T.)

SURTEES, the Right Rev. William Frederick, Lord Bishop Suffragan of Crediton (31, K.T.)

TYNER, the Right Rev. Richard, Lord Bishop of Clogher (18)

WILSON, the Right Rev. John Leonard, Lord Bishop of Birmingham (K.T.)

OTHER CLERGY

ABBOTT, the Rev. John Charles (18)

ADDIS, the Rev. Ellis Avenel (18)

ADDISON, the Ven. Archdeacon Lancelot Farquharson (18)

ALLAN, the Rev. Alexander Dean Hugh (30)

ALLENBY, the Rev. David Howard Nicholas, S.S.M. (18)

AMES, the Rev. Edward Francis Welldon (18)

AMIES, the Rev. Daniel John (18)

ANDERSON, the Rev. John (18)

ARMITAGE, the Rev. James (18)

ARMSTRONG, the Rev. Arthur Evelyn (K.T.)

ARMSTRONG, the Ven. Archdeacon Mervyn (18)

ASKINS, the Very Rev. William James (30)

ASTBURY, Canon Harold Stanley (18)

BABINGTON, the Very Rev. Richard (18)

BAILEY, the Rev. John Henry Shackleton (31)

BALL, the Rev. Robert George (18)

BANNISTER, the Rev. Lambrock Flower Long (K.T.)

BARNETT, the Rev. Edward John Gaitskell (18)

BARRETT, the Ven. Archdeacon William Rothwell (30)

BARTELS, the Rev. Reginald Cain (18)

BASKIN, the Rev. John Evett D'Acre (18)

BATCHELOR, Canon Alfred Williams (30)

BATTERSBY, the Rev. Alfred (18)

BATTERSBY, the Rev. Gerald William (18, K.T.)

BAYLIS, the Rev. Harry (31, K.T.)

BEAUFOY, the Rev. Mark Raymond (18)

BELL, the Rev. Charles Louis (18, K.T.)

BENNETT, Preb. Bernard Callender (18, K.T.)

BENNETT, the Rev. Reginald Ward (18, K.T.)

BENNETT, Canon Stamford Herbert Alfred (18)

BEZZANT, Canon James Stanley (18)

BIRCH, the Ven. Francis Butler Cregoe (18)

BIRD, Canon Richard (18)

BLEASE, the Rev. John Thomas (18, K.T.)

BLOWEY, the Rev. Harry Francis Tozer (31, K.T.)

BOLTON, Canon Charles Arnold (31, K.T.)

BOOTY, the Rev. Jack Grattan (30, K.T.)

BORDER, the Rev. Joseph Thomas Ross (18)

BORRETT, the Rev. Charles Walter (18)

BOURCHIER, the Rev. Chancellor Wilfrid La Rive (18)

BOURNE, the Rev. William Temple (18, K.T.)

BOYLDEW, the Rev. William Edward McCaughan (18)

BRACEWELL, Canon William (31)

BRAHAM, the Rev. Norman (18)

BRALEY, Canon Evelyn Foley (18, K.T.)

BREENE, the Rev. Chancellor Richard Simmons (28)

BRERETON, Canon Philip Harrington Lloyd (18, K.T.)

BRETTON, the Rev. William Frederick (18)
BRIGGS, the Rev. Joseph William (31, K.T.)
BRITTON, the Rev. Frederic Henry (18)
BROADHURST, the Rev. John James (18)
BROOKE, the Rev. John (18)
BROWN, the Rev. Cyril Alfred (30)
BROWN, The Rev. Cyril James (18)
BROWN, the Rev. Herbert Stanley (30)
BROWN, the Rev. Philip Stanley (30)
BROWN, the Rev. William Arthur James (18, K.T.)
BROWN-BERESFORD, the Rev. James Henry (18)
BROWNE, the Rev. Francis Bernard Ross (K.T.)
BROWNE, the Ven. Archdeacon Thomas Robert (18)
BRUCE, the Rev. Francis Rosslyn Courtenay (30)
BULL, the Ven. Archdeacon Charles Ernest Samuel (18)
BURGESS, the Rev. Leonard Arthur (18)
BURNE, the Rev. Harry (K.T.)
BURROWS, Canon Frederick (30, K.T.)
BUTTERFIELD, the Rev. Roland Potter (18)
BUTTERWORTH, Canon John Ivan Spenser (K.T.)
BUTTON, the Rev. Kenneth Francis (18)

CALDICOTT, Canon Joseph George (18)
CALLOW the Rev. Victor Allen (18, K.T.)
CAMPBELL, the Rev. Robert (18)
CANTLOW, Canon Joseph Charles (30, K.T.)
CARDELL-OLIVER, the Rev. Ivan Alexander (18)
CARDEN, Preb. Stanley Roots (18, K.T.)
CAREW, the Rev. Eustace Harold (18)
CARPENTER, Canon Leavett Charles Carpenter (30)
CARRICK, the Rev. Francis Robert Powles (18)
CARSON, the Rev. John Henry (18)

CARVER, the Rev. Alfred Basil (18)
CASHMORE, the Rev. Cyril (18, K.T.)
CASHMORE, Canon Thomas Herbert (18, K.T.)
CATLEY, the Rev. Alfred Mollett (18)
CATTELL, Canon Frederick Laughton (30)
CHAFFEY, the Rev. Kenneth Arthur (18)
CHAMBERLAIN, Canon George Ashton (18)
CHANCE, Canon Albert Edward (K.T.)
CHAPMAN, Canon John Roland (18)
CHARLES, the Rev. Austin Clelland Flowerday (18)
CHATFIELD, the Rev. Benjamin George (18)
CHAYTOR, the Rev. Henry John (18)
CHISHOLM, the Ven. Archdeacon Alexander (31)
CLACY, the Rev. Thomas William (18)
CLARENDON, the Rev. William Randal Slacke (30, K.T.)
CLARKE, the Rev. Harold Walton (18)
CLARKE, the Ven. Archdeacon Maurice (30)
CLARKE, the Rev. Oliver White (18, K.T.)
CLARKE, the Rev. Wilfred Landsell (K.T.)
CLARKE, the Rev. William Edgar (18)
CLOUGH, the Rev. Percy William Gliddon (K.T.)
COCKS, Canon William (18, K.T.)
COLYER, the Rev. Frederick John (K.T.)
COOPER, the Rev. Oscar William Charles (18)
COOPER, the Ven. Archdeacon Samuel James (18)
CORY, the Rev. Canon Alexander (18)
COTTAM, the Rev. Frank (18, K.T.)
CRANSWICK, the Rev. Rupert Loraine (18)
CRESSWELL, the Rev. Cyril Leonard (18)
CRICK, the Very Rev. Thomas, Dean of Rochester (18)

DANGERFIELD, the Rev. Arthur Thomas (K.T.)
DART, Canon John Lovering Campbell (30, K.T)
DATSON, the Rev. John Harold (18)
DAVIES, the Rev. Benjamin (18)
DAVIES, the Rev. David (30)
DAVIES, the Very Rev. David Jones, Dean of Wellington (18)
DAVIES, Canon John Caradog (30)
DAVIES, the Rev. Meredith (K.T.)
DAYNES, Canon Francis John (18)
DEANE, the Rev. Ronald Peter (18)
DENMAN, the Rev. Ronald (18)
DOBBIN, Canon William Hume (18)
DODD, Canon James (31)
DOVE, the Rev. Frederick John (18)
DOWNHAM, the Rev. Edward (K.T.)
DUMPHREYS, the Rev. William Hugh Stewart (18)
DUNN, the Rev. Albert Reginald (30)
DYSON, Canon Oswald (18, K.T.)

ECCLES, the Rev. Lionel Gilbert Frank St. John (18)
EDDLESTON, the Rev. William (18, K.T.)
EDWARDS, the Rev. Alfred Herbert (18)
EDWARDS, the Rev. Frank Llewellyn (18)
EDWARDSON, the Rev. Joseph (K.T.)
ELDRIDGE-DOYLE, Canon Claude James (18)
ELLIOTT, Canon William Henry Hatchard (30)
ELWELL, the Rev. George Henry Willmott (30)
ESSAME, the Rev. William Guthrie (18)
ETHELL, the Rev. Thomas Frederick (18, K.T.)
EVANS-PROSSER, the Rev. Raymond Alfred (30)
EVERITT, the Rev. Thomas Augustus (18, K.T.)
EZZY, the Rev. Roy Albert (18)

FARLIE, the Rev. Stanley (18)
FARNELL, the Rev. Alan James (18)

FARROW, Canon Alfred Ellis (30)
FAVELL, the Rev. William (K.T.)
FERRARO, Preb. Francis William (18, K.T.)
FIRTH, the Rev. John (K.T.)
FISHER, the Rev. Francis Vivian (18)
FITZHERBERT, the Ven. Archdeacon Henry Edward (18)
FLYNN, the Rev. Thomas Henley (K.T.)
FORTESCUE, the Ven. Archdeacon Cecil Francis (30)
FOSTER, Canon Henry Clapham (18)
FOWLER, the Rev. Richard Harold (30, K.T.)
FOX, the Rev. Charles Alfred (18)
FRANKLAND, the Rev. John Naylor (30, K.T.)
FRANKLIN, the Rev. Henry Laurence (18)
FRENCH, the Rev. Victor John (18)
FROSSARD, the Very Rev. Edward Louis (18)
FRY, the Rev. John George (18, K.T.)

GARDINER, Canon Sydney Reade (18)
GASKING, the Rev. Clement Augustine (30)
GERRY, the Rev. Allan Ronald (18, K.T.)
GIBSON, the Rev. John Paul Stewart Riddell (18)
GICK, the Rev. Arthur Eldon (28)
GILBERT, the Rev. Frederic James (18)
GILL, the Rev. Robert Henry (18, K.T.)
GILLETT, the Rev. James (30, K.T.)
GILSON, the Rev. George Cameron (30)
GODBER, the Rev. William Thomas (K.T.)
GOODALL, the Rev. Joseph Brittain (30)
GORRIE, the Rev. Leslie Manifold (30)
GORSE, the Rev. Henry (18)
GOULD, the Rev. William Leonard Powell (30, K.T.)
GRAHAM, Canon Henry Burrans (18, K.T.)
GRAHAM, the Rev. Nathaniel Robert Albert (18)

GRAY, Canon James (30, K.T.)
GREENUP, the Rev. Geoffrey Frederick (30, K.T.)
GREENWOOD, the Rev. Arthur John (K.T.)
GREEVES, the Rev. Alfred Theodore Wellesley (K.T.)
GREGORY, the Rev. John Benjamin Evans (18, K.T.)
GREGORY, the Rev. Wallie Milton Vivian (18, K.T.)
GRIFFITH - GREEN, the Rev. Charles Beauchamp (18)
GROOM, the Rev. William Herbert (18, K.T.)
GROSVENOR, Major the Rev. John Ernest (33, K.T.)
GROVES, the Rev. Gerald William Norris (18, K.T.)
GROVES, the Rev. Sidney John Selby (18, K.T.)
GUEST - WILLIAMS, the Rev. Alyn Arthur (30, K.T.)

HADFIELD, the Rev. Frederic Walter (18)
HALEWOOD, the Rev. Peter Bolland (18, K.T.)
HALL, the Rev. George Roland (30, K.T.)
HALL, the Rev. William John (18)
HALLIWELL, Canon Thomas (18)
HARFITT, the Rev. Frederick Harry Emmanuel (18)
HARRISON, Preb. John Ellis Scott (18)
HART, the Rev. Howard Percy (18)
HARTFORD, Canon Richard Randall (18)
HARTWIG, Canon Vernon Desmond (18)
HARVEY, the Rev. Thomas Sidney (18)
HAWKINS, the Rev. Ralph Gordon (18)
HAWORTH, the Rev. Harry Cecil (18, K.T.)
HAYDOCK, the Rev. William (18)
HEARD, the Rev. Alexander St. John (K.T.)
HERBERT, the Rev. Thomas Davies (18, K.T.)
HESELTON, the Rev. Rodolphus Thomas (18, K.T.)
HEWITT, the Ven. Archdeacon Alexander Chichele (30)
HEYDON, the Rev. Francis Garland William Woodard (18)

HIBBERT, Canon Harold Victor (18)
HICKSON, the Rev. Wilmot Thomas (K.T.)
HILL, the Rev. James Llewellyn Grice (18)
HOBSON, the Rev. John (18)
HODGE, the Rev. Herbert Alfred (18)
HOLLAND, the Rev. John Sharples (18)
HOLLOWAY, the Rev. Algernon James (K.T.)
HOLMES, the Rev. Melville Edward (K.T.)
HONE, the Rev. Ernest Archibald (K.T.)
HOPKINS, the Rev. Alexander Charles (30)
HOULDEN, the Rev. William Ernest Leonard (18)
HOWELLS, the Very Rev. Adelukun Williamson Fowell Olumide (18)
HUGHES, Canon David (K.T.)
HUGHES, the Rev. William James (K.T.)
HULLEY, Flt. Lt. the Very Rev. Charles Edward (K.T.)
HUMPHREYS, the Very Rev. Thomas Sutcliffe (18)
HURST, the Rev. Harry Thorley (30)

IBBOTSON, the Rev. Alick (K.T.)
IRESON, Canon Arthur Stanley (18)
IRVINE, the Rev. Thomas Thurstan (18)
IRWIN, the Rev. Samuel Francis (18)
ISBISTER, the Rev. Sydney Charles Molson (18, K.T.)

JAMES, the Rev. Arthur Dyfrig (18)
JAMESON, the Rev. Bert Desmond (18)
JAYAWARDENA, the Rev. Basil Stanley Herbert (K.T.)
JENKINS, the Ven. Archdeacon Allan McQuire (18)
JENKINS, the Rev. John Lewis (K.T.)
JOHN, the Rev. Arthur Gwynne (K.T.)
JOHN, the Rev. William Raymond (18)
JOHN, the Rev. Winston Gwynne (18)

CHRISTIAN BY DEGREES

JOHNSON, Canon William
Robert (18)
JOLLY, Canon Frederick George
(18)
JONES, the Rev. Arthur Edward
(18)
JONES, Canon Arthur Oswald (18,
K.T.)
JONES, the Rev. Edward Ellis (30)
JONES, the Rev. Edward Harries
(18)
JONES, the Rev. Eric Bertram
(K.T.)
JONES, Canon Gerald Ernest
(18)
JONES, the Rev. Gryffydh Watcyn
(K.T.)
JONES, the Very Rev. Herbert
Arthur (18, K.T.)
JONES, the Rev. Horace Edwin
(30, K.T.)
JOSE, the Rev. Jack Rowse (18)
JOURDAN, the Rev. George
Viviliers (18)
JUDD, Preb. Arnold Frederick
(18)

KAA, the Rev. Te Angahiku Te
Hihi Kakahukiwi (18)
KAY, Canon Kenneth (18)
KAYLL, the Rev. Arthur Gregory
(18)
KEAR, the Rev. Ivor Evans (18)
KEIGHTLEY, the Rev. Frederick
Richardson (18)
KELLY, Canon David (18)
KENNEDY-NEWMAN, the Rev.
Frank (18, K.T.)
KERR, the Rev. Cecil Maurice
(18, K.T.)
KING, the Rev. Cuthbert (30,
K.T.)
KING, the Rev. Edwin (18)
KIRKPATRICK, the Rev. Robert
(18)
KITCHENER, the Rev. Harold
(18, K.T.)
KRISHNASWAMY, the Rev. Paul
Aiyaiyengar (18, K.T.)

LACKEY, the Rev. William (30,
K.T.)
LAMB, the Rev. Percy Cecil
Chalmers (18)
LAMPE, the Rev. Geoffrey
William Hugo (18)
LANCASTER, the Rev. Lyonel
Lewis (347)
LANCE, the Rev. Raymond
Sullivan Knox (K.T.)

LANGDON, the Rev. Lewis
Samuel (K.T.)
LANGDON, the Rev. Percy
George (30)
LANGDON, the Rev. William
Ancell Martin (K.T.)
LANGLEY, the Rev. Llewellyn
William Charles (18)
LANGTON, the Rev. Hugh
Banastre (18)
LATTER, the Rev. Kenneth
Alfred (18, K.T.)
LAWRENCE, the Rev. Marcus
Hughes (K.T.)
LAWSON, the Rev. Julius Thomas
Svend (18, K.T.)
LEE, Canon William Henry Askins
(18)
LEIGH, the Rev. Richard Kenyon
(18)
LeMASURIER, the Rev. Arthur
George (K.T.)
LEONARD, the Rev. Francis
Joseph (18)
LEWIS, the Rev. Jenkin Lewis
Dyfed (30, K.T.)
LEWIS, the Rev. John Rapley (18)
LEWIS-CROSBY, the Very Rev.
Ernest Henry (30)
LINTON, the Rev. Sydney (18)
LIPSCOMB, the Rev. Gun Hatt
(18, K.T.)
LISTER, Canon John George (18,
K.T.)
LITTLER, the Rev. Oscar (18,
K.T.)
LLOYD, the Rev. Benjamin (18,
K.T.)
LLOYD, the Rev. John Godfrey
(K.T.)
LOUND, the Rev. William Edward
Ashworth (18)
LOUGHEED, Preb. Britain (18)
LOWMAN, the Rev. Edward
Sydney Charles (18)

McFALL, the Very Rev. Thomas
Henry Crampton (18)
McGARVEY, the Rev. Samuel
Rentoul (18)
MACK, the Rev. Devereux Robert
John (18)
MACKAY, Canon Colin
Campbell (K.T.)
McKELVIE, the Rev. Robert
Fritz Stanley (18, K.T.)
MACKENZIE, the Rev. Ramsay
Malcolm Bolton (30)
MACKRELL, the Rev. Arthur
Thomas John (K.T.)

McLEOD, the Rev. Douglas (18)

McLEOD, the Rev. Wellington Alexander (18)

McTIGHE, the Very Rev. Robert (18)

MALCOLM, the Ven. Archdeacon Douglas Blomfield (18)

MANGOLD, the Rev. Arthur James (18)

MANN, the Rev. Edwin Eustace de Lacy (18)

MANNING, Preb. William Robert Fitzgerald (18)

MANTON, the Rev. William (18, K.T.)

MARSHALL, Canon Guy (K.T.)

MARTYR, the Rev. James Graham de Garlieb (K.T.)

MASSIAH, the Rev. Henry (32)

MELHUISH, the Rev. John (18)

MELVILLE, the Rev. Harold Augustine (18)

MEREDITH, the Rev. Ronald Duncan d'Esterre (K.T.)

METTRICK, the Rev. Francis (18)

MILLER, the Rev. Donald Campbell (30)

MOERAN, Preb. William Graham (18)

MOIR, the Rev. Edwin Cecil (18)

MONEY, Canon William Taylor (32, K.T.)

MONK, the Rev. Arthur Sydney (30, K.T.)

MOORE, the Rev. Joseph William Ball (18, K.T.)

MORAN, Canon Walter Isidore (K.T.)

MORCOM-HARNEIS, the Rev. Theophilus William (18)

MORRAN, Canon Lionel Manus (18)

MORRIS, Canon Richard Stafford (30, K.T.)

MORTLOCK, Canon Charles Bernard (18, K.T.)

MOSS, the Rev. William Stanley (18)

MOSS-BLUNDELL, the Rev. Reginald Seymour (18)

MOSSE, the Rev. Charles Herbert (32, K.T.)

MOYES, the Rev. Clifford Leigh (30)

MUMFORD, the Rev. William Hugh Nottage (18)

MUNRO, Canon Alexander Robert Stewart (18)

MYRES, the Rev. Miles Weight (33, K.T.)

NAPIER-MUNN, the Rev. William Ernest (18)

NAYLOR, the Very Rev. Alfred Thomas Arthur (30, K.T.)

NIBLOCK, the Rev. Gordon (K.T.)

NICHOLAS, the Rev. Samuel Richard Stephen (18)

NORTON, the Rev. Herbert Arthur John Rubens (18)

O'BRIEN, the Rev. Ronald Arthur (18)

OSMAN, the Rev. Alfred Lancaster (18)

OWEN, Canon Gwilym

PAGE, the Rev. Gerald Webster (18)

PALLOT, the Rev. Elias George (30, K.T.)

PARRY, the Rev. Haydn Alexander (18)

PARRY-WILLIAMS, the Rev. Ezra Charles William (K.T.)

PATON-WILLIAMS, Canon Francis (30, K.T.)

PATTERSON, the Rev. Robert Dixon (18)

PAYNTER, Canon Francis Samuel (32, K.T.)

PEACOCK, Canon Wilfrid Morgan (30. K.T.)

PENNEY, the Rev. Arthur Edwin (18)

PERCIVAL, the Rev. Sidney Theodore (32, K.T.)

PERKINS, the Rev. Harry (K.T.)

PHILLIMORE, the Rev. Edward Granville (18, K.T.)

PHIPPS-WILLIAMS, the Rev. Henry (18)

PHYTHIAN-ADAMS, Canon William John Telia Phythian (K.T.)

PICKLES, Canon Harold (30, K.T.)

PIKE, the Rev. Frederick Aneurin (18)

PIRANI, the Rev. Maurice Russell (18)

PIZEY, the Rev. Edward John (18, K.T.)

PLAISTOWE, the Rev. Ronald Percy Frank (18)

POLLARD, the Rev. Francis Albert (K.T.)

POPHAM, Canon Frederick Stephen (30, K.T.)

POWELL, the Rev. Francis George (30, K.T.)
POYNTZ, the Rev. James (18)
PRATT, the Rev. Francis William (K.T.)
PRATT, the Ven. Archdeacon Isaac Henry (28)
PRATT, the Rev. John Francis Isaac (18)
PRENTIS, the Rev. Thomas David (18)
PREST, the Rev. Walter (18)
PRIOR, Canon William Henry (18)
PUGH, Preb. James Ernest (18, K.T.)
PURVIS, the Rev. John Stanley (18, K.T.)

READ, the Rev. Frank (18)
REED, the Rev. Lancelot George (30)
REINDORP, the Rev. Hector William (31)
RICHARDS, the Rev. Robert William Bruce (18)
RIDINGS, the Rev. Alfred (K.T.)
RILEY, the Rev. John Edward (18, K.T.)
RIMMER, Canon Joseph Stuart (30, K.T.)
ROACH, the Rev. John Edward Wynne (18, K.T.)
ROAKE, the Rev. Albert Henry (30)
ROBERTON, the Rev. Edward Heton (32)
ROBERTS, the Rev. Norman Lee (18)
ROBERTS, the Rev. Samuel James (18)
ROBERTS, Canon Windsor (30, K.T.)
ROBERTSON, the Ven. Archdeacon Charles Shearer (30, K.T.)
ROBERTSON, the Rev. Michael William (18)
ROBINSON, Canon Walter Sydney (18)
ROBSON, Canon James Russel (31, K.T.)
ROFFE-SILVESTER, the Rev. Charles Geoffrey (18, K.T.)
ROGERS, the Very Rev. Edgar (32, K.T.)
ROGERS, the Ven. Archdeacon Reginald Pearson (30, K.T.)
ROGERS, the Rev. Thomas Alfred (30)

ROOKE, the Rev. George William Emmanuel (18)
ROPER, Canon George Hamilton (18)
ROYLE, the Rev. Edward (K.T.)
ROYSE, the Ven. Archdeacon Thomas Henry Foorde Russell Buckworth (18)
RUSSELL, the Rev. Morris Charles (K.T.)
RUSSELL-CHAPMAN, the Rev. Walter William (18, K.T.)

SALT, the Rev. Selwyn Marson Ivon (18)
SANSOM, Canon Joseph Donald (18)
SARA, the Rev. George Claud (18)
SAUNDERS, the Rev. Kenley Frederick (18)
SAUNDERS, the Rev. William Daniel (30, K.T.)
SAUNDERSON, the Rev. Harry Vincent (18)
SAWYER, the Rev. William Ellis (18)
SCANLON, the Rev. Thomas Henry (18)
SCOTT, the Rev. Malcolm de Burgh (30)
SEARS, the Ven. Archdeacon Frederick William (18)
SEATON, Canon John Alderson (18)
SEMPLE, the Rev. Edgar George (30)
SENIOR, the Rev. Sam (18)
SHARPE, Canon Thomas Gordon (18)
SHAW, Canon Kenneth Edwin (18)
SHELMERDINE, Preb. Thomas Greatorex (K.T.)
SIDWELL, the Rev. Walter Thomas (18)
SIMONS, the Rev. Lewis Christmas (18, K.T.)
SIMPSON, the Rev. Fred Stanley Wood (K.T.)
SIMPSON, the Rev. Percy John Frank (30, K.T.)
SINGLETON, the Rev. Thomas Bayden (31)
SKENE, Canon Frederick Norman (30)
SKEY, the Very Rev. Oswald William Laurie (18)

SKIPWITH, the Rev. Osmund Humbertson (18)

SLATOR, the Rev. William Thompson Howard (18)

SMALLFIELD, the Rev. William Mandeno (18)

SMART, the Rev. Donald Arthur (K.T.)

SMETHURST, Canon Arthur Frederick (18, K.T.)

SMITH, the Rev. Leslie Percival Gordon (K.T.)

SMITH, the Rev. Stanley (18)

SMYTH, Canon Alfred Victor (18)

SNELL, Preb. Leland John Blashford (18)

SNOWDEN, the Rev. Henry Charles (K.T.)

SOADY, the Rev. Francis Benney (18)

SOMERVILLE, the Rev. Kenneth Brooks (18)

SOWDEN, the Rev. Jack Leslie (18)

SPENCER-HALL, the Ven. Archdeacon Walter Charles (18)

STALEY, Canon James Edwin (18, K.T.)

STANTON, Canon Robert James (18)

STEAD, Canon Francis Thomas (30, K.T.)

STEVENS, the Rev. Joseph (18)

STEVENSON, the Rev. Ronald (K.T.)

STEWART, the Rev. Reginald Boylette (30)

STOPFORD, the Rev. James Stanley Bird (30, K.T.)

STOTE-BLANDY, the Rev. Gordon Blandy (18)

SUTTON, the Rev. Alan Walker (K.T.)

SUTTON, the Rev. Francis Joseph (31, K.T.)

TAYLOR, Canon Thomas Whitehead (18)

THOMAS, the Ven. Archdeacon John Christopher Columbus (18)

THOMAS, Canon Walter George (18)

THOMSON, Canon Andrew Nathaniel (18)

THURLOW, the Rev. Alfred Gilbert Goddard (18)

TILL, the Rev. Kenneth James (K.T.)

TINDALL, the Rev. Horace George (18)

TOBIAS, the Rev. Chancellor John (28)

TOBIAS, the Rev. Matthew (18)

TOOP, the Rev. William John (18, K.T.)

TOPHAM, Canon John (18)

TOWNSEND, the Rev. Francis Algernon (18)

TREACHER, Preb. Hubert Harold (18)

TRIVETT, the Very Rev. Alexander Christopher Sargent (K.T.)

TRUTWEIN, the Rev. Percy William (18)

TURNER, the Rev. Everett George (30)

TYDEMAN, the Rev. Richard (18)

UPRICHARD, Canon Leonard Victor (18)

VAUGHAN, Canon George (K.T.)

VERITY, the Rev. Richard Ridley (30, K.T.)

VICKERY, Canon Hadden Kingston (18)

WALDEGRAVE, Canon George Turner (33, K.T.)

WALDEN-ASPY, the Rev. Frederick Charles (30)

WALKER, Canon John Arthur (K.T.)

WALLER, the Rev. Charles Lansley (31)

WALLER, the Ven. Archdeacon John Thomas (31)

WALLIS, the Rev. Montague Calverley (30, K.T.)

WALTON, the Rev. John William (18)

WARING, the Rev. Thomas Power (18)

WATKINS, the Rev. Thomas George David (K.T.)

WEAVER, the Rev. Frederick William (K.T.)

WEBB, the Rev. Alexander Lewis (18)

WEBBER, the Rev. Thomas Arthur (K.T.)

WEIR, the Rev. Robert Edward (18)

WESTON, the Rev. Donald Reginald (18, K.T.)

WHEATLEY, the Rev. James Edward (18)
WHEELER, the Rev. George Edward (18)
WHEELER, the Rev. Malcolm John Stuart (18)
WHITE, the Very Rev. John Lawrence (18)
WHITEHOUSE, Canon Victor Harold (K.T.)
WHITING, the Rev. Thomas Edward (18)
WHITTLE, The Ven. Archdeacon John Tyler (K.T.)
WIBBY, the Rev. William Edward (32, K.T.)
WICKING, the Rev. David Henry (18)
WILKINSON, the Rev. James Percy (30, K.T.)
WILLIAMS, Canon Anthony Lewis Elliott (K.T.)
WILLIAMS, the Ven. Archdeacon Archibald Morlais (18)
WILLIAMS, the Rev. Bernard Prior (30)
WILLIAMS, Canon Clifford George (18)
WILLIAMS, the Rev. David Francis (18)
WILLIAMS, the Rev. Howell Saunders (18)
WILLIAMS, the Rev. John Henry (18)
WILLIAMS, the Rev. John James (18)

WILLIAMS, the Rev. Kenneth Edward Chilton (18)
WILLIAMS, the Rev. William David Conwyl (18)
WILLIS, the Rev. Harold Stanley (18)
WILSON, the Rev. David Frederick Ruddell (30, K.T.)
WILSON, the Rev. Hugh McDowall (18)
WILSON, the Rev. William Wyatt (K.T.)
WOOD, the Rev. Charles Henry Joseph (K.T.)
WOOD, the Rev. Edward Francis (18)
WOODFIELD, the Rev. Harry (18, K.T.)
WRAITH, the Rev. Lawrence Victor (18)
WRIGHT, the Rev. Albert Alexander (18)
WRIGHT, the Rev. Edwin Rudland (K.T.)
WRIGHT, the Rev. William Roland Henry (30, K.T.)

YOUNG, the Ven. Archdeacon Frank Sydney (30)

(There are also in these same degrees 102 Free Church Ministers).

APPENDIX C

A List of the Members of the Thirty-third Degree of the Ancient and Accepted Rite for England and Wales (1954).

The Supreme Council of the Thirty-third Degree.

Most Puissant Sovereign Grand Commander
SIR TREVOR JOCELYN MATTHEWS

Very Puissant Lieutenant Grand Commander
ARTHUR LIONEL FITZROY COOK

Grand Marshal
SIR ERIC STUDD, O.B.E.

Grand Chancellor
MAJOR ROBERT LIDSAY LOYD, O.B.E., M.C.

Grand Captain General
MAJOR SIR THOMAS GABRIEL LUMLEY LUMLEY-SMITH, D.S.O.

Grand Treasurer General
CECIL FRANCIS CUMBERLEGE

Grand Chamberlain
CAPT. THE RIGHT HON. HARRY FREDERICK COMFORT CROOKSHANK, M.P.

Grand Prior
THE REV. CANON GEORGE TURNER WALDEGRAVE, M.B.E.

Grand Secretary General
COL. ERNEST GEORGE DUNN, D.S.O.

Honoris Causa (in order of appointment)

JOHN H. COWLES (*Southern Jurisdiction, U.S.A.*)
MELVIN M. JOHNSON (*Northern Jurisdiction, U.S.A.*)
THE EARL OF STAIR (*Scotland*)
DOUGLAS FRASER, Q.C. (*Canada*)
H.M. KING GUSTAF VI ADOLF (*Sweden*)
RAYMOND F. BROOKE (*Ireland*)
JUDGE THOMAS J. HARKINS (*Southern Jurisdiction, U.S.A.*)
CLARENCE MACLEOD PITTS (*Canada*)

CHRISTIAN BY DEGREES

Members of the Thirty-third Degree (Grand Inspectors General)

ADAMS, Col. Cecil Clare
ALBAN, Sir Frederick John, C.B.E.
ALDERSON, Gerald Graham
ALEXANDER OF TUNIS, Field-Marshal the Earl of, K.G., G.C.B., G.C.M.G., M.C.
ALLEN, Col. Sir Stephen Shepherd, K.B.E., C.M.G., D.S.O.

BARNE, the Right Rev. George Dunsford, D.D., C.I.E., O.B.E.
BRAITHWAITE, Vice-Admiral Lawrence Walter, C.M.G.
BRIDGE, George Edmund Walker
BROWNE, Bertie Frederick

CAMPBELL, Sir Archibald Young Gipps, K.C.I.E., C.B.E.
CHITTY, Lieut.-Col. John Walter, M.B.E.
CLARK, Milbourne Edward
CLARK, Robert Harrison George
COBURN, Alvin Langdon
CORAH, Sir John Harold
CRANSTOUN-DAY, Thomas Nathaniel

DALE, Ernest Edward
DENTITH, Arthur William
DICK, Robert Peter
DIXON, Robert Wilkin Ernest
DYER, Col. George Nowers, C.B.E., D.S.O.

ELLIS, Joseph Arthur
EVANS, John Howell

GIRLING, William James, C.B.E.
GROSVENOR, Major the Rev. John Ernest, M.B.E.

HARRIS, the Lord, M.C.
HATCH, Harry
HENEAGE, Lieut.-Col. the Lord, O.B.E.
HOLLAND, Sir Robert Erskine, K.C.I.E., C.S.I., C.V.O.
HOST, William James

JENNINGS, Edward Edgar
JONES, Eustace Alfred

LAING, Alexander Mossman
LEICESTER-WARREN, Major Cuthbert

MACCLYMONT, Colin Alexander
MALLENDER, Capt. Basil Arthur
MATHEWS, Hamilton Bartlet
MYRES, the Rev. Miles Weight, D.D.

NORMAN, Brig.-Gen. Claude Lumsden, D.S.O., M.V.O.

PERCIVAL, William Howes
PERRAM, Charles Herbert
POLLOCK, Archibald Barr

RICKARD, Col. Frank Martyn
RODGERS, the Rev. William
ROWLATT, Major Henry Napier
ROYSE, Alfred Ernest
RUSSELL, George

SOMERS, Seth Smith, O.B.E.
SMITH, Henry Clifford
SPENCE, Sir Reginald Arthur
STOW, Ernest Charles Sergeant, O.B.E.
STUDD, Bernard Cyril

THIRKILL, Sir Henry, C.B.E., M.C.
TILLEY, Albert
TURNER, Frank Douglas

VIVIAN, James Howard

WALTHALL, Brig.-Gen. Edward Charles Walthall Delves, C.M.G. D.S.O.
WALTON, Col. Frederick, M.C.
WATCH, Engr. Lieut.-Comdr. Harold Victor Hume
WHITE, Sir Sydney Arthur, K.C.V.O.

INDEX